Needlecraft
Stitch Directory

First published in 2012 by
Jacqui Small llp
An imprint of Aurum Press
7 Greenland Street
London NW1 0ND

Copyright © RotoVision SA 2012
www.rotovision.com

Art Director: Emily Portnoi
Cover design: Emily Portnoi
Design concept: Emily Portnoi
Artworking: Emma Atkinson
Stitch illustrations: Emily Portnoi and Emma Atkinson,
based on sketches by Sarah Whittle
Stitch photography: Simon Punter
Commissioning Editor: Isheeta Mustafi
Needlework on p. 3: Carina Envoldsen-Harris
Needlework on p. 4: Katrien van Deuren
Needlework on p. 6: Amy B. Friend
Typeset in Avenir, Caecilia Com, and Gentium

ISBN: 978 1 906417 80 2

A catalogue record for this book is available from
the British Library.

2014 2013 2012
10 9 8 7 6 5 4 3 2 1

Printed in China

Needlecraft
Stitch Directory

A visual reference of over 50 needlecraft styles
and the stitches that go with them

Sarah Whittle

jacqui
small

STYLE DIRECTORY

Introduction.............................7

CHAPTER 1
Surface embroidery.........................10

CHAPTER 2
Counted-thread work.....................38

CHAPTER 3
Quilting, patchwork
and appliqué.............................54

CHAPTER 4
Other techniques..................80

STITCH DIRECTORY

CHAPTER 5
Basic stitches.........................92

CHAPTER 6
Line stitches...........................104

CHAPTER 7
Crossed stitches.......................118

CHAPTER 8
Isolated stitches 132

CHAPTER 9
Straight stitches 142

CHAPTER 10
Buttonhole stitches 156

CHAPTER 11
Chain stitches................................168

CHAPTER 12
Pulled and drawn
stitches 180

CHAPTER 13
Canvaswork stitches.............192

CHAPTER 14
Other stitches 210

Working techniques.....................228

Glossary..232
Contributors/photographers.............236
Index...238

INTRODUCTION

Whether you are a beginner looking for a new challenge or an experienced pro wishing to rediscover a forgotten skill, this book has something for everyone. The first section of this book will introduce you to some well-known techniques, such as freestyle embroidery, cross-stitch, canvaswork and appliqué, as well as some not-so-well-known techniques, such as sashiko quilting and huck embroidery. Throughout this first section, the Style Directory, you will find inspirational galleries from contemporary practitioners to inspire your own creations.

In the second section, the Stitch Directory, you are provided with more than 130 stitches, with easy step-by-step diagrams and clear instructions to follow. Individual entries also give advice on appropriate threads and fabrics, and list the technique(s) that each stitch is suitable for.

This book will lead you on a journey of discovery into the fascinating world of needlecraft.

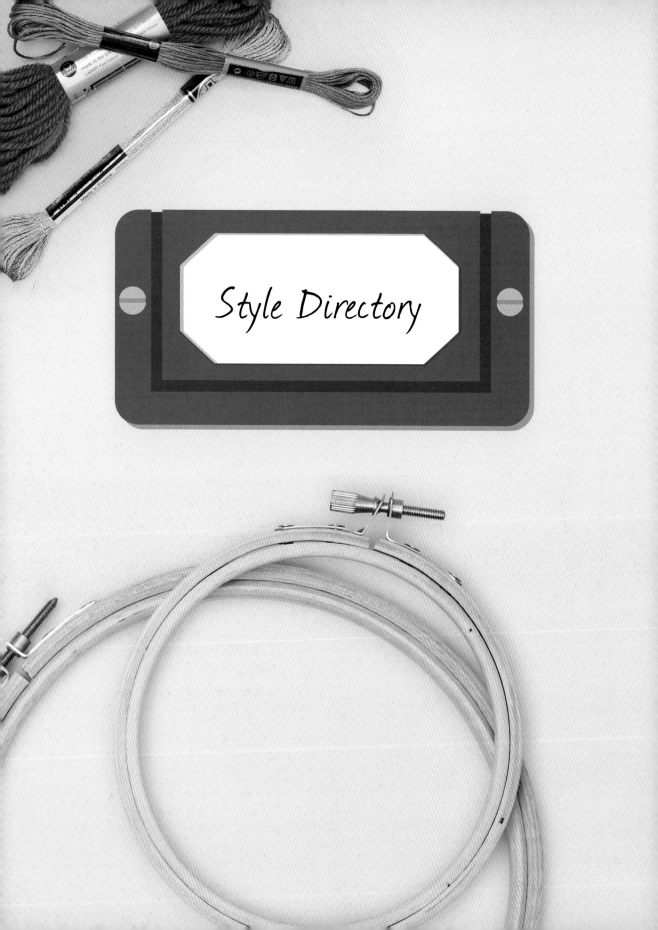

Style Directory

CHAPTER 1
Surface embroidery   10

Freestyle embroidery	12
Whitework	14
Mountmellick	16
Broderie anglaise	17
Crewelwork	18
Goldwork	20
Free machine embroidery	22
Beadwork	24
Shadow embroidery	26
Ribbon work	27
Redwork	28
Candlewicking	29
Couching and laid work	30
Cutwork	32
Brazilian embroidery	34
Silk shading	35
Net embroidery	36
Stumpwork	37

CHAPTER 2
Counted-thread work   38

Blackwork	40
Cross-stitch	42
Canvaswork	44
Assisi	46
Bargello	47
Hardanger	48
Drawn-thread work	49
Drawn-fabric work	50
Chicken scratch	51
Huck embroidery	52
Hedebo embroidery	53

CHAPTER 3
Quilting, patchwork
and appliqué   54

Hand quilting	56
Machine quilting	58
Sashiko quilting	60
Trapunto quilting	61
Corded quilting	62
Tied quilting	63
Patchwork	64
Crazy patchwork	66
Seminole patchwork	67
Hand appliqué	68
Raw-edge appliqué	70
Needle-turned appliqué	71
Shadow appliqué	72
Hawaiian appliqué	73
Machine appliqué	74
Stained-glass appliqué	76
Fused appliqué	77
Reverse appliqué	78
Suffolk puffs	79

CHAPTER 4
Other techniques   80

Needle lace	82
Punch needle	83
Smocking	84
Tatting	86
Needle felting	88

1: SURFACE EMBROIDERY

When you think of surface embroidery, you might imagine sumptuous fabrics encrusted with stitches in silken and metallic threads. This may be true of historical embroideries, but today, surfaces for embroidery are limited only by your imagination. They may include paper, leather, metal, ceramics, wood, plastic and even toast!

Through the centuries a variety of methods and techniques have been used to embellish clothing and household items. Fashions have come and gone, but the techniques and skills have pretty much stayed the same. Surface embroidery covers a range of techniques, including freestyle embroidery, crewelwork, stumpwork, beadwork and whitework. All of these techniques can be applied to items for the home, personalized gifts, clothing or even your own individual and unique artwork.

2

3

1

1 *Freestyle embroidery (Liz Bookey): linen; DMC embroidery cotton*

2 *Freestyle embroidery (Carina Envoldsen-Harris):
cotton fabric; DMC embroidery cotton*

3 *Free machine embroidery (Bonnie P. Dulude – Pastiche Studio):
water-soluble stabilizer; silk thread*

4 *Hand embroidery with beads (MimiLove): canvas; embroidery cotton;
cotton fabric; DMC embroidery cotton*

Contemporary practitioners are pushing the boundaries of embroidery, whether as a craft, hobby or art form. These stitchers are using surface embroidery techniques as a springboard for their own creativity, putting a unique modern stamp on this traditional craft. Learning these same techniques will give you, too, the ability to transform any boring bit of fabric into a work of art.

FREESTYLE EMBROIDERY

Also known as: free embroidery

Freestyle embroidery is simply embroidery that is worked freely on the surface of a piece of fabric, either following a design or pattern or just mark making in different stitches. Unlike with counted-thread embroidery techniques, you are not restricted to where on the fabric you have to stitch – there is no counting of threads involved; you are truly 'free' to embellish your fabric in whatever way you wish.

There are hundreds of stitches that can be used in freestyle embroidery, from basic outline stitches for simple motifs to more complex stitches, which can add depth and texture to an otherwise plain and uninteresting fabric. If you are new to embroidery then it would be best to begin by mastering the techniques covered in the Basic Stitches chapter in the second section of this book (p. 92).

Ideas for freestyle embroidery can come from anywhere: patterns you see around the house, a child's drawing or the outline of a leaf you find on the pavement. If your response to this is to say, 'Hey, I can't draw,' have no fear – there are plenty of great new patterns on the market for you to choose from!

RELATED STITCHES

(p. 94)	Backstitch
(p. 100)	Blanket stitch
(p. 99)	Buttonhole stitch
(p. 95)	Chain stitch
(p. 97)	Feather stitch
(p. 101)	Fly stitch
(p. 134)	French knot
(p. 96)	Lazy daisy stitch
(p. 94)	Running stitch
(p. 151)	Satin stitch
(p. 95)	Split stitch
(p. 98)	Stem stitch

FABRICS: Plain-weave fabrics are used for freestyle embroidery – usually cotton, linen or silk. With freestyle embroidery you can experiment on a multitude of surfaces, including paper, metal, plastic, wood and even slate. (For hard materials, holes are made first and stitches are then worked in and out of these.) The possibilities are endless!

THREADS: Embroidery cotton (six-stranded cotton, as it is also known), stranded silk and cotton pearl (perlé) are the main thread types used, although there are many different types and textures of threads that can be utilized instead.

Freestyle embroidery and watercolour (MimiLove): canvas; embroidery cotton, beads

Freestyle embroidery (Carina Envoldsen-Harris): linen; DMC embroidery cotton

Freestyle embroidery (Shannon Genova-Scudder): cotton; DMC embroidery cotton

NEEDLES: Crewel needles, which are pointed and have a large eye to take different thread thicknesses, are used for this type of embroidery.

OTHER EQUIPMENT: To keep your stitches even and prevent your work distorting, it is best to use an embroidery hoop or frame, which will keep the fabric taut. The choice is yours, though – some embroiderers prefer to work without a hoop. You will also need a small pair of embroidery scissors, fabric or dressmaker's scissors for cutting fabric and a fabric marker pen (fading or water-soluble) for transferring designs.

COMMON APPLICATIONS: Freestyle embroidery can be used to embellish garments, household items such as cushions, table linen and bedding, and for creating your own unique artworks.

WHITEWORK

'Whitework' is the general term used to describe embroidery worked in white thread on a white fabric. Unlike blackwork (another counted-thread technique, but one that uses small patterns to form a design), whitework uses many freestyle, raised and textured embroidery stitches to cover the fabric's surface. This work encompasses many different surface embroidery techniques, including Mountmellick, broderie anglaise, candlewicking and cutwork (all covered individually in this chapter). Whitework is also used in counted-thread work – for example, Hardanger, Hedebo embroidery, drawn-thread work and drawn-fabric work.

Whitework was very popular from the seventeenth to the nineteenth century. Women at home would use it to decorate christening robes, wedding dresses, nightdresses, handkerchiefs, tablecloths and bedspreads with designs featuring plants, fruit and flowers – creating heirloom pieces that would be passed down through generations. Early French whitework was worked on fine calico or net so that the embroidery stood out from the background. Ireland also became famed for its whitework, which was produced by a skilled workforce made up of peasants.

RELATED STITCHES

(p. 94)	Backstitch
(p. 99)	Buttonhole stitch
(p. 158)	Buttonhole stitch with picot
(p. 159)	Double buttonhole bar
(p. 134)	French knot
(p. 189)	Hemstitch
(p. 96)	Lazy daisy stitch
(p. 153)	Padded satin stitch
(p. 94)	Running stitch
(p. 151)	Satin stitch
(p. 159)	Single buttonhole bar
(p. 98)	Stem stitch

FABRICS: Whitework embroidery can be worked on linen, cotton sateen, calico and netting.

THREADS: A variety of threads can be used for this work, including embroidery cotton, silk or cotton pearl (perlé), coton à broder and non-mercerized cotton for Mountmellick work (p. 16). The choice of thread is dependent on the type of fabric and the purpose of the piece.

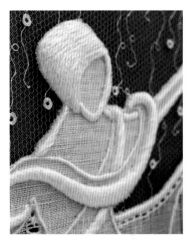

Whitework, pleating and hand embroidery (Karen Ruane): calico and silk; cotton pearl (perlé) and coton à broder

Fine whitework based on the designs and illustrations of Erté and Leon Bakst (Katie Pirson): linen batiste and conservation net; Maderia cotona nos. 30, 50 and 80, stranded cotton, floche à broder and coton à broder

Fine whitework based on the designs and illustrations of Erté and Leon Bakst (Katie Pirson): linen batiste and conservation net; Maderia cotona nos. 30, 50 and 80, stranded cotton, floche à broder and coton à broder

NEEDLES: Crewel, chenille, tapestry and darning needles can be used for these techniques. The choice will depend on both the type of thread and the fabric being used.

OTHER EQUIPMENT: You will also need a small pair of embroidery scissors, an embroidery hoop to keep the fabric taut and prevent your stitches puckering and a fabric marker pen (fading or water-soluble) for transferring your designs.

COMMON APPLICATIONS: Whitework is still used today as it was traditionally – on personal items such as christening robes and handkerchiefs, as well as home décor, including bedspreads, blankets, cushions and table linen.

MOUNTMELLICK

Also known as: Mountmellick work

This style of embroidery is a form of whitework and takes its name from the town of Mountmellick in Ireland. First introduced in around 1825 by a Quaker woman called Johanna Carter, it was soon being worked by young girls and women to earn a living.

Mountmellick has a heavier, coarser appearance than other forms of whitework, and can usually be identified by its typical use of fruit and flower motifs. Mountmellick work also often has a knitted fringe edge.

Mountmellick (Sophie Long): heavy cotton sateen; Mountmellick threads nos. 1–4

RELATED STITCHES

(p. 99)	Buttonhole stitch
(p. 97)	Feather stitch
(p. 134)	French knot
(p. 153)	Padded satin stitch
(p. 151)	Satin stitch
(p. 98)	Stem stitch

FABRICS: This embroidery is usually worked on a firm, tightly woven white cotton sateen.

THREADS: Mountmellick traditionally uses a heavyweight white matt embroidery cotton or a non-mercerized knitting cotton.

NEEDLES: Chenille embroidery needles are used for this work, as they are long and sharp, with a large eye. Darning needles, which are long and have a long eye, are also used.

OTHER EQUIPMENT: To keep your stitches even and prevent your work distorting, it is best to use an embroidery hoop or frame, which will keep the fabric taut. You will also need a small pair of embroidery scissors.

COMMON APPLICATIONS: Mountmellick can be used to decorate nightdresses, tablemats, tablecloths, sachets, bed linen and pillows.

BRODERIE ANGLAISE

Also known as: eyelet embroidery and Madeira work

Broderie anglaise is a very pretty variety of cutwork, featuring characteristic small round or oval eyelets. This technique was frequently used in the eighteenth and nineteenth centuries to embellish nightwear, underwear, baby clothes and household linen. Designs are generally simple; they are often floral in nature and usually limited to borders and trimmings.

Traditional broderie anglaise was most often worked on white or very pale blue fabric; modern forms are now worked in other colours, too. However, the colour of the thread always matches the colour of the fabric.

Broderie anglaise with lace (Karen Ruane): cotton fabric and lace; stranded cotton

RELATED STITCHES

(p. 99)   *Buttonhole stitch*
(p. 153)   *Padded satin stitch*
(p. 94)   *Running stitch*
(p. 151)   *Satin stitch*

FABRICS: The fabrics used for broderie anglaise include cambric, calico, cotton, lawn and very fine linen.

THREADS: Stranded cotton or embroidery silk and cotton pearl (perlé) can all be used for this technique.

NEEDLES: The most suitable needle for broderie anglaise is a crewel needle.

OTHER EQUIPMENT: You will need a pair of small, sharp embroidery scissors, an embroidery hoop or frame, a fabric marker pen (fading or water-soluble) and a stiletto for making holes.

COMMON APPLICATIONS: Broderie anglaise is still used to create traditional-looking bed linen, baby clothing, cot quilts, christening robes, nightwear and underwear.

CREWELWORK

Also known as: Jacobean embroidery

Crewelwork is embroidery worked in wool. It developed in Europe in the seventeenth century, where it was used for wall panels, bed hangings, upholstery and curtains. The technique was particularly popular in England during this period, which is why it also came to bear the alternative name of 'Jacobean embroidery'. Its popularity also reached the American colonies of the time. Strong, brightly coloured wools were used to depict stylized motifs inspired by nature – birds, fruit, leaves, flowers and animals and, typically, the 'tree of life', which took the form of an embellished, many-branched tree. Oriental fabrics imported from China, India and Persia also influenced early designs.

Traditional crewelwork used woollen threads to produce a slightly raised effect on linen fabric, with the texture of the fabric adding to the overall appearance. Today linen is still a common choice, although modern embroiderers may often choose other background fabrics and threads. A variety of freestyle embroidery stitches can be used for the designs.

RELATED STITCHES

(p. 99)	Buttonhole stitch
(p. 95)	Chain stitch
(p. 101)	Coral stitch
(p. 102)	Cretan stitch
(p. 101)	Fly stitch
(p. 134)	French knot
(p. 100)	Herringbone stitch
(p. 154)	Long and short stitch
(p. 151)	Satin stitch
(p. 95)	Split stitch
(p. 217)	Square laid filling stitch
(p. 98)	Stem stitch

FABRICS: Plain-coloured linen twill and linen union fabrics are usually used for crewelwork, although modern choices may include cotton or silk dupion. If heavier threads are used, the fabric will need to be strong enough to support the stitches.

THREADS: Specialist crewel wools are thicker than ordinary stranded cotton. They come in a range of colours and are usually two-ply in thickness, although a lot of modern crewelwork designs tend to be stitched in silk or stranded cotton.

Hand-embroidered crewelwork (Katrina Herron): canvas; DMC embroidery cotton

Hand-embroidered crewelwork (Katrina Herron): canvas; DMC embroidery cotton

NEEDLES: Crewel needles are used for this type of embroidery. They are sharp, with large eyes, and can cater for different thread thicknesses.

OTHER EQUIPMENT: You will also need a small pair of embroidery scissors, an embroidery hoop to keep your fabric taut and a fabric marker pen (fading or water-soluble) for transferring designs.

COMMON APPLICATIONS: Crewelwork is most often used for home décor – cushions, wall hangings, fire screens and foot stools.

GOLDWORK

Also known as: metal thread embroidery

Goldwork is the art of embroidering with metal threads. Despite its name, it does also incorporate other metals, including silver and copper. This is a sumptuous, highly textured form of embroidery, which has been used throughout the centuries for religious vestments, royal dress and military costumes. English goldwork dates back more than 1,000 years, and can be seen on examples of *Opus Anglicanum* (literally, 'English work'), the famous English school of embroidery of the twelfth to the fourteenth century. The Syon Cope (a priest's cape), in the collection of the Victoria and Albert Museum, London, is one of the few remaining examples of this work.

Couching and laid work (p. 30) are the techniques most often used in goldwork. This is because a lot of the threads used in goldwork are too thick to be sewn through the fabric and are therefore better laid on the fabric's surface using the couching method.

Modern goldwork embroidery uses a variety of metal threads such as gimp, purl gold, bullion and plate. Goldwork is a highly skilled technique, which takes a lot of practice to master.

RELATED STITCHES

(p. 98)	Basic couching
(p. 212)	Bokhara couching
(p. 214)	Pendant couching
(p. 215)	Puffy couching
(p. 213)	Romanian couching
(p. 214)	Trailing couching

FABRICS: Goldwork embroidery is traditionally worked on a silk velvet fabric. Silk fabrics can be backed with calico fabric for added support. Church linen, which is 100 per cent linen, can also be used. Metallic kid leather is used for flat areas of a design, usually worked over a felt padding. Felt is also used for working raised areas of goldwork.

THREADS: A variety of threads are available for goldwork, including gimp, purl gold, rough purl, pearl purl, smooth purl, bright check purl, smooth passing, twist, broad plate and bullion. Colours range from gold, copper, silver and gilt to many other colours. A fine silk thread is then used for couching.

'Plunging'

The tail ends of laid threads can be tidied by 'plunging' them through to the back of fabric, out of sight. Leaving the tying thread at the back of the fabric, make a hole in the fabric with a large chenille needle. Cut the couched (p. 30) thread, leaving a short tail, thread it through the needle and pull it through to the back of fabric. This tail can then be folded back and secured with the tying thread.

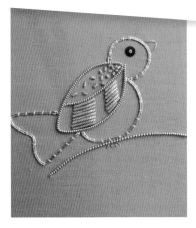

Goldwork (Katie Pirson): Edinburgh linen; Japanese thread, smooth purl, bright check purl, Elizabethan twist, soft string padding, felt padding, Pearsall's embroidery silk and metal threads

Goldwork, couching, cutwork and chipping (Lizzy Lansberry): cotton fabric; polyester machine thread, Japanese thread, bright check purl, pearl purl, metallic machine embroidery thread and spangles

Silk shading and goldwork (Katie Pirson): silk dupion; goldwork threads and DMC embroidery cotton

NEEDLES: Crewel needles and beading needles can be used for goldwork embroidery; both are available in various sizes. A large-size darning or chenille needle is used for 'plunging' (see box above) threads to the back of the fabric. Many stitchers also find a curved quilting needle and a leather needle useful.

OTHER EQUIPMENT: You will also need a small pair of embroidery scissors, an embroidery hoop to keep your fabric taut, a fabric marker pen (fading or water-soluble) for transferring designs, a velvet board used for cutting purls, beeswax for coating threads to add strength and a pair of tweezers.

COMMON APPLICATIONS: Goldwork appears most often on ecclesiastical embroideries – church vestments and altar cloths – as well as on clothing, embroidered art and cushions.

FREE MACHINE EMBROIDERY

Also known as: free-motion embroidery

Free machine embroidery is a fast and effective way of creating freestyle embroidery with a domestic sewing machine. It is a technique that is growing in popularity because it allows the embroiderer to create needle-painted (p. 35), illustrative designs with ease. With the presser foot removed and the feed dogs lowered, fabric can be moved in any direction to either fill a large area or to draw or sketch a design.

The feed dogs are what allow a sewing machine to control the fabric as it passes underneath the presser foot, thus creating an even stitch. Some machines have a lever for lowering the feed dogs; others have a cover that fits over them. The machine's stitch width and length are set to zero before commencing sewing, so by moving the fabric in any direction, you have total control over the length of your stitches.

Free machine embroidery uses two basic machine stitches – straight or zig-zag – and interesting effects can be achieved by changing either the top or bottom tensions of the machine.

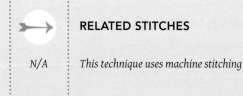

RELATED STITCHES

N/A

This technique uses machine stitching

FABRICS: A variety of fabrics can be used for free machine embroidery, including silk noile, linen and cotton calico. Some embroidery artists use a heavy cotton canvas or sailcloth as a background fabric. Specialist fabrics such as vanishing muslin and cold- and hot-water-soluble fabrics are used for creating the more intricate patterns of machine lace. Interfacing or fabric stabilizer is used for support. Paper can also be used for experimentation.

Free machine embroidery (Emily Mackey – Maxemilia): silk fabric; cotton threads

Appliqué and free machine embroidery (Laura Amiss): felt and print on art canvas; cotton threads

Free machine embroidery, log cabin patchwork and raw-edge appliqué (Kajsa Wikman): linen tea towel and cotton wadding; sewing threads

THREADS: Silk or viscose are the best threads to use for this technique. You can also use general-purpose sewing threads. Invisible nylon threads can be used in the bottom spool so that the design will only be visible on the right side of the fabric.

NEEDLES: Machine needles are available in different sizes and for different fabrics. Choose a suitable needle for the fabric you are using.

OTHER EQUIPMENT: You will also need a small pair of embroidery scissors, an embroidery hoop to keep your fabric taut, a fabric marker pen (fading or water-soluble) for transferring designs, an unpicker (stitch ripper) for unpicking errors and dressmaker's scissors.

COMMON APPLICATIONS: Free machine embroidery is commonly used to decorate T-shirts, bags, purses, cushions, tea cosies, tea towels and table linen, and to create embroidered artwork.

BEADWORK

Also known as: bead embroidery

Beads have been used to decorate fabric since ancient Egyptian times, and beadwork embroidery in particular often features on the traditional textiles of India, Africa and North America. This ancient craft is the art of applying beads to a surface fabric. It differs from other forms of beadwork, in which beads are usually woven – on or off a loom – or supported by wires.

In beadwork embroidery glass, pearl and semi-precious beads are either applied individually or in strings, which are then couched to the surface of the fabric. Beads can be applied as decorative elements in conjunction with other embroidery stitches to fill a design, or used as an outline. Even an entire design can be worked in glass seed beads. This technique is very time consuming and takes a lot of patience – seed beads are tiny! Beadwork can also be applied as a motif to a backing fabric, which is then cut out and applied to the chosen item with fabric glue or using appliqué techniques.

RELATED STITCHES

(p. 94)   *Backstitch*
(p. 98)   *Basic couching*

FABRICS:
A variety of fabrics can be used for beadwork embroidery, including silk, satin, velvet, linen and cotton calico.

THREADS: This work requires a thread that is strong enough to support the weight of the beads. Beading thread is generally silk, cotton or synthetic.

NEEDLES: Specialist beading needles are used to apply the beads to fabric. They are long, pointed, very fine and have a small eye, making it easy to pass through the tiny seed beads. Beading needles are available in various sizes.

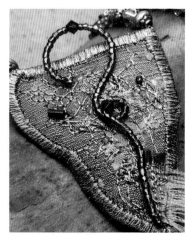

Beadwork (Eleanor Pigman): batik fabric; seed beads

Beadwork and free machine embroidery (Bonnie P Dulude – Pastiche Studio): silk; silk and metallic threads

Beadwork (Brenda Kee): silk dupion; metallic threads

OTHER EQUIPMENT: You will also need seed beads, which come in sizes 15/0, 11/0 and 8/0: 15/0 beads are about 1.5mm in size, 11/0 beads are about 1.8mm or 2.0mm and 8/0 seed beads are about 3.0mm. You will also need a small pair of embroidery scissors, an embroidery hoop to keep your fabric taut, a fabric marker pen (fading or water-soluble) for transferring designs, a velvet board for laying out your beads, beeswax for coating threads to add strength and a pair of tweezers.

COMMON APPLICATIONS: Beadwork can be used to embellish clothing and personal accessories such as bags and purses, or to create embroidered art.

SHADOW EMBROIDERY

Colour choice

It is best to stick to strong colours for shadow embroidery as paler colours will not stand out as well.

Also known as: shadow work

Shadow embroidery is a very delicate form of embroidery that uses sheer fabrics and closed herringbone stitch. The stitches are worked on the back, or wrong, side of the fabric and show through to the front, giving a shadowy effect. This technique was especially popular in the eighteenth century, when it was worked white on white and known as shadow work. Shadow embroidery is believed to be of Indian origin.

Modern shadow work is worked in coloured threads on either white or pale-coloured sheer fabrics. Designs for this type of embroidery are mainly floral, although fruit and berries are also popular.

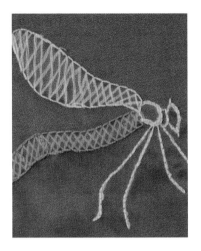

Shadow embroidery (Sarah Whittle): crystal organza; cotton embroidery thread

FABRICS: The sheer fabrics most often used for shadow embroidery are organdie, voile, chiffon, organza and georgette.

THREADS: Stranded silk or cotton threads are used for this technique.

NEEDLES: Shadow embroidery usually requires fine needles, such as sharps or crewel needles.

OTHER EQUIPMENT: You will also need a small pair of embroidery scissors and a fabric marker pen (fading or water-soluble) for transferring designs. An embroidery hoop is essential to keep your fabric taut while working.

COMMON APPLICATIONS: This type of work appears on lingerie, nightdresses, children's clothing, sachets and even curtains.

RELATED STITCHES

(p. 128)   *Closed herringbone stitch*
(p. 134)   *French knot*
(p. 99)   *Holbein stitch*
(p. 94)   *Running stitch*

RIBBON WORK

Also known as: silk ribbon embroidery

This is the beautiful art of embroidering with silk ribbons. It is a form of dimensional embroidery and is used to depict naturalistic forms such as flowers and leaves.

Ribbon work dates back to the seventeenth century, when it was a popularly used form of decoration on coats and gowns. In the nineteenth century, it was commonly used to embellish an even wider range of items, including clothing, bags, shawls, hats and household items.

Samples of ribbon work can be found in the cultures of China, Europe and America, among others.

Ribbon work (Brenda Kee): silk dupion; silk ribbon

FABRICS: Any type of fabric can be used for this work, including satin, silk dupion, linen, cotton calico or velvet.

THREADS: Silk ribbons are best for this work, although synthetic ribbons can also be used. The most popular ribbon widths are 4 and 7mm (⅛ and ¼in). Other threads such as cotton pearl (perlé), stranded silk or cotton are also required for other areas of a design.

NEEDLES: Chenille and tapestry needles are usually used for ribbon work because they are thicker, have larger eyes and easily produce holes in the fabric to pass the ribbon through. Crewel needles are also used.

OTHER EQUIPMENT: You will also need a small pair of embroidery scissors and a fabric marker pen (fading or water-soluble) for transferring designs. An embroidery hoop is essential to keep your fabric taut.

COMMON APPLICATIONS:
Ribbon work is used most often on clothing and fashion accessories such as bags and shawls. It is also used to make framed pictures.

RELATED STITCHES

(p. 134)	*French knot*
(p. 96)	*Lazy daisy stitch*
(p. 98)	*Stem stitch*
(p. 146)	*Straight stitch*

REDWORK

Also known as: Turkey redwork

This embroidery technique uses red thread to embroider simple line drawings or designs. Redwork originated in Turkey, although it then went on to become very popular in the 1800s in America. A particular colour process was used to create a colourfast dye for the thread; the resulting thread became known as 'Turkey red', hence this technique's other name.

Due to its simplicity, redwork embroidery was an inexpensive form of decoration. Designs were printed onto small calico squares, which sold for a penny and became known as 'penny squares'.

Typical subjects for redwork include nursery rhymes, flowers and animals.

Redwork (Yuki Sugashima): linen; embroidery cotton and metallic embroidery thread

FABRICS: Cotton calico is still used for this work.

THREADS: The best thread for redwork is embroidery cotton (six-stranded cotton).

RELATED STITCHES

(p. 94)	Backstitch
(p. 134)	French knot
(p. 95)	Split stitch
(p. 98)	Stem stitch
(p. 146)	Straight stitch

NEEDLES: Crewel needles are used because they are pointed, have a large eye and are also available in different sizes.

OTHER EQUIPMENT: You will also need a small pair of embroidery scissors, an embroidery hoop to keep your fabric taut and a fabric marker pen for transferring designs.

COMMON APPLICATIONS: Today, redwork is generally used to decorate table linen, tea towels, pillowcases and quilt blocks.

CANDLEWICKING

Also known as: tufting

Candlewicking is a type of whitework embroidery (p. 14) that forms loops or knots of thread on the surface of the fabric. The base fabric generally used is a softly woven cotton or unbleached cotton calico. Candlewicking then covers this with floral or geometric forms to produce a richly textured effect.

Candlewicking is so called because workers of the technique originally used cotton wick – more commonly used for candle making – to create their stitches. This work became particularly popular in America in the nineteenth century, where it was mostly used for making bedspreads.

Candlewicking (Sara Adnum):
calico; embroidery cotton

FABRICS: Fabrics suitable for candlewicking include soft cotton twill and unbleached cotton calico.

THREADS: The range of threads appropriate for this technique include traditional candlewick, cotton pearl (perlé), crochet cotton, coton á broder and three-ply mercerized cotton.

NEEDLES: Chenille needles are usually used for candlewicking because they are long, sharply pointed and have a large eye.

OTHER EQUIPMENT: You will also need a small pair of embroidery scissors, an embroidery hoop to keep your fabric taut and a fabric marker pen for transferring designs.

COMMON APPLICATIONS: As traditionally, candlewicking is still mostly used for bedspreads and cushion covers.

→ RELATED STITCHES

(p. 136)	Colonial knot
(p. 94)	Backstitch
(p. 95)	Split stitch
(p. 98)	Stem stitch

COUCHING AND LAID WORK

Also known as: laid-thread work

Couching and laid work are very similar embroidery techniques, both of which have been around for centuries. Couching comes from the French word *coucher*, which means 'to lie down'. Threads are laid on the surface of the fabric and then tied down with small stitches. The tying stitches can either be worked in the same colour or a contrasting colour for a more decorative effect. Couching and laid work are used for embroidering with textured threads, metallics, ribbons or cords that cannot be drawn through the fabric.

The difference between these two techniques is that couching is usually used for outlining simple designs, whereas in laid work, groups of threads are laid down side by side or in grid-like patterns to fill a space. The threads are then held in place with either slanted or criss-cross stitches.

Goldwork (p. 20) utilizes both couching and laid thread work as an economical way of using precious metals like gold and silver. Laid work is also commonly used in crewelwork embroidery (p. 18).

RELATED STITCHES

(p. 98)	Basic couching
(p. 218)	Battlement filling
(p. 212)	Bokhara couching
(p. 216)	Couched circles
(p. 214)	Pendant couching
(p. 215)	Puffy couching
(p. 217)	Square laid filling
(p. 214)	Trailing couching

FABRICS: Any fabric suitable for the type of threads being laid can be used for couching and laid work, including linen, cotton, silk, satin and velvet.

THREADS: A variety of threads can be used for these techniques. For the laid threads experiment with metallics, cords, ribbons and textured threads, including knitting wools. For the tying threads, use stranded cotton, silk or cotton pearl (perlé). The choice of thread is dependent on the type of fabric and what it will be used for.

Decorative couching stitches

As well as small, straight or criss-cross stitches, a number of other stitches can be used to couch threads. Try the following for a variety of different results: blanket stitch, Cretan stitch, feather stitch, herringbone stitch and open chain stitch.

Couching and freestyle weaving (Brenda Kee): cotton, linen, raffia and lace; gold cording and embroidery thread

Couching and goldwork (Lizzy Lansberry): silk dupion; embroidery thread, passing thread, pearl purl and twist

Couching (Sam Gillespie): natural linen; embroidery thread and DMC threads

NEEDLES: Crewel or chenille needles can be used for both techniques. They are sharply pointed, have large eyes and are suitable for different thread thicknesses.

OTHER EQUIPMENT: You will also need a small pair of embroidery scissors, an embroidery hoop to keep your fabric taut and prevent your stitches puckering, a stiletto (which is used for piercing holes in the fabric when you want to take the laid thread through to the back of the fabric) and a fabric marker pen (fading or water-soluble) for transferring designs.

COMMON APPLICATIONS: Couching and laid work appears on wall hangings, bedspreads, blankets, cushions, clothing, quilts and patchwork.

CUTWORK

In cutwork embroidery, parts of the design are literally cut away from the base fabric either before or after the motif has been stitched. This gives a lace-like appearance to the finished piece. The more areas of background fabric that are cut away, the lacier the effect. Cutwork embroidery is traditionally a whitework technique (p. 14), meaning that it is produced in white thread on a white background. Modern cutwork designs, however, are often stitched in coloured threads too.

Examples of cutwork include broderie anglaise (p. 17), which is the English version of cutwork, developed around 1850; Reticella, which was popular in Venice between the fifteenth and seventeenth centuries; Renaissance cutwork, which is stitched entirely in buttonhole stitch (p. 99); and Richelieu cutwork, which was named after Cardinal Richelieu of France and is characterized by the addition of picots (p. 158) to bars of buttonhole stitch worked between design areas.

RELATED STITCHES

(p. 99)	Buttonhole stitch
(p. 158)	Buttonhole stitch with picot
(p. 159)	Double buttonhole bar
(p. 94)	Running stitch
(p. 159)	Single buttonhole bar

FABRICS: A stiff, firm linen or cotton must be used for this type of embroidery so that the material does not fray when the chosen areas are cut away.

THREADS: Embroidery thread, silk or cotton pearl (perlé) are all suitable threads for cutwork embroidery. The choice of thread is dependent on the heaviness of the fabric.

NEEDLES: Crewel needles are used for this work. They are sharply pointed, have large eyes and are suitable for different thread thicknesses.

Cutwork hint

Care should be taken when cutting away areas of fabric. Work from the reverse side of the fabric and start cutting at the centre of the shape, working outwards to the corners, keeping as close to the stitching as possible.

Cutwork, appliqué and hand embroidery (Karen Ruane): silk dupion and cotton stripe lace; cotton pearl (perlé) and coton á broder

Cutwork and hand embroidery (Karen Ruane): silk dupion and printed cotton; stranded cotton and cotton pearl (perlé)

Cutwork and fine whitework based on the designs and illustrations of Erté and Leon Bakst (Katie Pirson): linen batiste and conservation net; Madeira cotona nos. 30, 50 and 80, stranded cotton, floche à broder and coton à broder

OTHER EQUIPMENT: You will also need a small pair of embroidery scissors, an embroidery hoop to keep your fabric taut and a fabric marker pen (fading or water-soluble) for transferring designs.

COMMON APPLICATIONS: Cutwork is commonly used on household table linen, bedding sheets and clothing such as nightwear and children's dresses.

BRAZILIAN EMBROIDERY

Also known as: Brazilian dimensional embroidery

Brazilian embroidery differs from other surface embroidery techniques in that it uses Z-twist rayon threads. These are twisted in the opposite direction to cotton threads, which have an S twist. This means that some of the stitches used in Brazilian embroidery are worked backwards so that the fibres of the thread do not unravel.

Rayon threads have a high sheen. They were originally manufactured in Brazil, although they are now made in the United States too. Usual subjects for this type of embroidery include flowers and plants, worked so that they create a three-dimensional effect.

Brazilian embroidery and Mediterranean double-knotted lace stitch (Loretta Holzberger): raw silk; EdMar Brazilian embroidery threads

FABRICS: This embroidery requires a firmly woven fabric such as trigger cloth, which is a polyester and cotton mix.

THREADS: The Z-twist rayon threads used in Brazilian embroidery come in different thread weights, from fine to extra heavy, and with different twists.

RELATED STITCHES

(p. 98)   *Basic couching*
(p. 134) *Bullion knot*
(p. 98)   *Stem stitch*

NEEDLES: Millinery needles are used in Brazilian embroidery, as they are long and straight with a round eye. This makes them easier to pass through twists of threads when working stitches that wrap around the needle. Tapestry needles are used for working stitches that do not pass through the fabric because they are blunt-ended and will not split the threads.

OTHER EQUIPMENT: To prevent your work distorting and to keep stitches even, it is best to use an embroidery hoop. You will also need a small pair of embroidery scissors and a fabric marker pen (fading or water-soluble) for transferring designs.

COMMON APPLICATIONS: Brazilian embroidery is commonly used to create realistic, three-dimensional pictures or to embellish cushions and clothing.

SILK SHADING

Also known as: long-and-short-stitch embroidery and needle painting

Silk shading is the art of 'painting with the needle' to create naturalistic forms. It is a beautiful technique in which threads of silk or cotton are blended together on a silk background to form shaded areas of light and dark. Popular subjects for silk shading include flowers, plants, fruit and animals. Silk shading is attributed to the Chinese, who used fine silk threads to produce exquisite pictures and costumes.

Long and short straight stitches are worked in rows, and colours are carefully blended together to produce the shaded effect. By choosing a colour palette close to the subject matter, realistic pictures can be produced.

Silk shading (Mary Brown): silk dupion; stranded cottons

FABRICS: Fabrics used for silk shading include silk, cotton sateen, cotton calico and linen.

THREADS: This type of embroidery is usually worked in stranded silk or stranded cotton.

NEEDLES: Sharply pointed crewel needles are suitable for silk shading. These have a large eye to take one or more strands of thread.

OTHER EQUIPMENT: To prevent your work distorting and to keep stitches even, it is best to use an embroidery hoop. You will also need a small pair of embroidery scissors and a fabric marker pen (fading or water-soluble) for transferring designs.

COMMON APPLICATIONS: Silk shading is used to create realistic 'painted' pictures, both as artwork and also applied to cushions, bags and table linen.

RELATED STITCHES

(p. 154)	Long and short stitch
(p. 151)	Satin stitch
(p. 98)	Stem stitch

NET EMBROIDERY

Net embroidery is a very delicate, lace-like embroidery, worked on white or black net or tulle fabric. A marker pen is used to draw a design on paper and the net is then placed on top of this, and the design followed. If black net is used and the design is not visible, it can be worked by counting the mesh instead. Net embroidery became popular from the early nineteenth century when it was seen on veils and gowns. Said to have been perfected in Limerick, Ireland, it was known there as Limerick lace and Carrickmacross.

Designs are usually geometric or floral in nature. The outline of the design is worked first using a blunt needle in a running or stem stitch, then certain areas are covered with filling stitches. Never use a knot; simply darn in the ends of the threads instead.

Net embroidery using fly stitch, French knots, split stitch and wheatear stitch (Lucy Portsmouth): white tulle and cream organza; Anchor and DMC stranded cotton

FABRICS: A good-quality hexagonal net or tulle fabric should be used for net embroidery because cheaper nets will tear easily.

RELATED STITCHES

(p. 151)	*Darning stitch*
(p. 94)	*Running stitch*
(p. 98)	*Stem stitch*

THREADS: This type of work requires a fine silk embroidery thread.

NEEDLES: A blunt-ended tapestry needle is best for net embroidery.

OTHER EQUIPMENT: A pair of small, sharp embroidery scissors, a marker pen and paper for creating a pattern.

COMMON APPLICATIONS: Net embroidery appears on nightwear, underwear, veils and wedding gowns.

STUMPWORK

Also known as: raised embroidery

This old embroidery technique dates back to the seventeenth and eighteenth centuries, when it was used to decorate boxes, mirror frames and panels with biblical scenes. It is a form of raised embroidery, suited to creating the three-dimensional figures, plants and animals that were all popular subjects for this technique. Raised areas of stumpwork are created by padding or stuffing behind the stitches with felt, leather or, historically, even wood.

Other areas of stumpwork embroidery may include the use of wires – for example, to depict the wings of insects. The techniques of needle-made lace and appliqué are also widely used for this work.

Stumpwork and hand embroidery (Waterrose): canvas fabric; stranded cotton

FABRICS: Background fabrics include duchess satin, silk dupion or cotton; wings, etc use silk organza; padded areas use felt or kid leather.

RELATED STITCHES

(p. 94)	Backstitch
(p. 98)	Basic couching
(p. 212)	Bokhara couching
(p. 99)	Buttonhole stitch
(p. 167)	Ceylon stitch
(p. 138)	Cup stitch
(p. 115)	Ladder stitch
(p. 177)	Raised chain stitch
(p. 131)	Raised herringbone stitch
(p. 98)	Stem stitch
(p. 140)	Woven picot

THREADS: Stranded silk, stranded cotton, metallic, rayon threads and monofilament (a transparent thread used for invisible sewing) can all be used for stumpwork.

NEEDLES: Suitable needles include crewel, chenille, sharps, beading and blunt-ended tapestry needles – in varying sizes for different threads and thicknesses.

OTHER EQUIPMENT: You will also need a small pair of embroidery scissors, tweezers, an embroidery hoop, stumpwork wires or beading wire (available in various gauges), a fabric marker pen for transferring designs, toy stuffing for padded areas and beads.

COMMON APPLICATIONS: Stumpwork is used to create three-dimensional pictures or decorative objects.

2: COUNTED-THREAD WORK

The name provides the clue with this type of work – it is embroidery that is created by counting the threads of the ground fabric. Dating back hundreds of years, counted-thread work is gaining popularity with a new generation of embroiderers who are experimenting with old, traditional techniques and developing new and innovative ways of working.

The most popular forms of counted-thread work are canvaswork and cross-stitch, both of which are currently experiencing a revival among a younger, hipper generation of stitchers. Unlike freestyle embroidery, where you work freely over the fabric, counted-thread work designs are charted on graph paper or using computer software, with each square of a chart representing a stitch. Most designs are worked from the centre of the fabric outwards, either on canvas, even-weave fabric or Aida cloth.

The following pages will introduce you to some of the most popular counted-thread embroidery techniques and allow you to discover how some of today's modern stitchers are using these techniques to create wonderful artwork and accessories for home and fashion.

1

1 *Huck embroidery (Kumi Nakagame – K-Style Shonan): Japanese Swedish weaving cloth; DMC pearl cotton*

2 *Cross-stitch (Sam Gillespie): 28-count fabric on buttons; DMC embroidery cotton*

3 *Chicken scratch (Kristena Derrick): gingham cotton; cotton embroidery thread*

4 *Needlepoint (NeedleYou): 14-count interlock canvas; Patternayan Persian wool*

BLACKWORK

Also known as: Spanish work

This traditional counted-thread embroidery technique uses black thread on natural cream or white fabric to form small repeating patterns that create different tones within design areas. Blackwork became very popular in England during the Tudor and Elizabethan periods; many famous portraits from this time show subjects wearing shirts, bodices, caps and smocks embellished with black silk thread. First introduced to Spain by the Moors who settled there around AD711, it is thought to have been brought to England by Henry VIII's Spanish wife, Catherine of Aragon, thus inheriting the name of 'Spanish work'.

Blackwork embroidery was traditionally used to work geometric patterns to fill scrolling designs of flowers, leaves and fruit on even-weave fabric. Although it is usually considered a counted-thread technique, modern stitchers now use a variety of stitches and techniques, as well as coloured threads, to create their own exciting interpretations.

RELATED STITCHES

(p. 201)	Algerian eye stitch
(p. 94)	Backstitch
(p. 120)	Single cross-stitch
(p. 120)	Half cross-stitch
(p. 121)	Three-quarter cross-stitch
(p. 99)	Holbein stitch
(p. 98)	Stem stitch

FABRICS: Blackwork is traditionally worked on even-weave linen, but Aida cloth can also be used. Even-weave linen is made up of single threads in a regular mesh, which keeps the stitches even. Even weaves are used for counted-thread techniques, and for drawn and pulled work (pp. 49 and 50).

Aida is a coarse, open-mesh fabric that is described in terms of its 'count', or the number of holes per 2.5cm (1in). It is available in a range of counts from 8, the coarsest, to 20. The most popular count is 14. Blackwork can also be worked on plain weaves, including cotton calico and silk.

Colour tip

Tonal effects can be achieved by altering the number of threads in your needle or by using threads of different thicknesses.

Blackwork using cross-stitch (Kristy Kizzee): 14-count Aida cloth; DMC threads

Blackwork, appliqué and hand quilting (Sami Teasdale – Teasemade): gingham, linen, tana lawn, Aida, wadding; cotton pearl (perlé)

Blackwork using backstitch (Amanda Miller): calico; DMC threads

THREADS: Embroidery cotton (six-stranded cotton), silk threads, cotton pearl (perlé), sewing cotton and soft embroidery cotton can all be used for blackwork.

NEEDLES: Tapestry needles are most commonly used for this style of embroidery because their blunt tips do not split the fabric. If you are not stitching on an even-weave fabric, a crewel needle is the best needle to use – its sharp point will enable you to pierce the fabric easily.

OTHER EQUIPMENT: To prevent your work distorting and to keep stitches even, it is best to use an embroidery hoop to keep the fabric taut. You will also need a small pair of embroidery scissors.

COMMON APPLICATIONS: Blackwork can be seen today on cushions, samplers, framed pictures, table linen and ornaments.

CROSS-STITCH

Also known as: sampler stitch

Cross-stitch is one of the oldest embroidery techniques there is. It dates back to the days of ancient Egypt, and can be seen in the work of many cultures and countries, from Scandinavia to Greece and India. It was most often used to adorn clothing and household linen.

A simple cross-stitch is easy to learn; it consists of two diagonal stitches worked in a cross. Designs are then created by following a charted design or pattern, most often on even-weave or Aida cloth. Aida is the most popular choice – both with beginners and more experienced stitchers – because the holes in the fabric are so easy to count. Cross-stitch can also be stitched onto plain-weave fabric with the aid of waste canvas (see below).

Cross-stitch embroidery can be used for creating simple motifs, decorative borders and more complex pictorial images, and it is currently back in vogue with contemporary embroiderers, who are adopting cross-stitch as a way of expressing popular culture.

RELATED STITCHES

(p. 94)   Backstitch
(p. 120)   Single cross-stitch
(p. 134)   French knots
(p. 120)   Half cross-stitch
(p. 100)   Herringbone stitch
(p. 99)   Holbein stitch
(p. 123)   Marking cross-stitch
(p. 121)   Three-quarter cross-stitch

FABRICS: Cross-stitch embroidery can be worked on even-weave linen, in anything from a 6 to 36 count, or Aida cloth, which is available in 8 to 18 count. The most popular counts for cross-stitch are 22-count even-weave fabric and 14-count Aida fabric. The count refers to the number of threads or holes per 2.5cm (1in) in either direction. Other surfaces available are perforated paper and plastic canvas for making three-dimensional objects. Waste canvas is a special fabric that pulls apart when wet, and so can be used as a 'removable' guide when working counted-thread designs on plain-weave fabrics.

Cross-stitch (Claudia Dominguez): natural linen covering buttons; embroidery cotton

Cross-stitch (Claudia Dominguez): natural linen; embroidery cotton

Cross-stitch (Michele Outland – Return to Me): cotton canvas; DMC cotton thread

THREADS: Embroidery cotton (six-stranded cotton) Is usually used for cross-stitch embroidery. Stranded silk, Flower Thread, cotton pearl (perlé) and metallic threads can also be used.

NEEDLES: Tapestry needles are usually used for cross-stitch. They are blunt-ended so will not split the threads of the fabric. They also have a large eye to take different thread thicknesses.

OTHER EQUIPMENT: To prevent your work distorting and to keep stitches even, it is best to use an embroidery hoop to keep your fabric taut. You will also need a small pair of embroidery scissors, a pair of dressmaker's scissors for cutting fabric and masking tape for binding fabric edges.

COMMON APPLICATIONS: Cross-stitch can be used to embroider cushions, decorative ornaments, bookmarks, bags, purses, jewellery and table linen.

CANVASWORK

Also known as: canvas embroidery and needlepoint

Canvaswork, or needlepoint as it is also commonly known, dates back to the Middle Ages, although it became particularly popular during the seventeenth and eighteenth centuries, when it was used to decorate chairs, stools, fire screens and settees. Two well-known examples of canvaswork are Berlin wool work, which was popular in Victorian times and is worked in bright gaudy colours, and petit point, which is worked on a fine canvas fabric using very small stitches.

This counted-thread technique is worked on an open-mesh canvas fabric. The stitches are usually worked in tapestry wool, Persian wool or crewel wool. Other embroidery threads, such as cotton or silk, can be used too – especially when working on small projects.

Needlepoint stitches can completely cover the background fabric, which is why this technique is often confused with tapestry. The main stitch used here is tent stitch, which can be used in conjunction with other more complex stitches to create designs, or entirely on its own, simply using changes in thread colour to create the desired effect.

RELATED STITCHES

(p. 201)	Algerian eye stitch	(p. 207)	Jacquard stitch
(p. 209)	Brick stitch	(p. 201)	Leviathan stitch
(p. 197)	Brighton stitch	(p. 196)	Milanese stitch
(p. 206)	Byzantine stitch	(p. 200)	Moorish stitch
(p. 195)	Cashmere stitch	(p. 203)	Mosaic stitch
(p. 199)	Chequer stitch	(p. 207)	Parisian stitch
(p. 199)	Condensed Scotch stitch	(p. 205)	Pineapple stitch
(p. 203)	Cushion stitch	(p. 202)	Rhodes stitch
(p. 208)	Florentine stitch	(p. 198)	Scotch stitch
(p. 204)	Gobelin filling stitch	(p. 204)	Slanted gobelin stitch
(p. 209)	Greek stitch	(p. 194)	Tent stitch
(p. 202)	Hungarian diamond stitch	(p. 205)	Upright gobelin stitch

Needlepoint (NeedleYou): 14-count interlock canvas; Patternayan Persian wool

Needlepoint (NeedleYou): 14-count interlock canvas; Patternayan Persian wool

FABRICS: Canvaswork is worked on a single-or double-mesh canvas fabric. Popular choices include single-mesh (mono) canvas, ranging from 10 count (coarse) to 22 count (fine); interlock single canvas, which is more stable and does not pull out of shape easily, in 10 to 22 count; double-mesh (Penelope) canvas in 7 to 10 count; and rug canvas, which is available in 3 to 6 count. The count refers to the number of threads or holes per 2.5cm (1in) in either direction.

THREADS: Two-ply Persian wool, four-ply tapestry wool and two-ply crewel wool can all be used for canvaswork.

NEEDLES: Tapestry needles are the best choice for canvaswork; they are blunt-ended and so do not split the threads of the fabric, and have a large eye to take different thread thicknesses.

OTHER EQUIPMENT: To prevent your work distorting and to keep stitches even, it is best to use an embroidery hoop to keep your fabric taut. You will also need a small pair of embroidery scissors, a pair of dressmaker's scissors for cutting fabric and masking tape for binding any fabric edges.

COMMON APPLICATIONS: Canvaswork can be used on anything from cushions to rugs, decorative objects, bookmarks, bags, covered buttons, purses and belts.

ASSISI

Assisi embroidery is a form of cross-stitch in which the background area is embroidered, leaving just the area of the design itself unstitched. This style of embroidery originated in medieval Italy in the town of Assisi, where it was traditionally worked in red or blue on a cream linen fabric. Traditional designs were heraldic in character, featuring mythical beasts and birds.

The main stitches used for this technique are cross-stitch and Holbein stitch. The standard working method is to begin by stitching the design outline in Holbein stitch – usually worked in a darker colour – and then filling in the background with cross-stitch, although modern styles of Assisi incorporate a whole variety of different stitches.

Assisi and freestyle embroidery (Annet Spitteler): quilter's cotton; embroidery cotton

FABRICS: Assisi embroidery can be worked on even-weave linen, available in 6 to 36 count, or Aida fabric, which is available in 8 to 18 count. The most popular counts are 22 count even-weave fabric and 14-count Aida fabric. The count refers to the number of threads or holes per 2.5cm (1in) in either direction.

THREADS: Embroidery cotton (six-stranded cotton) and cotton pearl (perlé) can be used for Assisi embroidery.

NEEDLES: Tapestry needles are best for Assisi work – their blunt tips will not split the threads of the fabric.

OTHER EQUIPMENT: To prevent your work distorting and to keep stitches even, it is best to use an embroidery hoop to keep your fabric taut. You will also need a small pair of embroidery scissors, graph paper for charting designs, a pair of dressmaker's scissors for cutting fabric and masking tape for binding fabric edges.

COMMON APPLICATIONS: Assisi embroidery is usually worked on cushions, decorative objects, bookmarks, framed artwork, bags and purses.

RELATED STITCHES

(p. 120)	*Single cross-stitch*
(p. 134)	*French knot*
(p. 120)	*Half cross-stitch*
(p. 99)	*Holbein stitch*
(p. 121)	*Three-quarter cross-stitch*

BARGELLO

Also known as: flame stitch, Florentine work and Hungarian point

Bargello embroidery is said to have originated in Hungary and then arrived in Florence, Italy, in the fifteenth century. This embroidery takes its name from the Bargello Palace in Florence, now a national museum and home to some early Hungarian examples of this work.

This very distinct counted-thread technique is worked on canvas entirely in Florentine stitch. Stitches are worked horizontally from the centre of the canvas and in a vertical direction, forming a distinctive zig-zag, flame-like pattern. One of the main features of Bargello work is the beautiful shading and blending of colours, which were traditionally muted pinks, greens and browns.

Bargello (Margaret Burns): 12-count mono mesh canvas; tapestry wool

FABRICS: Bargello embroidery is worked on single-mesh (mono) canvas. An interlocking canvas is best to use, as it does not pull out of shape easily. This is available in counts from 10 (coarse) to 22 (fine). The count refers to the number of threads or holes per 2.5cm (1in) in either direction.

THREADS: Four-ply tapestry wools and two-ply crewel wools can be used for Bargello embroidery. Silk threads can also be used on finer canvas.

NEEDLES: Tapestry needles are best for Bargello work – their blunt tips will not split the threads of the fabric.

OTHER EQUIPMENT: To prevent your work distorting and to keep stitches even, it is best to use an embroidery hoop to keep your fabric taut. You will also need a small pair of embroidery scissors, a fabric marker pen, a pair of dressmaker's scissors for cutting canvas and masking tape.

COMMON APPLICATIONS: Bargello is particularly suited to cushions, furniture decorations and personal accessories such as bags.

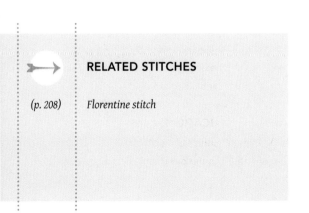

RELATED STITCHES

(p. 208)   *Florentine stitch*

HARDANGER

Originating in Hardanger, Norway, this style of embroidery is a form of drawn-thread work (p. 49) and cutwork embroidery (p. 32), usually worked in white thread on white fabric. Groups of satin stitches are worked together, which are known as 'kloster blocks'.

Kloster blocks are formed by working an irregular number of satin stitches (usually five), in geometrical patterns – either squares, triangles, oblongs or diamonds. Each group of stitches is worked over four horizontal threads and four vertical threads. The tops or bottoms of the vertical threads are then cut away or withdrawn after the stitches are worked to form openwork spaces. Areas of open threads are left and further decorated with other stitches, such as overcast bars and needleweaving.

Hardanger (Sonja Pharr Poor): 28-count linen; cotton pearl (perlé)

FABRICS: Hardanger embroidery is worked on even-weave linen fabric. Popular counts include 22 count, 24 count or 28 count. The count refers to the number of threads or holes per 2.5cm (1in) in either direction.

RELATED STITCHES

(p. 225)   *Kloster blocks*
(p. 224)   *Needleweaving*
(p. 191)   *Overcast bars*
(p. 191)   *Woven bars*

THREADS: Cotton pearl (perlé) can be used for the kloster blocks and embroidery thread for the overcast bars and needleweaving.

NEEDLES: Tapestry needles are usually used for Hardanger; they are blunt-ended so they will not split the threads of the fabric.

OTHER EQUIPMENT: To prevent your work distorting and to keep stitches even, it is best to use an embroidery hoop to keep your fabric taut. You will also need a small pair of embroidery scissors and a pair of tweezers to help remove threads.

COMMON APPLICATIONS: Hardanger generally features on tablemats, tablecloths, napkins, pillowcases and sheets.

DRAWN-THREAD WORK

In this counted-thread embroidery technique, certain warp or weft threads are withdrawn from the fabric to create an open, lacy foundation on which to work stitches. Unlike drawn-fabric work (p. 50), where the stitches are pulled together to form holes, the threads here are withdrawn before the stitching commences. There are many forms of drawn-thread work, with examples dating back as early as the sixteenth century. Over time, different variations of the technique developed in Spain, Italy, Cyprus, Sicily and Russia.

Hemstitching is a form of drawn-thread work, as are both Hardanger (left) and needleweaving. Drawn-thread work is usually worked in white thread on white fabric and is typically used for borders on household linen. For an explanation of how to work a drawn-thread border, see p. 230.

Drawn-thread work and pulled-thread work (Lizzy Lansberry): Edinburgh linen; lace thread, stranded cotton, coton á broder and floche à broder

FABRICS: Drawn-thread work is usually worked on an even-weave linen fabric, which is available from 18 count to 36 count. The count refers to the number of threads or holes per 2.5cm (1in) in either direction.

THREADS: Cotton pearl (perlé) or embroidery cotton (six-stranded cotton) is usually used for this work.

NEEDLES: Tapestry needles are best for drawn-thread work – their blunt tips will not split the threads of the fabric.

OTHER EQUIPMENT: An embroidery hoop will keep your fabric taut and your stitches even. You will also need embroidery scissors, and tweezers to remove threads.

COMMON APPLICATIONS: Drawn-thread work is used to decorate tablemats, tablecloths, napkins, pillowcases and sheets.

RELATED STITCHES

(p. 189)	Hemstitch
(p. 190)	Ladder hemstitch
(p. 224)	Needleweaving
(p. 191)	Overcast bars
(p. 190)	Serpentine stitch
(p. 191)	Woven bars

DRAWN-FABRIC WORK

Also known as: openwork and pulled work

Drawn-fabric work is sometimes confused with drawn-thread work (p. 49); here, however, the stitches are pulled together to create an open, lacy effect rather than being removed from the fabric altogether. Drawn-fabric work is also commonly referred to as 'openwork'. It is said to have developed both in the Middle East and Peru, with the earliest known examples dating back to AD1200. However, the technique did not become widely popular until the sixteenth and seventeenth centuries.

Pulled-thread stitches are worked on a loosely woven linen fabric and are pulled tightly together to form decorative holes. Drawn-fabric work usually uses the same colour for both thread and fabric, for example white on white. This means that the pulled stitches are not usually visible but rather 'sink' into the fabric, leaving a pattern of holes.

Whitework, based on the designs of Margaret MacDonald Mackintosh, including net darning, cutwork, ladder stitch, padded satin stitch, counted satin stitch, trailing stitch, pulled-thread work, French knots and eyelets (Katie Pirson): Charlotte linen; cotton pearl

RELATED STITCHES

(p. 186)	Algerian eye stitch
(p. 182)	Cobbler stitch
(p. 186)	Coil stitch
(p. 188)	Four-sided stitch
(p. 183)	Pin stitch
(p. 185)	Pulled honeycomb stitch
(p. 184)	Punch stitch
(p. 185)	Ringed backstitch
(p. 187)	Single faggot stitch
(p. 187)	Three-sided stitch
(p. 188)	Wave filling stitch

FABRICS: Drawn-fabric work is usually worked on a loosely woven linen fabric or scrim linen (a loosely woven lightweight linen, often used for curtains).

THREADS: Either cotton pearl (perlé) or crochet cotton are strong enough to resist breaking when the stitches are pulled tightly.

NEEDLES: Tapestry needles are best for this work – their blunt tips will not split the threads of the fabric.

OTHER EQUIPMENT: An embroidery hoop will keep your fabric taut and your stitches even. You will also need a small pair of embroidery scissors.

COMMON APPLICATIONS: Drawn-fabric work is usually seen on tablemats, tablecloths and bedspreads.

CHICKEN SCRATCH

Also known as: Amish embroidery, depression lace, gingham lace and snowflake embroidery

This counted-thread embroidery technique is said to have first taken hold in America, where it was presumably introduced by the early settlers. It is worked on gingham and creates a lace-like effect. Gingham is a checked fabric, which usually comes in red, green or blue.

Chicken scratch is traditionally worked in white thread for the filling stitches and outlined in the colour of the darkest check of the chosen gingham. The main stitch used in this type of embroidery is the double cross-stitch, which is a very simple one to master.

Chicken scratch (Kristena Derrick): gingham cotton; embroidery cotton

RELATED STITCHES

(p. 122)	*Double cross-stitch*
(p. 94)	*Running stitch*
(p. 141)	*Woven circles*

FABRICS: Gingham is usually available in 3mm or 6mm (¹/₈in or ¼in) checks.

THREADS: Embroidery cotton (six-stranded cotton) is the usual choice for this type of work.

NEEDLES: Chicken scratch is best worked with crewel or tapestry needles.

OTHER EQUIPMENT: To prevent your work distorting and to keep stitches even, it is best to use an embroidery hoop to keep your fabric taut. You will also need a small pair of embroidery scissors.

COMMON APPLICATIONS: Chicken scratch is commonly used on aprons, tablemats, tablecloths, pillows and cushions.

HUCK EMBROIDERY

Huck embroidery is a form of surface darning that was popular in the United States in the 1930s and 1940s. It was traditionally used mostly for tea towels, although it appears on a much wider range of items today.

Huck embroidery is worked on a special woven fabric (huck or huckaback, also called Monk's cloth) intended for the purpose. This has pairs of raised threads; the needle is passed under these raised threads without ever piercing the fabric.

Simple geometric and floral patterns are popular for this technique.

Huck embroidery (Katherine Kennedy): Huck towelling; cotton pearl (perlé)

FABRICS: Huck weave fabric (Swedish weaving cloth or Monk's cloth) is available by the metre or yard, half-metre or half-yard, or fat quarter.

THREADS: Embroidery cotton (six-stranded cotton) or cotton pearl (perlé) thread can be used for huck embroidery. Metallic threads are good for festive table linen.

NEEDLES: A blunt-ended tapestry needle is best.

OTHER EQUIPMENT: You will need a small pair of sharp embroidery scissors, graph paper and a pencil.

COMMON APPLICATIONS: Huck embroidery can be used on a range of items, from towels, Afghan blankets, table linen, table runners, curtains and decorative ornaments to cushions and pincushions.

RELATED STITCHES

(p. 151)   *Darning stitch*

HEDEBO EMBROIDERY

Also known as: Danish work

Hedebo embroidery originated in Copenhagen, Denmark. It was traditionally worked in white thread on white fabric and was used by peasants to decorate men's shirts, women's underwear and bedsheets. Early seventeenth-century versions of Hedebo embroidery were a cut and drawn-thread work style (p. 49). After evolving through many different changes in style, Hedebo finally developed into an open cutwork technique.

Areas of openwork (p. 32) are cut away and then filled with a variety of lacy stitches. Satin stitches are used for solid areas, while buttonhole stitches are used for edging the cut shapes. This is a similar technique to broderie anglaise (p. 17).

Hedebo embroidery (Belle Coccinelle): pure linen; Madeira cotton thread

RELATED STITCHES

(p. 99)	Buttonhole stitch
(p. 158)	Buttonhole with picot
(p. 159)	Double buttonhole bar
(p. 153)	Padded satin stitch
(p. 94)	Running stitch
(p. 151)	Satin stitch
(p. 159)	Single buttonhole bar

FABRICS: Hedebo embroidery is worked on even-weave linen or cotton fabric.

THREADS: Embroidery cotton (six-stranded cotton) or cotton pearl (perlé) embroidery thread can be used.

NEEDLES: Hedebo uses either a blunt-ended tapestry or crewel needle.

OTHER EQUIPMENT: You will need an embroidery hoop, a small pair of sharp embroidery scissors, a stiletto (for piercing the fabric) and a fabric marker pen (fading or water-soluble).

COMMON APPLICATIONS: Hedebo embroidery is usually seen on tablecloths, table runners, clothing, ornaments, pincushions, pillowcases and cushions.

Quilting, patchwork and appliqué have been around for centuries. The history of these techniques not only spans centuries but continents too, with examples ranging from ancient Egyptian relics and early Mongolian pieces to the work of Amish settlers in Pennsylvania. As a result, there are also many different variations on these techniques, most of which have probably passed down the generations, from mother to daughter.

Unlike surface embroidery techniques, which are a purely decorative way of embellishing fabric, quilting, patchwork and appliqué have often been used as functional crafts for creating warm clothing and bedding out of remnants of fabric. In mid-nineteenth-century America, quilting brought women together in quilting bees. Women would pool their efforts to complete quilts to commemorate an event or a family occasion, such as a wedding or birth.

Quilting bees are still popular today, although their function is now often more social than practical. Quilting itself has also come to be recognized as an artform, often displayed in museums and galleries.

1

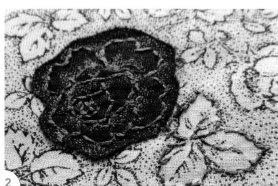

2

1 *Sashiko (Saké Puppets): cotton; sashiko thread*

2 *Hand appliqué (Claudia Dominguez): cotton; embroidery cotton*

3 *Machine quilting and patchwork (Emma How – Sampaguita Quilts): quilter's cottons; Gütermann 50wt cotton thread*

4 *Machine quilting and patchwork (Emma How – Sampaguita Quilts): quilter's cottons; Gütermann 50wt cotton and Superior Threads King Tut 40wt cotton thread*

5 *Hand-assembled and attached yo-yos (Katrina Herron): Anna Maria Horner 'Little Folks' voile; Gütermann hand-quilting cotton thread*

HAND QUILTING

Quilting involves joining three layers of fabric – a top layer, a middle layer of wadding and a background layer – and for hand quilting these are stitched by hand. The three layers are first pinned together and tacked using a contrasting thread. Tacking threads are worked horizontally, vertically and diagonally. The tacked fabric is then positioned in a hoop or quilting frame, right-side up, and all three layers are stitched together using a simple running or stab stitch (the needle is 'stabbed' into the fabric, then pulled through from the underside to complete one stitch at a time), in straight rows or decorative patterns.

Examples of hand quilting have been found in India, Europe and Persia dating back to the thirteenth century, and the practice continues today. Although time consuming compared to machine quilting, its advantages are that it is both leisurely and portable.

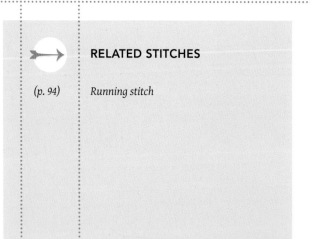

RELATED STITCHES

(p. 94)   *Running stitch*

FABRICS: Light- to medium-weight cotton or silk fabrics are generally used for hand quilting. Calico is usually chosen for the backing fabric.

THREADS: A 100 per cent cotton quilting thread is suitable for hand quilting. General-purpose sewing threads can also be used, but they are not as strong as quilting threads. A strong tacking thread is also needed.

Hand quilting and appliqué (Corey Voder): cotton and Essex linen; crochet thread

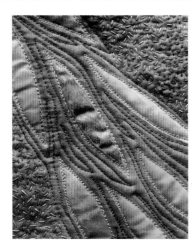

Hand quilting, machine quilting and appliqué (Fiona Dix): handpainted silk and felted merino wool; embroidery cotton

Hand quilting, machine quilting and appliqué (Fiona Dix): handpainted silk and felted merino wool; embroidery cotton

NEEDLES: You may use betweens or quilting needles suitable for the thread you are using – these have a small, round eye and so are well suited to working fine stitches in heavy fabrics.

OTHER EQUIPMENT: You will need a pair of dressmaker's scissors, a rotary cutter, a cutting mat, dressmaker's pins, tracing paper, a fabric marker pen or dressmaker's carbon paper and cotton or synthetic wadding. A hoop or quilting frame and a thimble are optional extras.

COMMON APPLICATIONS: Quilting can be used to make bedspreads, clothing, wall hangings, toys and decorative objects.

MACHINE QUILTING

Although a machine-worked quilt does not have the charm of a hand-stitched one, this is certainly a faster and less time-consuming technique. Any domestic sewing machine can be used for this method. Specialist quilting machines are available too, with features such as a better feed control and a longer extension table, but these machines do tend to be more expensive.

Machine quilting falls into two categories: machine-guided quilting (the feed dogs – see p. 232 – of the machine are raised) and free-motion quilting (the feed dogs are lowered or covered, depending on your machine).

Machine-guided quilting is worked using an open-toe embroidery foot or quilting foot. It is used for stitching straight and slightly curved lines with a short, straight stitch. Free-motion quilting uses a darning foot and can be worked freely over the surface of the fabric. It is a more expressive way of machine quilting and is used to create more freely flowing designs.

RELATED STITCHES

N/A

This technique uses machine stitching

FABRICS: Light- to medium-weight cotton or silk fabrics are generally used for machine quilting. Calico is usually chosen for the backing fabric.

THREADS: A 100 per cent cotton machine thread or a polyester blend is suitable for machine quilting. A strong tacking thread is also needed.

NEEDLES: The needle used in the machine needs to be suitable for your chosen fabric.

Machine quilting, trapunto quilting and needle-turned appliqué (Emma How – Sampaguita Quilts): quilter's cotton; Superior Threads Bottom Line (white) and Aurifil 50wt Cotton Mako

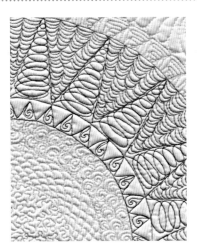

Machine quilting (Emma How – Sampaguita Quilts): quilter's cotton; Aurifil 50wt Cotton Mako

Machine quilting and patchwork (Emma How – Sampaguita Quilts): quilter's cotton; Gütermann cottons

OTHER EQUIPMENT: Apart from a sewing machine, you will need a pair of dressmaker's scissors, a rotary cutter, a cutting mat, dressmaker's pins, tracing paper, a fabric marker pen or dressmaker's carbon paper and cotton or synthetic wadding. A hoop or quilting frame is optional.

COMMON APPLICATIONS: Machine quilting is used to produce bedspreads, clothing, wall hangings and decorative objects.

SASHIKO QUILTING

Also known as: sashiko embroidery

Sashiko, meaning 'little stab' or 'stab stitch', is a form of quilting that originated in Japan in the eighteenth century. It was traditionally worked using running stitch to create patterns in white thread on an indigo blue fabric. The Japanese used this technique to hand sew layers of fabric together or to repair worn clothing, and inspiration for designs came from kimono fabrics, or directly from nature, often including clouds, bamboo, waves and flowers.

Sashiko is still used today, although it is now generally restricted to use as a decorative form of embroidery, used to embellish accessories and household items as well as quilts. It is often used in combination with patchwork and appliqué.

Sashiko (Saké Puppets): cotton and cotton canvas; sashiko thread

FABRICS: Fabric consisting of 100 per cent cotton or a cotton and linen mix can be used for sashiko quilting. Special pre-printed sashiko fabrics are also available, with designs already marked in place to follow.

THREADS: A 100 per cent cotton thread or specialist sashiko quilting threads can be used for this technique.

NEEDLES: Crewel needles can be used for sashiko quilting. Specialist sashiko needles can also be purchased. Both types have a larger eye to allow for heavier sashiko threads.

OTHER EQUIPMENT: You will need a pair of dressmaker's scissors, dressmaker's pins and a fabric marker pen or dressmaker's carbon paper for transferring designs to your fabric. You will also need wadding if making a quilt.

COMMON APPLICATIONS: Sashiko quilting can be used to make bedspreads, cushions, bags, purses, pincushions and table linen.

RELATED STITCHES

(p. 94)   *Running stitch*

TRAPUNTO QUILTING

Also known as: stuffed quilting

This form of stuffed work is similar to corded quilting (p. 62) but here the 'stuffing' is not restricted to parallel lines, so areas of padding can appear anywhere in a design. Trapunto quilting is traditionally worked by hand using two layers of fabric – usually white. The earliest examples are said to be Sicilian. This technique was often combined with corded quilting, so both methods are often referred to as 'Italian quilting'. Modern quilters generally use free machine embroidery (p. 22) to work their designs.

Designs are drawn on calico backing fabric and then stitched. A small hole is made in the calico for areas to be padded, stuffing is gently inserted, then the hole is stitched closed. The design appears in high relief on the right side.

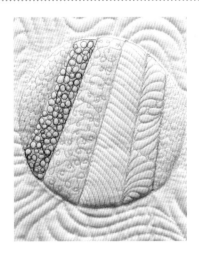

Machine quilting, trapunto quilting and needle-turned appliqué (Emma How – Sampaguita Quilts): white quilter's cotton; Superior Threads Bottom Line and Aurifil 50wt Cotton Mako

FABRICS: For trapunto work, calico can be used for the background fabric, and silk, cotton or linen for the top layer.

THREADS: A 100 per cent cotton thread or quilting thread can be used for hand-sewn quilting and a 100 per cent cotton or polyester machine thread can be used for machine-sewn versions.

NEEDLES: Hand quilting is best done using sharps or betweens. For machine quilting, the needle needs to be suitable for the type of fabric being used.

OTHER EQUIPMENT: You will need a pair of dressmaker's scissors, dressmaker's pins, a fabric marker pen, stuffing (cotton, wool or synthetic) and a sewing machine with a suitable foot.

COMMON APPLICATIONS: Trapunto quilting is used to make bedspreads, cushions, bags and purses, artwork and other decorative objects.

RELATED STITCHES

(p. 94)   *Running stitch*

CORDED QUILTING

Also known as: Italian quilting

This very old technique was once popular in Italy, hence its alternative name. It is a form of stuffed quilting similar to trapunto (p. 61) but instead of featuring flowing lines, it is created by working parallel lines of stitching, either by hand using a running or stab stitch (p. 94), or by machine.

The design is drawn on the background fabric – most often calico – the top layer of fabric is tacked to the back and then the stitching is worked through both layers. When the stitching is complete, a soft woollen cord is threaded through the double rows of stitching, with small loops left to prevent puckering. The design appears as a relief on the right side.

Boutis, a form of corded quilting, (Catherine Rosselle): cotton percale; glacé-finish cotton

FABRICS: Calico can be used for corded quilting background layers and a satin or silk fabric can be used for the top layer.

THREADS: A 100 per cent cotton thread or quilting thread can be used for hand-sewn corded quilting, and a 100 per cent cotton or polyester machine thread for machine-sewn versions. You will also need a soft woollen cord or woollen thread.

NEEDLES: Hand quilting is best done using sharps or betweens; a machine needle needs to be suitable for the type of fabric being used. You will also need a flat, blunt needle with a large eye for threading the cord.

OTHER EQUIPMENT: You will need a pair of dressmaker's scissors, dressmaker's pins, a fabric marker pen, stuffing (cotton, wool or synthetic) and a sewing machine with suitable foot.

COMMON APPLICATIONS: Corded quilting is used to produce bedspreads, cushions, bags and purses.

RELATED STITCHES

(p. 94)   *Running stitch*

TIED QUILTING

This traditional form of quilting consists of layers of fabric and wadding held together at spaced intervals with knotting rather than the usual stitching. The top layer can be pieced (made up of smaller pieces sewn together; see patchwork, p. 64) or left whole.

The top layer is marked with dots using a fabric marker pen, evenly spaced so that they are appropriate for the scale of quilt being made. All the layers are pinned together, then a 5mm (¼in) stitch is made at each of the marked dots. Each stitch can be worked individually, or stitched in rows, leaving the thread slack between each stitch. When all the stitches are complete, the threads between each are cut, leaving a long tail. Finally, the threads are tied in a double knot and trimmed.

Tied quilting and split-stitch embroidery (Saké Puppets): cotton; embroidery thread

FABRICS: Both plain and patterned cotton calico can be used for tied quilts.

THREADS: Embroidery cotton (six-stranded cotton) or wool threads can be used for working this technique, while general-purpose machine sewing threads can be used for finishing your quilt.

NEEDLES: Tied quilting is best done using a needle with a large eye, such as a crewel or chenille needle.

OTHER EQUIPMENT: You will need a pair of dressmaker's scissors, a craft knife or rotary cutter for cutting fabric, a pencil, dressmaker's pins, safety pins, a cutting mat, a ruler, a fabric marker pen, wadding and a sewing machine for finishing off.

COMMON APPLICATIONS: This technique is commonly used to make bedspreads and baby quilts.

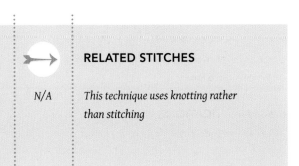

RELATED STITCHES

N/A

This technique uses knotting rather than stitching

PATCHWORK

Also known as: pieced work

Patchwork is the art of piecing together small bits of fabric in geometric patterns to form a cloth. It developed as an economical way of creating larger pieces by salvaging scraps that would otherwise be thrown away. Today's modern patchwork, however, generally uses shop-bought fabrics.

Patches can be joined together by hand or by machine. Hand piecing using a simple whip stitch gives a more traditional look, although machining is much quicker and easier, even allowing for several pairs of patches to be sewn together in one go. For easy management, patchwork is usually sewn in blocks. Each block is then sewn to subsequent blocks to form a whole design.

Patchwork is easy to learn but it takes a lot of careful planning, measuring and cutting, and paper templates must be accurate. Working over backing papers is a good way to make precise-angled shapes, particularly hexagons and triangles. These can be made from paper or thin card – a shape is cut, placed on the fabric, then cut out with an allowance around the edge, which is then folded in. The edges are stitched in place, then the papers are removed once all the pieces have been joined together.

RELATED STITCHES

N/A

This technique uses machine stitching

FABRICS: Many different fabrics can be used for patchwork, including plain and patterned cotton, calico, needlecord, organza, sateen, satin and silk.

THREADS: For machine stitching, a general-purpose cotton or rayon (viscose) machine thread can be used, while hand sewing is best done using a 100 per cent cotton thread.

Patchwork and freestyle embroidery (Amanda Cowell): various cotton fabrics and wool felt; embroidery thread

Patchwork (Mary Maulhardt Gaston – 'mary made me'): cotton; sewing threads

Patchwork (Roslyn Mirrington): linen/cotton blend fabric, quilting cottons, twill tape and piping; cotton machine thread and three strands of DMC embroidery cotton

NEEDLES: Sharps are the best needles to use if you are completing patchwork by hand; if working with a machine, the needle needs to be suitable for the type of fabric you are using.

OTHER EQUIPMENT: You will need a pair of dressmaker's scissors, a craft knife or rotary cutter for cutting fabric, a pencil, dressmaker's pins, a cutting mat, a metal ruler, tracing paper, paper or card for creating templates, a fabric marker pen and a sewing machine.

COMMON APPLICATIONS: Patchwork can be used to create all sorts of items, from cushions to wall hangings, bedspreads, clothing, decorative ornaments, toys and pincushions.

CRAZY PATCHWORK

Also known as: crazy quilting, puzzle patchwork and random patchwork

Crazy patchwork was a favourite pastime of the Victorians. It is an easy technique to learn: scraps of leftover fabrics in various textures and colours are applied to a background fabric in a random order to resemble something a bit like crazy paving.

The scraps or patches of fabric can be joined together using a sewing machine, or they can be hemmed and applied just like appliqué (p. 71) using slip stitch. To finish off, the patches can then be topstitched with decorative embroidery stitches such as herringbone, feather or chain stitch.

Crazy patchwork and ribbonwork (Annet Spitteler): cotton and linen; cotton pearl (perlé), embroidery cotton, metallic thread, silk ribbon

FABRICS: Any type of fabric can be used for crazy patchwork, including cotton, silk, velvet, organza and satin.

THREADS: For machine stitching, a general-purpose cotton or rayon (viscose) machine thread can be used, while embroidery cotton floss or silk can be used for the embroidery stitches.

RELATED STITCHES

(p. 95)   *Chain stitch*
(p. 97)   *Feather stitch*
(p. 100)   *Herringbone stitch*

NEEDLES: Your machine needle will need to be suitable for the type of fabric you are using. A crewel needle is best for working the embroidery stitches.

OTHER EQUIPMENT: You will need a pair of dressmaker's scissors, a craft knife or rotary cutter for cutting fabric, a pencil, dressmaker's pins, a cutting mat, metal ruler, tracing paper, a fabric marker pen and a sewing machine.

COMMON APPLICATIONS: Crazy patchwork works well for cushions, wall hangings, bedspreads, clothing, decorative ornaments and pincushions.

SEMINOLE PATCHWORK

This very distinctive patchwork was created in the nineteenth century by the Seminole Indians of the Everglades in Florida in the US. Seminole women used diagonal strips of leftover pieces of fabric to create jackets, skirts and other items of clothing, featuring dramatic geometric patterns. Items were first made by hand, then later by sewing machine.

The basic technique here is to sew long strips of fabric or ribbon together with a sewing machine, cut and rearrange the pieces into decorative patterns, stripes or chevrons, and then sew them back together again to form intricate designs.

Seminole patchwork dress (Kiloran Greenan): cotton; cotton threads

FABRICS: Plain cotton fabrics in bright colours can be used for Seminole patchwork.

THREADS: You should choose a general-purpose cotton machine thread that matches the colour of your fabric.

NEEDLES: The machine needle needs to be suited to the type of fabric you are using.

OTHER EQUIPMENT: You will need dressmaker's scissors, a craft knife or rotary cutter for cutting fabric, a pencil, dressmaker's pins, a cutting mat, a metal ruler, tracing paper, a fabric marker pen and a sewing machine.

COMMON APPLICATIONS: Seminole work appears on cushions, wall hangings, bedspreads, clothing and decorative ornaments.

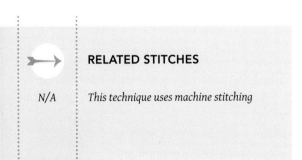

RELATED STITCHES

N/A

This technique uses machine stitching

HAND APPLIQUÉ

Also known as: applied work

Hand appliqué dates back to ancient Egyptian and Greek times, and is the method of applying fabric shapes to a background fabric using hand stitching or hand embroidery to create designs or patterns. This technique provides a means of decorating plain background fabrics with small remnants of more expensive fabrics.

Hand appliqué begins with the creation of a paper template of a design. This is then used as a cutting guide – the template is placed on the right side of the fabric, the shape is traced, then the design is cut out, leaving a 5mm (¼in) seam allowance all the way around. This seam allowance is then pressed under using an iron. (Some crafters like to press the seam allowance over the paper template.) Curved areas or corners are clipped so they lie flat.

Next, the edges of the shape are tacked using a running stitch, then the shape is applied to the background fabric using a slip stitch or a blanket stitch. Appliquéd pieces can then be further embellished with hand embroidery stitches.

RELATED STITCHES

(p. 98)	*Basic couching*
(p. 100)	*Blanket stitch*
(p. 99)	*Buttonhole stitch*
(p. 97)	*Feather stitch*
(p. 100)	*Herringbone stitch*
(p. 94)	*Running stitch*

FABRICS: A range of different fabrics can be used for appliqué, including plain and patterned cotton, calico, needlecord, gingham, organza, taffeta, felt, wool, sateen, satin and silk.

THREADS: For hand appliqué, a 100 per cent cotton thread that closely matches the colour of the fabric you are appliquéing can be used. Alternatively, embroidery thread can be used in a contrasting colour.

NEEDLES: A sharps needle is suitable for hand appliqué, while a crewel needle is best for working any hand embroidery stitches.

Hand appliqué (Alyssa Thomas): linen; DMC embroidery cotton

Hand appliqué and raw-edge appliqué (Carina Envoldsen-Harris): cotton fabric and Polyfil; DMC embroidery cotton

Hand appliqué and patchwork (Sara Adnum): pure cotton; embroidery thread

OTHER EQUIPMENT: You will need a pair of dressmaker's scissors, a craft knife or rotary cutter for cutting fabric, a pencil, dressmaker's pins, a cutting mat, a metal ruler, tracing paper, freezer paper for creating templates and a fabric marker pen.

COMMON APPLICATIONS: Appliqué can be used to decorate cushions, wall hangings, bedspreads, clothing, decorative ornaments and pincushions.

RAW-EDGE APPLIQUÉ

Also known as: raw-edged appliqué

As the name suggests, this is the method of applying fabric shapes with unfinished edges to a background fabric. A firm, closely woven fabric is usually used to limit fraying, but one of the nice features of this type of appliqué is that the edges of the fabric will softly fray when washed.

Shapes are traced onto your appliqué fabric or cut freehand, and then either pinned or bonded to the background fabric. Hand embroidery stitches or a sewing machine with an appliqué foot can used to secure these shapes to the background using a straight or zig-zag stitch. Free machine embroidery (p. 22) can also be used to 'draw' over the top of the fabric shapes to hold them in place.

Raw-edge appliqué and backstitch (Kajsa Wikman): cotton; sewing threads

FABRICS: Closely woven plain or patterned cotton fabrics can be used for raw-edge appliqué. Felt can also be used as it will not fray and needs little sewing.

THREADS: General-purpose machine threads or machine embroidery threads – cotton, silk or rayon (viscose) – can be used for this type of appliqué.

RELATED STITCHES

(p. 100)	*Blanket stitch*
(p. 99)	*Buttonhole stitch*
(p. 97)	*Feather stitch*

NEEDLES: You will need a machine needle suitable for the type of fabric you are stitching on.

OTHER EQUIPMENT: You will need a pair of dressmaker's scissors for cutting fabric, a pencil for drawing your design, a pair of small embroidery scissors, dressmaker's pins, tracing paper, fusible bonding web, an iron, a sewing machine with an appliqué foot and a fabric marker pen.

COMMON APPLICATIONS: Raw-edge appliqué is suited to cushions, wall hangings, bedspreads, tablecloths, clothing and decorative ornaments.

NEEDLE-TURNED APPLIQUÉ

Also known as: needle-turn appliqué

This traditional technique is used to apply fabric shapes to a background fabric using hand stitching. Shapes are traced onto fabric and cut out, leaving at least a 2.5mm ($^1/_8$in) seam allowance around the edge. Curved areas are clipped so that they will lie flat, and the fabric shapes are pinned to the background fabric. The seam allowance is then turned under using the tip of the needle as you sew.

The main stitch used for this type of appliqué is a slip stitch, which is an almost invisible stitch that 'disappears' into the fabric background.

Needle-turned appliqué (Claudia Dominguez): cotton and linen; embroidery thread

FABRICS: Plain or patterned cotton fabrics can be used for needle-turned appliqué.

THREADS: This type of appliqué requires a fine cotton sewing thread in the same colour as your appliqué shapes.

NEEDLES: Sharps are used for hand sewing appliqué; they are long and sharp, and available in various sizes. Choose a suitable needle size for the fabric and thread you are using.

OTHER EQUIPMENT: You will need an embroidery hoop or frame, a pair of dressmaker's scissors for cutting fabric, a pencil for drawing your design, a pair of small embroidery scissors, dressmaker's pins, tracing paper and a fabric marker pen.

COMMON APPLICATIONS: Needle-turned appliqué can be seen on anything from cushions to wall hangings, bedspreads, tablecloths, clothing and decorative ornaments.

RELATED STITCHES

N/A   *Slip stitch*

SHADOW APPLIQUÉ

Also known as: shadow quilting

Shadow appliqué is similar to shadow embroidery (p. 26) but instead of stitches creating a shadow effect, appliqué shapes are sandwiched between layers of transparent fabric to create a muted effect. The fabric shapes can be plain or patterned cotton.

Using the fused appliqué method (p. 77), appliqué shapes are first bonded to the bottom layer of transparent fabric. Another layer of transparent fabric is laid over the top of the previous layer. The layers are tacked together using a running stitch around the edges, and hand embroidery stitches or a machine zig-zag stitch are then worked around the edges of the appliquéd shapes.

Shadow appliqué (Diem Chau): organza and porcelain plate; polyester thread

FABRICS: Organza, crystal organza and silk organdie are generally used for the transparent layers and plain or patterned cotton fabrics are used for the appliqué shapes.

THREADS: Embroidery cotton (six-stranded cotton) or silk can be used for shadow appliqué.

NEEDLES: Sharps are used for hand sewing appliqué and crewel needles are used for hand embroidery. Both of these are available in various sizes. Choose a suitable needle size for the fabric and thread you are using.

OTHER EQUIPMENT: You will also need an embroidery hoop, a pair of dressmaker's scissors for cutting fabric, a pencil for drawing your design, a pair of small embroidery scissors, dressmaker's pins, tracing paper, fusible web, a fabric marker pen and a sewing machine.

COMMON APPLICATIONS: Shadow appliqué is suitable for cushions, wall hangings, bedspreads, tablecloths, clothing and decorative ornaments.

→ RELATED STITCHES

(p. 100)	*Blanket stitch*
(p. 99)	*Buttonhole stitch*
(p. 95)	*Chain stitch*
(p. 94)	*Running stitch*
(p. 95)	*Split stitch*
(p. 98)	*Stem stitch*

HAWAIIAN APPLIQUÉ

Also known as: Hawaiian quilting

This decorative form of appliqué was introduced to the Hawaiian islands by American missionary women in the nineteenth century. Hawaiian appliqué is worked using silhouetted designs in flat colours, which are cut in a similar way to paper snowflakes. The designs are worked from the centre outwards to cover an entire piece.

Designs were traditionally worked in two plain colours, using techniques similar to all quiltmaking; however, modern Hawaiian quilts incorporate batik fabrics, which give them a dramatic effect.

Hawaiian appliqué (Tanya Grin): cotton; quilting thread

FABRICS: Hawaiian appliqué is usually produced using plain cotton fabrics.

THREADS: A quilting thread is suitable for this type of appliqué.

NEEDLES: Sharps are used for hand sewing appliqué and betweens are used for quilting.

OTHER EQUIPMENT: You will also need an embroidery hoop, a pair of dressmaker's scissors for cutting fabric, a pencil for drawing your design, a pair of small embroidery scissors, dressmaker's pins, tracing paper, a fabric marker pen and wadding.

COMMON APPLICATIONS: Hawaiian appliqué is often seen on cushions, wall hangings and bedspreads.

RELATED STITCHES

(p. 100)   *Blanket stitch*
(p. 99)   *Buttonhole stitch*

MACHINE APPLIQUÉ

Like hand appliqué, machine appliqué is the method of applying fabric shapes to a background fabric to form a design or pattern. Machine appliqué, however, is an especially fast and fun method of creating a design. All you need for this is a sewing machine that has a zig-zag stitch, some fusible web (with a special paper backing for drawing on) and some fabric.

Designs for machine appliqué are traced onto the fusible web, cut out and then ironed onto the appliqué fabric. The design is then carefully cut out. Once this has been done, the paper backing can be peeled off the fusible web and the appliqué design ironed onto the background fabric.

Using a sewing machine set to straight stitch or zig-zag, the design is then stitched around the edges. Free-motion stitching can also be used for this – simply lower the feed dogs (p. 22) so you are free to feed the fabric through the machine manually.

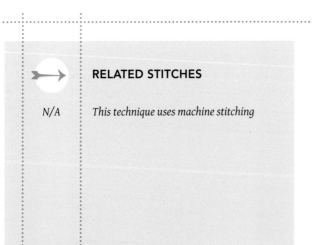

RELATED STITCHES

N/A   *This technique uses machine stitching*

FABRICS: Fabrics used for machine appliqué should be light- to medium-weight and closely woven. Many different types can be used, including plain and patterned cotton, calico, needlecord, gingham, organza, taffeta, felt, wool, sateen, satin and silk.

THREADS: For machine appliqué, a general-purpose 100 per cent cotton thread in the same or a contrasting colour can be used. Machine embroidery threads can also be used.

Free-motion machine appliqué, raw-edge appliqué and backstitch (Kajsa Wikman): cotton; sewing threads

Free-motion machine appliqué, raw-edge appliqué and cross-stitch (Kajsa Wikman): linen and cotton; sewing threads

Machine appliqué and fabric fusing (Janet Reddick): cotton; Coats & Clark thread

NEEDLES: Your machine needle needs to be suitable for the fabric you are using.

OTHER EQUIPMENT: You will need a pair of dressmaker's scissors, a pair of small, sharp scissors, a craft knife or rotary cutter for cutting fabric, a pencil, a cutting mat, fusible bonding web (such as Bondaweb), an iron and a sewing machine with an appliqué foot.

COMMON APPLICATIONS: Machine appliqué can be used to decorate cushions, wall hangings, bedspreads, clothing, table linen, pincushions and decorative ornaments.

STAINED-GLASS APPLIQUÉ

This form of appliqué consists of thin strips of black fabric or bias binding surrounding fabric shapes, creating the effect of leading and coloured glass in a stained-glass window. The 'glass' fabric shapes of your design can be appliquéd to your background fabric either by hand or machine, or by using the fused appliqué method (p. 77). The black or dark fabric strips are then appliquéd on top.

Bold, simple designs work best for this technique. Take inspiration for your designs from actual stained-glass windows, or simply refer to design books on the subject.

Paper-pieced stained-glass appliqué (Becky Meece): cottons; sewing threads

FABRICS: Many different plain or patterned fabrics can be used for creating stained-glass appliqué, such as cotton calico, silk, satin and polyester/rayon (viscose).

THREADS: For hand-sewn appliqué a 100 per cent cotton sewing thread is best, while machine sewing can be done using a 100 per cent cotton thread or a polyester mix.

RELATED STITCHES

(p. 100)   *Blanket stitch*
(p. 99)   *Buttonhole stitch*

NEEDLES: Sharps needles are used for general sewing and are available in various sizes, so they are the best choice for stained-glass appliqué.

OTHER EQUIPMENT: You will also need dressmaker's scissors for cutting fabric, a pencil for drawing your design, a pair of small, sharp scissors, a rotary cutter or craft knife for cutting out your appliqué shapes, a cutting mat and fusible bonding web (such as Bondaweb), a sewing machine, dressmaker's pins and tracing paper.

COMMON APPLICATIONS: Stained-glass appliqué is most often used on cushions, decorative ornaments and bedspreads.

FUSED APPLIQUÉ

This quick and easy form of appliqué involves bonding fabric shapes onto the surface of another fabric using paper-backed fusible web. The shape is drawn onto the paper side and then ironed onto your appliqué fabric. Once the shape has been cut out, the paper backing is peeled off the fusible web and the shape is then ironed onto the main fabric.

The raw edges can then be covered using a machine zig-zag stitch, or they can be finished off with hand embroidery stitches, including buttonhole stitch, blanket stitch, feather stitch or couching.

Fused appliqué, raw-edge appliqué and free-motion machine appliqué (Kajsa Wikman): linen and cotton; sewing threads

FABRICS: Many different plain or patterned fabrics can be used for creating fused appliqué, such as cotton calico, silk, satin, polyester/rayon (viscose), wool, felt and linen.

THREADS: Both cotton and silk embroidery thread can be used for this work.

NEEDLES: This sort of appliqué is best done using a crewel needle.

OTHER EQUIPMENT: You will also need a pair of dressmaker's scissors for cutting fabric, a pencil for drawing your design, a pair of small, sharp scissors, a rotary cutter or craft knife for cutting out your appliqué shapes, a cutting mat, fusible bonding web (such as Bondaweb) and an iron.

COMMON APPLICATIONS: Fused appliqué can be used on cushions, decorative ornaments, tablecloths, bedspreads and clothing.

RELATED STITCHES

(p. 98)	Basic couching
(p. 100)	Blanket stitch
(p. 99)	Buttonhole stitch
(p. 95)	Chain stitch
(p. 97)	Feather stitch
(p. 100)	Herringbone stitch

CHAPTER 3: QUILTING, PATCHWORK AND APPLIQUÉ

77

REVERSE APPLIQUÉ

To create reverse appliqué, two or more layers of fabric are laid on top of one another and then the layers are cut away in designs or patterns to reveal the fabric below. The raw edges are then either covered with buttonhole stitches or turned and hemmed. You can work reverse appliqué by hand or machine.

This type of appliqué is said to have originated in Inuit and Aleut cultures. Examples of reverse appliqué can also be seen on early eighteenth-century American quilts.

Reverse appliqué (Mary Gaston): wool felt; sewing thread

FABRICS: Any plain or patterned fabric can be used for creating reverse appliqué, such as 100 per cent cotton calico, silk, satin, polyester/rayon (viscose), wool, felt and linen.

THREADS: For hand-sewn appliqué, a 100 per cent cotton sewing thread should be used. For machine sewing, use a 100 per cent cotton thread or a polyester mix.

NEEDLES: Sharps needles are used for general sewing and are available in various sizes – these are the best choice for reverse appliqué.

OTHER EQUIPMENT: You will also need a pair of dressmaker's scissors for cutting fabric, a vanishing fabric marker for drawing your design and a pair of small embroidery scissors.

COMMON APPLICATIONS: Reverse appliqué works well on cushions, decorative ornaments, tablecloths, bedspreads and clothing.

RELATED STITCHES

(p. 99) *Buttonhole stitch*

SUFFOLK PUFFS

Also known as: yo-yos

Suffolk puffs, or yo-yos, as they are commonly called, are created from circles of fabric gathered at the edges with running stitch. The gathering pulls the fabric into the centre of the circle, forming a 'puff'.

Suffolk puffs can be used as simple decorations, sewn together to form a continuous fabric using quilting and patchwork techniques or appliquéd to the surface of a fabric. They are easy and fast to make, in various sizes, colours and fabrics. A Suffolk puff can be further decorated by adding a button or bead to the centre.

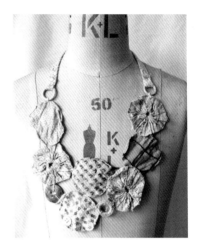

Suffolk puffs (Viv Sliwka): vintage American Suffolk puffs

FABRICS: Any plain or patterned fabric can be used to make puffs, including soft 100 per cent cotton, silk, satin, polyester/rayon (viscose), voile and organza.

THREADS: A strong general-purpose sewing thread used double is needed to stand up to the process of gathering the puffs.

RELATED STITCHES

(p. 94)   *Running stitch*

NEEDLES: Sharps needles are used for general sewing and are available in various sizes – these are the best choice for making Suffolk puffs.

OTHER EQUIPMENT: You will also need a pair of dressmaker's scissors for cutting fabric, paper to create a template and a round object in different sizes to trace around, such as a cup or round biscuit cutter.

COMMON APPLICATIONS: Suffolk puffs can be used on cushions, decorative objects, tablecloths, bedspreads and even jewellery.

4: OTHER TECHNIQUES

This chapter contains a number of specialist needlecraft techniques that cannot be categorized into any specific section. They are nevertheless all fascinating techniques, which take skill and patience to learn.

Needle lace and tatting are old techniques that use loops and knots of thread to construct free-form pieces, which resemble lace.

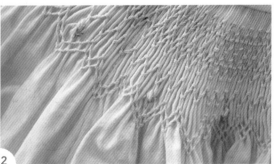

Smocking is the art of gathering large widths of fabric into folds and pleats and decorating them with hand embroidery stitches. This beautiful technique works well with softly draping fabrics.

Needle felting and punch needle are similar techniques. Both take threads and fibres and merge them into the background of another fabric, creating painterly effects.

1 Brazilian embroidery and stumpwork needle lace (Loretta Holzberger): linen/rayon linen-look fabric; EdMar rayon embroidery threads

2 Smocking (Marie Grace Smith): cotton; sewing threads

3 Free machine lace embroidery (Susie Cowie): water-soluble base; rayon thread

4 Needle felting and embroidery (Catherine Parsons): wool felt and merino wool; embroidery thread and silk ribbons

4

NEEDLE LACE

Also known as: needle-made lace

Needle lace was developed in Italy in the seventeenth century. Unlike traditional lace, which is made with bobbins, needle lace is made with a needle and thread.

The design is first drawn on stiff paper or card, which is then attached to fabric. The outline of the design is then couched with thread. This is the foundation on which a series of buttonhole stitches are worked to fill in the design. Once the design is complete, the foundation stitches are released and the lace can be removed.

Needle lace, mixed fabric work, hand appliqué, hand crochet and machine embroidery (Firuzan Göker): vintage and new silk; silk ribbon, silk machine thread, cotton crochet thread, white fibre thread and silk embroidery thread

FABRICS: Needle lace uses a firm, medium-weight cotton fabric for the foundation fabric.

THREADS: Cordonnet crochet cotton, quilting cotton and tatting cotton can be used for the foundation and the filling stitches, while a general-purpose 100 per cent cotton sewing thread can be used for the tying thread.

NEEDLES: Sharps can be used for couching, while a blunt tapestry needle is best for working buttonhole stitches.

OTHER EQUIPMENT: You will also need a pair of small, sharp embroidery scissors, thick paper or card and paper scissors. A thimble and a pillow for working hands free are both optional.

COMMON APPLICATIONS: Needle lace is used to create free-form decorative ornaments, artwork, jewellery and other three-dimensional objects.

RELATED STITCHES

(p. 98) *Basic couching*
(p. 99) *Buttonhole stitch*

PUNCH NEEDLE

Also known as: punch, punch work and Russian embroidery

This three-dimensional form of embroidery, which uses a special tool called a punch needle, is said to have originated in Russia. It is used to create bold designs and pictures that resemble painted pictures.

The punch tool, which is pointed and hollow with an eye, is threaded with embroidery thread, silk ribbon, or any thread that will thread through it. The design is traced on the back of the fabric and filled in by pushing the tool – held perpendicular to the fabric – through the back of the fabric, creating a tufted loop of thread on the surface. A simple running stitch is used but this is only visible on the back of the fabric.

Punch needle (Erin Flanagan Lind): weaver's cloth and reeded raw silk (for backing); DMC thread, DMC metallic thread and Gentle Art hand-dyed thread

FABRICS: Weaver's cloth, which is a cotton and polyester mix, is usually used for punch needle ombroidery.

THREADS: Both embroidery thread and silk ribbon cotton pearl (perlé) can be used for this sort of work.

NEEDLES: Punch needles are available in different sizes. The most common sizes are small (takes one strand of embroidery thread), medium (takes two or three strands), and large (takes all six strands). There are also special punch needles available for silk ribbon and for creating rugs.

OTHER EQUIPMENT: You will need an embroidery hoop or stretching frame, a pair of small, sharp embroidery scissors, a punch needle threader, a fabric marker pen (vanishing or water-soluble), dressmaker's carbon paper for transferring designs, tracing paper and a spooler/yarn holder.

COMMON APPLICATIONS: Punch needle work can be applied to decorative ornaments, pincushions, cushions, rugs, brooches and pictures.

→ **RELATED STITCHES**

(p. 94)   *Running stitch*

SMOCKING

Smocking is an ancient technique that dates back to the Saxons. It is a decorative method of gathering a large width of fabric into narrow folds or pleats. In England, the smock was a loose-fitting garment worn by agricultural workers in rural areas. The yoke of this garment was gathered, with the bottom half being left free and loose to allow for movement. The same gathering technique is still used for clothing today, particularly for children.

Smocking is created by first marking the reverse of the fabric with rows of dots in a grid pattern. Commercial transfer patterns are available, or a fabric marker pen and a ruler can be used. The fabric is then gathered into 'tubes' using a gathering stitch. (For a full explanation of how to prepare fabrics for smocking, see p. 228.) Decorative embroidery stitches are then added to the finished fabric, such as honeycomb stitch and surface honeycomb stitch. Once the decorative stitches are completed, the gathering stitches are removed.

RELATED STITCHES

(p. 220) *Honeycomb stitch*
(p. 221) *Surface honeycomb stitch*

FABRICS: Light- and medium-weight plain and patterned cotton fabrics can be used for smocking. This technique works best on soft fabrics that drape well.

THREADS: You should use cotton embroidery threads for the decorative embroidery stitches and a 100 per cent cotton general-purpose sewing thread or tacking thread for the gathering stitches.

Smocking (Marie Grace Smith): cotton;
sewing threads

Smocking (Susan Bischoff): vintage kimono
fabric; single strand DMC embroidery cotton

NEEDLES: A sharps needle can be used for the gathering stitches and a crewel needle for the decorative embroidery stitches.

OTHER EQUIPMENT: You will also need a pair of small, sharp embroidery scissors, dressmaker's scissors, a fabric marker pen, a metal ruler and a commercial smocking transfer (if using).

COMMON APPLICATIONS: Modern smocking is often featured on cushions, bags, scarves and jewellery, as well as on baby garments and little girls' dresses.

TATTING

Tatting is thought to have developed around 200 years ago, from rope work created by sailors. Tatting is a form of lace constructed out of a series of knots and loops. The knots and loops are formed into circles and semi-circles; these were traditionally made into lace edgings, doilies and collars. Tatting is very similar to macramé, which is also created by knotting thread. Tatting is currently experiencing a revival with modern crafters, who are using it to create wonderful jewellery and free-form decorative objects.

There are three forms of tatting. The first is worked with a tatting needle. The second kind is 'cro-tatting', which is a combination of needle tatting and crochet. The third, and traditional, method uses a thread and shuttle.

N/A	**RELATED STITCHES**
	This technique uses knots and loops rather than stitches

THREADS: Tatting threads come in a variety of thicknesses and colours, and are usually made of cotton, rayon (viscose) or polyester.

NEEDLES: Specialist tatting needles in a range of different sizes are available for needle tatting. Tatting shuttles are 5–7cm (2–3in) long and come in metal and a variety of other materials.

: *Tatting (Anne Bruvold): Gestal Maxi thread*

: *Tatting (Anne Bruvold): Gestal Maxi thread*

OTHER EQUIPMENT: You will also need tatting snips, cutters, a shuttle winder, a crochet hook and spare bobbins to create your work.

COMMON APPLICATIONS: Tatting can be used to make necklaces, earrings, bracelets, rings, decorations and cushions.

NEEDLE FELTING

This dry felting method is a popular needlecraft technique, and is a very fun and easy alternative to wet felting. Needle felting uses barbed felting needles to bind wool fibres together to form three-dimensional objects and two-dimensional pictures. Needle felting can be worked with one felting needle or several felting needles grouped together in a special hand-held tool. Three-dimensional objects can be formed over polystyrene forms.

Two-dimensional needle felting is created by felting wool fibres on a wool felt background fabric. It can be worked by hand using felting needles or by machine using an embellisher. An embellisher is similar to a sewing machine but it does not have any thread. Instead, it has a number of special needles that needle-felt wool or any other fabric to a background fabric. This provides a faster, if somewhat less traditional, method of working.

N/A

RELATED STITCHES

This technique binds fibres rather than using stitches

FABRICS: Wool fabrics are used for the background of two-dimensional needle-felted pictures.

THREADS: Merino wool roving for needle felting is available in many different colours. Wool yarn and cut-out felt shapes can also be needle-felted.

NEEDLES: Specialist needle-felting needles come in different gauges, one of the most popular sizes being a 38 gauge.

Needle felting (Katrina Herron): roving fibre and found acorn tops

Needle felting and embroidery (Catherine Parsons): wool felt and merino wool; embroidery thread and silk ribbon

Needle felting (Daria lvovsky): organic wool wadding and silk

OTHER EQUIPMENT: You will also need a needle-felting brush/mat or piece of foam, and a needle-felting tool, which can hold three or more needles.

COMMON APPLICATIONS: Needle felting is generally used to create three-dimensional decorative objects, hot water bottles, cushions, bags and purses and two-dimensional pictures.

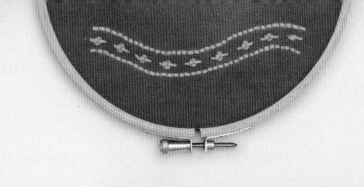

Stitch Directory

CHAPTER 5
Basic stitches 92

Running stitch	94
Backstitch	94
Split stitch	95
Chain stitch	95
Lazy daisy stitch	96
Feather stitch	97
Stem stitch	98
Basic couching	98
Holbein stitch	99
Buttonhole stitch	99
Blanket stitch	100
Herringbone stitch	100
Fly stitch	101
Coral stitch	101
Cretan stitch	102
Chevron stitch	103

CHAPTER 6
Line stitches 104

Scroll stitch	106
Open Cretan stitch	106
Thorn stitch	107
Double knot stitch	107
Basque stitch	108
Pekinese stitch	108
Single feather stitch	109
Closed feather stitch	109
Double feather stitch	110
Reversed fly stitch	111
Closed fly stitch	112
Double fly stitch	113
Loop stitch	114
Ladder stitch	115
Plaited braid stitch	116
Sorbello stitch	117

CHAPTER 7
Crossed stitches 118

Single cross-stitch	120
Half cross-stitch	120
Three-quarter cross-stitch	121
Tied cross-stitch	121
Double cross-stitch	122
Marking cross-stitch	123
Long-armed cross-stitch	124
Upright cross-stitch	124
Star stitch	125
Ermine stitch	125
Tied herringbone stitch	126
Laced herringbone stitch	126
Threaded herringbone stitch	127
Double herringbone stitch	127
Closed herringbone stitch	128
Herringbone ladder stitch	129
Interlaced herringbone stitch	130
Raised herringbone stitch	131

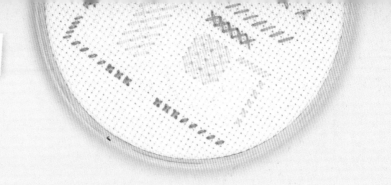

CHAPTER 8
Isolated stitches 132

French knot	134
Bullion knot	134
Chinese knot	135
Four-legged knot	135
Colonial knot	136
Square boss stitch	136
Detached wheatear stitch	137
Tête-de-boeuf stitch	137
Cup stitch	138
God's eye stitch	139
Woven picot	140
Woven circles	141

CHAPTER 9
Straight stitches 142

Whipped running stitch	144
Laced running stitch	144
Interlaced running stitch	145
Seed stitch	145
Straight stitch	146
Arrowhead stitch	146
Fern stitch	147
Leaf stitch	147
Vandyke stitch	148
Basket stitch (1)	149
Zig-zag stitch	150
Darning stitch	151
Satin stitch	151
Japanese darning	152
Padded satin stitch	153
Encroaching satin stitch	153
Long and short stitch	154
Brick stitch (1)	154
Plate stitch	155
Whipped satin stitch	155

CHAPTER 10
Buttonhole stitches 156

Tailor's buttonhole stitch	158
Buttonhole with picot	158
Single buttonhole bar	159
Double buttonhole bar	159
Up and down buttonhole stitch	160
Buttonhole wheels	161
Buttonhole flowers	161
Buttonhole filling stitch	162
Double blanket stitch	163
Overlapping blanket stitch	163
Crossed blanket stitch	164
Long and short blanket stitch	164
Closed blanket stitch	165
Knotted blanket stitch	165
Antwerp edging stitch	166
Ceylon stitch	167

CHAPTER 11
Chain stitches 168

Cable chain stitch	170
Feathered chain stitch	171
Broad chain stitch	172
Double chain stitch	173
Open chain stitch	174
Zig-zag chain stitch	174
Twisted chain stitch	175
Magic chain stitch	175
Rosette chain stitch	176
Raised chain stitch	177
Crested chain stitch	178
Heavy chain stitch	179

CHAPTER 12
Pulled and drawn stitches 180

Cobbler stitch	182
Pin stitch	183
Punch stitch	184
Ringed backstitch	185
Pulled honeycomb stitch	185
Coil stitch	186
Algerian stitch	186
Single faggot stitch	187
Three-sided stitch	187
Four-sided stitch	188
Wave filling stitch	188
Hemstitch	189
Serpentine stitch	190
Ladder hemstitch	190
Overcast bars	191
Woven bars	191

CHAPTER 13
Canvaswork stitches 192

Tent stitch	194
Cashmere stitch	195
Milanese stitch	196
Brighton stitch	197
Scotch stitch	198
Condensed Scotch stitch	199
Chequer stitch	199
Moorish stitch	200
Algerian eye stitch	201
Leviathan stitch	201
Rhodes stitch	202
Hungarian diamond stitch	202
Cushion stitch	203
Mosaic stitch	203
Slanted gobelin stitch	204
Gobelin filling stitch	204
Upright gobelin stitch	205
Pineapple stitch	205
Byzantine stitch	206
Jacquard stitch	207
Parisian stitch	207
Florentine stitch	208
Brick stitch (2)	209
Greek stitch	209

CHAPTER 14
Other stitches 210

Bokhara couching	212
Romanian couching	213
Trailing couching	214
Pendant couching	214
Puffy couching	215
Basket stitch (2)	215
Couched circles	216
Square laid filling	217
Battlement filling	218
Couched filling stitch	219
Honeycomb stitch	220
Surface honeycomb stitch	221
Eyelet wheels	222
Turkey work	223
Needleweaving	224
Kloster block	225
Shisha stitch	226

5: BASIC STITCHES

There are hundreds of embroidery stitches to go along with the different embroidery styles and techniques. If you are new to surface embroidery, this can be very daunting and you may wonder what stitches to use, how to use them and where. Just as a painter has a basic colour palette, an embroiderer has a set of basic stitches that he or she can use to create the simplest of embroideries or the most complex of artworks.

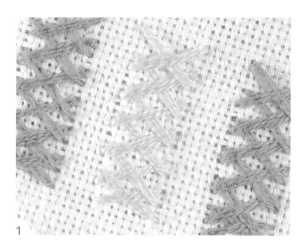

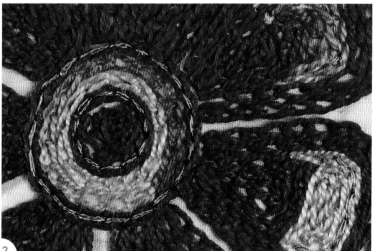

1 *Herringbone stitch (p. 100)*

2 *Chain stitch (p. 95)*

For example, the humble backstitch can be used to create an outlined design just as complex as a sophisticated line drawing, while a herringbone stitch worked on its own or decorated with other threads can produce a striking, colourful border for a skirt or tablecloth.

A common misconception is that surface embroidery is expensive. This is not the case! An array of beautiful, vivid designs can be worked with just a couple of skeins of thread and some plain cotton calico. Practise the 16 basic stitches on the following pages to begin your journey!

3

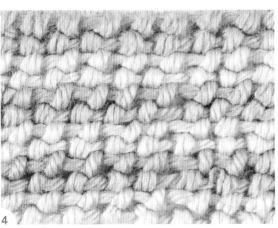

4

FABRICS: Any type of plain- or even-weave fabric can be used to work the basic stitches in this chapter. For practising, I recommend using a plain cotton calico as it is inexpensive and a good cloth to work your stitch samplers. It is readily available and provides a firm base fabric that can then be dyed or hand-painted. You can also experiment with these stitches on a variety of other surfaces, including paper, plastic, wood and even metal (create holes first, and work your stitches through these).

THREADS: There are many types and makes of embroidery cotton, or six-stranded cotton as it is also known. This is cheap and readily available, but do experiment with other threads such as tapestry wools, cotton pearl (perlé) – a single thread with a sheen – metallic threads or silk to see what kinds of textures you can create.

NEEDLES: Crewel needles are the most popular choice for the majority of surface embroidery techniques, though if you are using an even-weave fabric such as Aida cloth, a blunt-ended tapestry needle would be more appropriate as it does not split the threads of the fabric.

OTHER EQUIPMENT: Depending on the type of fabric you are stitching, an embroidery hoop may help to keep your fabric taut and your stitches even. You will also need a small pair of sharp embroidery scissors. For marking guidelines on your fabric, you will need a fabric marker pen; these are usually water-soluble or fading (within 48 hours).

3 *Stem stitch (p. 98)*

4 *Coral stitch (p. 101)*

RUNNING STITCH

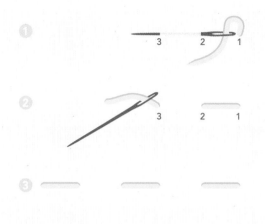

BACKSTITCH
Also known as: point de sable

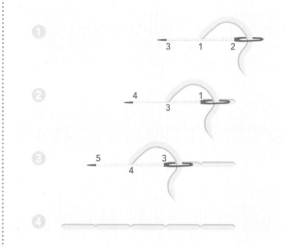

METHOD AND USES

This is the simplest and most basic of stitches and can be used on its own or as a foundation for other stitches. It is also frequently used in general sewing as a tacking stitch. Stitches are worked by passing the needle in and out of the fabric and should all be of an equal length.

Bring your needle up at 1, down at 2 and up at 3, then repeat this along your line. You can decorate basic running stitch by interlacing, lacing or whipping another thread through it.

FABRIC

Plain- or even-weave fabrics

Related techniques:
Quilting (p. 54), smocking (p. 84), freestyle embroidery (p. 12)

Similar stitches:
Interlaced running stitch (p. 145), laced running stitch (p. 144), whipped running stitch (p. 144)

METHOD AND USES

The simple backstitch is one of the most versatile stitches of all: it can be used as an outline stitch, as a foundation for other embroidery stitches such as Pekinese stitch and for ordinary sewing. Worked on its own using straight, even stitches, backstitch resembles a machine-worked stitch.

Bring the needle up at 1, down at 2, then up at 3. To start the next stitch, insert the needle at 1 again, then emerge at 4. Insert the needle at 3, then emerge at 5. Repeat along the line, keeping the length of each stitch as consistent as possible.

FABRIC

Plain- or even-weave fabrics; canvas

Related techniques:
Assisi (p. 46), blackwork (p. 40), cross-stitch (p. 42) freestyle embroidery (p. 12), crewelwork (p. 18)

Similar stitches:
Holbein stitch (p. 99), Pekinese stitch (p. 108)

SPLIT STITCH
Also known as: Kensington outline stitch

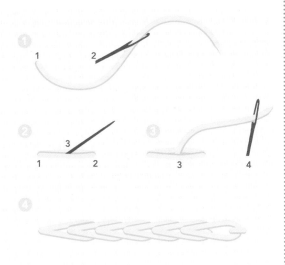

CHAIN STITCH
Also known as: point de chaînette and tambour stitch

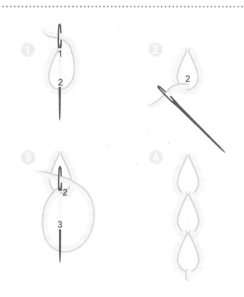

METHOD AND USES

Split stitch is used in most types of embroidery. It resembles chain stitch, and is great for straight and curved lines – especially outlines. When worked side by side in rows it also makes a smooth filling. You will need to use a thread that will split easily.

Working left to right, bring your needle up at 1, insert it again to the right of this at 2, then pull through firmly. Next, bring your needle up through the middle of the stitched thread at 3 and insert it again at 4. Repeat along your row or outline as required.

FABRIC

Plain- or even-weave fabrics

METHOD AND USES

This is one of the oldest embroidery stitches. It is useful for both straight and curved lines, and as a solid filling.

Working top to bottom, begin by bringing your needle up at 1, pulling the thread through. Reinsert your needle at 1 again, allow the tip to emerge at 2, then loop the thread under your needle, as shown. Pull the thread through the loop, but do not pull too tightly. Insert your needle at 2 again, start to emerge at 3, then loop your thread under the needle as before.
Pull through again, then repeat down your line.

FABRIC

Plain- or even-weave fabrics

Tip
Jazz up your chain stitch by decorating it with backstitch or whip stitch; this works especially well with gold metallic thread.

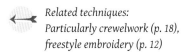
Related techniques:
Particularly crewelwork (p. 18),
freestyle embroidery (p. 12)

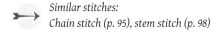
Similar stitches:
Chain stitch (p. 95), stem stitch (p. 98)

Related techniques:
Particularly crewelwork (p. 18),
freestyle embroidery (p. 12)

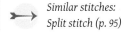
Similar stitches:
Split stitch (p. 95)

LAZY DAISY STITCH

Also known as: daisy stitch, detached chain stitch and single chain stitch

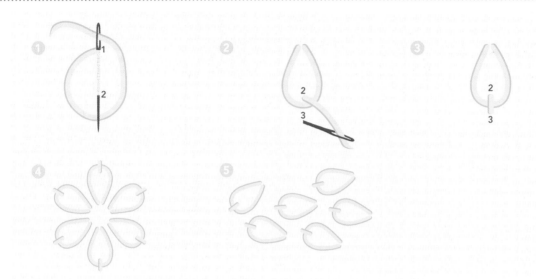

METHOD AND USES

This easy and versatile stitch is comprised of a single chain stitch. It is used singly to represent small leaves and buds. It is also often worked in circles to create flowers, which is the explanation for its name. Lazy daisy stitch can also be worked on its own as a filling stitch – stitches can be either grouped close together or scattered to fill an area.

Start by bringing your needle up at 1, then reinsert it at the same place, looping the thread round, as shown. Next, bring your needle up at 2, keeping the thread beneath the needle, then pull it through. To finish, take your needle down at 3, just below 2, making a small, straight stitch to hold the loop in place.

Step 4 above illustrates lazy daisy stitch arranged neatly in a circle to form a flower, while step 5 shows the same stitch scattered randomly as a filling.

FABRIC

Plain- or even-weave fabrics

Related techniques:
Freestyle embroidery (p. 12)

Similar stitches:
Chain stitch (p. 95)

FEATHER STITCH
Also known as: briar stitch and single coral stitch

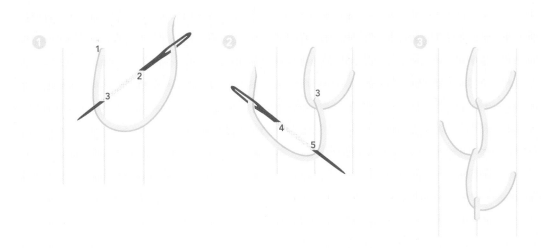

METHOD AND USES

Feather stitch is a decorative line stitch used for borders and straight or curved lines. It makes a lovely feathery line, which, once mastered, is quick to work. Have a go in different thread thicknesses or maybe layer rows over each other to create dense foliage or coral effects. You could also add other stitches, such as French knots (p. 134), to create a rambling rose effect.

You may find it easier to mark three lines as a guide. Begin at the top and work downwards. First, bring your needle up at 1, then down at 2 and up at 3, with your thread tucked beneath the needle, as shown.

Try to keep the distance between 1 and 2 equal to that between 2 and 3. Pull the needle through. Next, take your needle down at 4, then emerge at 5, again with the thread beneath the needle. Pull through.

Continue to create stitches, working from right to left then left to right down your row. Secure the last loop with a small tying stitch.

FABRIC

Plain- or even-weave fabrics

Related techniques:
Appliqué (p. 68), crazy patchwork (p. 66),
freestyle embroidery (p. 12)

Similar stitches:
Closed feather stitch (p. 109), double feather stitch
(p. 110), feathered chain stitch (p. 171), single feather
stitch (p. 109)

STEM STITCH

Also known as: crewel stitch

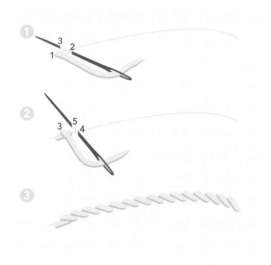

METHOD AND USES

This frequently used line stitch follows curves and intricate details well. As its name suggests, it is used to represent flower stems. It is also used for filling and shading.

Working left to right, simply stitch in a forwards–backwards motion along your line. Bring your needle up at 1, down at 2 and up at 3, halfway between 1 and 2 and above the thread. Pull your thread through, take your needle down at 4 and bring it up at 5, next to 2, above the stitch. Begin each stitch halfway along the previous one. Each stitch should be of equal length.

FABRIC

Plain- or even-weave fabrics

 Related techniques:
Particularly crewelwork (p. 18)

 Similar stitches:
No notable matches

BASIC COUCHING

Also known as: plain couching

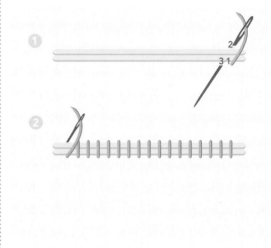

METHOD AND USES

Couching (from the French *coucher* – 'to lay down') attaches a thicker 'laid' thread (metallic, cord, ribbon, etc) to fabric using tiny stitches in a finer thread to define outlines and curves, fill motifs or edge appliqué shapes.

Place the laid thread on your fabric. For neat ends, you can bring this thread to the surface using a large-eyed needle. Bring your couching thread up at 1, down at 2, up at 3, holding the laid thread with your thumb. Repeat at regular intervals, then finish by taking both the laid and couching threads to the back of your fabric.

FABRIC

Plain- or even-weave fabrics. Use a hoop to keep fabric taut and prevent laid thread bunching up.

 Related techniques:
Appliqué (p. 68), freestyle embroidery (p. 12), goldwork (p. 20), couching and laid work (p. 30)

 Similar stitches:
Romanian couching (p. 213), puffy couching (p. 215), pendant couching (p. 214), Bokhara couching (p. 212)

HOLBEIN STITCH

Also known as: double running stitch

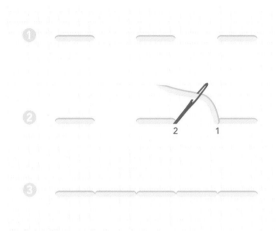

BUTTONHOLE STITCH

Also known as: button stitch

METHOD AND USES

Holbein stitch is a simple running stitch worked in two passes. It is used for outlining designs.

Start by working a row of running stitches. Keep the length and spaces between the stitches even. When you have completed your row, turn your work around and work back along the row, filling in the spaces with a second group of running stitches, emerging at 1 and then inserting the needle at 2, and so on. The appearance of both sides of the fabric will be exactly the same. The second row can be worked in a contrasting colour.

FABRIC

Best on even-weave linen and Aida

 Related techniques:
Assisi (p. 46), blackwork (p. 40),
cross-stitch (p. 42)

 Similar stitches:
Running stitch (p. 94)

METHOD AND USES

This stitch – used for straight lines and curves – is similar to blanket stitch, but here stitches are worked closer together to create a firm edge for buttonholes and for cutwork. Always keep the twisted edge to the middle, where the buttonhole slit will be cut. When used for cutwork, it is the lower twisted edge that the fabric is cut away from.

Bring your needle up at 1, down at 2 and up at 3 with the thread beneath the needle. Pull through and insert at 4 to repeat.

FABRIC

Plain- or even-weave fabrics

 Related techniques:
Appliqué (p. 68), cutwork (p. 32), drawn-thread
work (p. 49)

 Similar stitches:
Blanket stitch (p. 100), closed buttonhole stitch
(p. 165), double buttonhole bar (p. 159), single
buttonhole bar (p. 159), tailor's buttonhole stitch
(p. 158), up and down buttonhole stitch (p. 160)

BLANKET STITCH
Also known as: open buttonhole stitch

HERRINGBONE STITCH
Also known as: Russian cross-stitch and Russian stitch

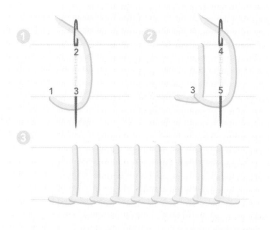

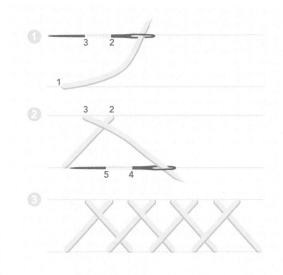

METHOD AND USES

Blanket stitch is worked in the same way as buttonhole stitch but with spaces in between each stitch. It is great for edgings (usually blankets) and straight or curved borders.

Using two guidelines, work left to right. Bring the needle up at 1, take it down at 2, then up at 3, looping the thread under the needle. Pull through. Insert the needle at 4 and emerge at 5 to create the next stitch, then repeat along your line. Secure the last loop with a small stitch.

FABRIC

Plain- or even-weave fabrics

METHOD AND USES

This relatively quick line stitch forms a decorative criss-cross border. It can be combined with other stitches, such as buttonhole stitch (p. 99). It is also used as an insertion stitch to join fabric pieces together. Work left to right.

Using two guidelines, bring your needle up at 1, down at 2, then up at 3. Next, take your needle down at 4 and up at 5. Begin again on the top row. Vary the angle of your stitches to space crosses further apart or closer together.

FABRIC

Plain- or even-weave fabrics, including ginghams, stripes

 Related techniques:
Freestyle embroidery (p. 12)

 Similar stitches:
Closed herringbone stitch (p. 128), double herringbone stitch (p. 127), herringbone ladder stitch (p. 129), interlaced herringbone stitch (p. 130), raised herringbone stitch (p. 131), threaded herringbone stitch (p. 127), tied herringbone stitch (p. 126)

 Related techniques:
Most embroidery styles, including appliqué (p. 68)

 Similar stitches:
Buttonhole stitch (p. 99), crossed blanket stitch (p. 164), double blanket stitch (p. 163), knotted blanket stitch (p. 165), long and short blanket stitch (p. 164)

FLY STITCH
Also known as: open loop stitch and Y-stitch

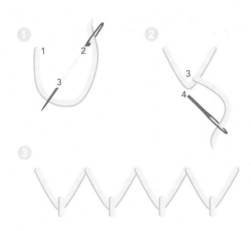

CORAL STITCH
Also known as: beaded stitch, coral knot and knotted stitch

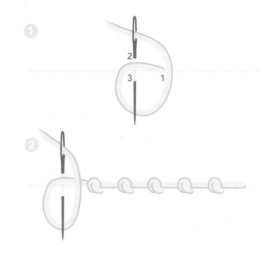

METHOD AND USES

Fly stitch can be made with a short or long tail; a long tail forms the letter 'Y', hence this stitch's alternative name. Fly stitch can be used scattered randomly, in horizontal or vertical lines or as a filling stitch. It also creates effective foliage and birds.

Working in any direction, bring your needle up at 1, then down at 2, leaving a loop of thread. Next, emerge at 3, inside this loop, then insert the needle at 4 to create a small, straight stitch to secure the loop. If working in a line, bring your needle up at 2 again to start the next stitch.

FABRIC
Plain- or even-weave fabrics

METHOD AND USES

Coral stitch can be used for outlines or fillings to give your work a beaded look.

Working right to left, bring your needle up at 1, lay your thread on top of the fabric, holding it down with your thumb. If it helps you keep your line straight, draw a guideline. Next, move a short distance to the left and pick up a small stitch between 2 and 3, under the thread. Make sure the thread is looped under the needle, as shown, then pull the thread through to form a knot. Continue working along the line in the same way.

FABRIC
Plain- or even-weave fabrics

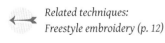

Related techniques:
Freestyle embroidery (p. 12)

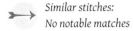

Similar stitches:
No notable matches

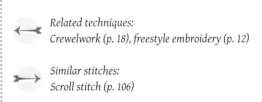

Related techniques:
Crewelwork (p. 18), freestyle embroidery (p. 12)

Similar stitches:
Scroll stitch (p. 106)

CRETAN STITCH

Also known as: closed Cretan stitch, long-armed feather stitch and Persian stitch

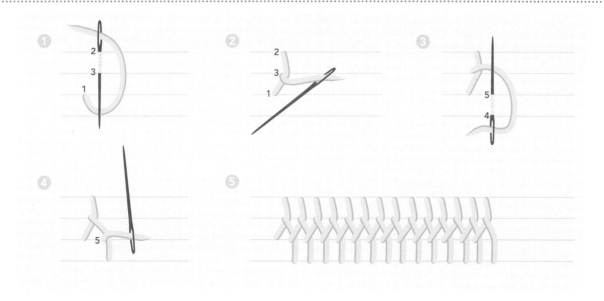

METHOD AND USES

Originating on the island of Crete, this centuries-old stitch can be worked either closed or open by placing the stitches close together or further apart, respectively. Shown here is a closed version; an open version is covered in Chapter 6. Cretan stitch is useful for creating leaves and feathers and has a lovely plaited appearance down its centre line.

Start by marking four parallel guidelines on your fabric. Next, working from left to right, bring your needle up at 1, down at 2 and then up halfway between these points, at 3. Before completing the stitch, make sure the thread is underneath the tip of your needle. Pull through.

Now insert your needle at 4 on the bottom guideline and emerge at 5 directly above this. Again, keeping your thread beneath the needle, pull through, then pass the needle over the top of this stitch to continue with the next stitch to the right. Continue working stitches along your line as desired.

FABRIC

Plain- or even-weave fabrics

Related techniques:
Freestyle embroidery (p. 12), crazy patchwork (p. 66)

Similar stitches:
Feather stitch (p. 97), open Cretan stitch (p. 106)

CHEVRON STITCH

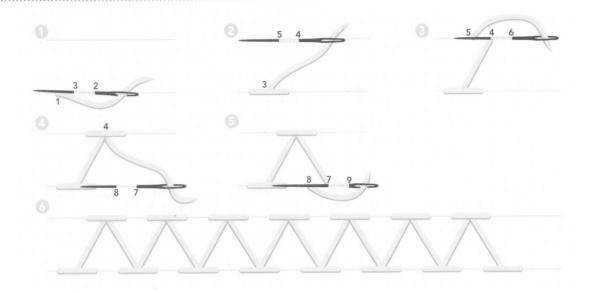

METHOD AND USES

This line, border and filling stitch is similar to herringbone stitch in its construction. It forms a zig-zag pattern from a series of straight stitches. Unless you are working on an even-weave fabric, in which case you can count the threads, it is best to draw two guidelines first to help keep your stitches even.

Working from left to right, bring your needle up on the lower line at 1, take it down again at 2, then back up at 3. The needle should emerge above the stitch and halfway between 1 and 2.

Next, on the upper line take your needle down at 4, to the right of 2 and up at 5. Now take your needle down at 6 and back up at 4, below the stitch you have just formed. On the bottom line take your needle down at 7 and up at 8, then down at 9 and up at 7 again. Continue working along your line in the same way.

FABRIC
Plain- or even-weave fabrics

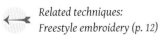

Related techniques:
Freestyle embroidery (p. 12)

Similar stitches:
Herringbone stitch (p. 100)

6: LINE STITCHES

The stitches in this chapter create decorative lines that follow a straight or curved line. They can be used to add simple but effective designs and detailing to household items such as cushions, tablecloths and towels, as well as clothing; if you are new to embroidery, they provide a very easy way to freshen up shop-bought items. You can use them singly or group different stitches together, using a variety of threads.

Line stitches can be used in rows or slanted to create interesting effects. Try overlaying stitches or using contrasting thread thicknesses to build up textures, too.

1 *Double knot stitch (p. 107)*

2 *Loop stitch (p. 114)*

1

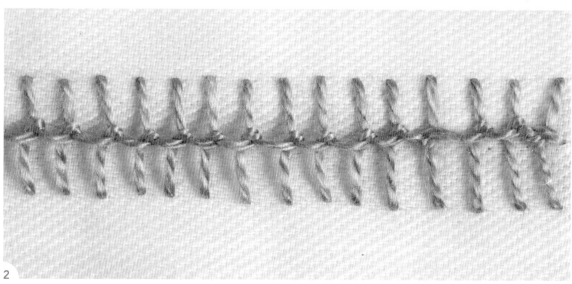

2

FABRICS: Any type of plain- or even-weave fabric can be used to work the 16 line stitches on the following pages. For practising, as with basic stitches, I recommend using a plain, inexpensive cotton fabric, such as a calico, which can be dyed or hand painted if you wish.

THREADS: Embroidery cotton (six-stranded cotton), tapestry wools, cotton pearl (perlé), soft cotton, metallic or silk threads can be used.

NEEDLES: Large-eyed crewel needles are the most useful as they come in a variety of sizes.

3

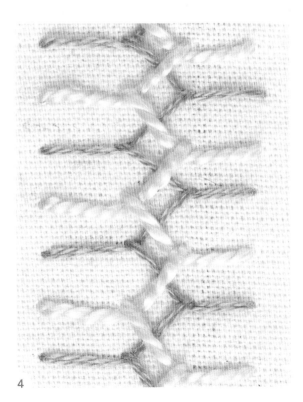

4

OTHER EQUIPMENT: You will need a small pair of sharp embroidery scissors. For marking guidelines on your fabric, you will need a fabric marker pen – these are usually water-soluble or fading. A hoop or frame is optional.

3 *Pekinese stitch (p. 108)*

4 *Open Cretan stitch (p. 106)*

SCROLL STITCH
Also known as: single knotted line stitch

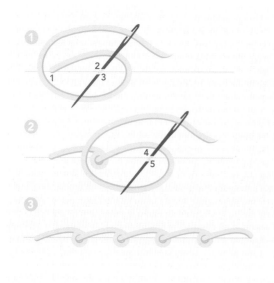

METHOD AND USES

Scroll stitch is ideal for depicting waves or rippled water. It can be worked close together or spaced apart, in straight lines or curved.

If working in a straight line, mark a guideline. Working left to right, bring your needle up at 1 then take a small stitch diagonally between 2 and 3. Wrap your thread around and under the needle. Pull through gently to form a knot. Repeat, inserting the needle at 4 and emerging at 5, then continue along your line as required. Fasten off the last scroll with a small stitch a short distance from your last knot.

FABRIC

Plain- or even-weave fabrics

Related techniques:
Freestyle embroidery (p. 12)

Similar stitches:
Coral stitch (p. 101)

OPEN CRETAN STITCH

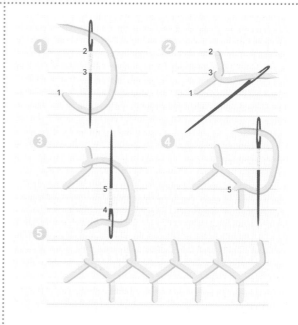

METHOD AND USES

This variation on Cretan stitch is worked in an open manner. It can be worked singly or with other stitches, or used as a filling stitch. Interesting borders can also be created with overlapping rows in threads of contrasting thicknesses.

Mark guidelines on your fabric. Working left to right, bring your needle up at 1, down at 2 and up at 3; your needle should point straight down, with the thread beneath it. Pull through gently. Take your needle down at 4 and up at 5 and, with your thread beneath, pull through. Continue working from top to bottom along your lines.

FABRIC

Plain- or even-weave fabrics

Related techniques:
Freestyle embroidery (p. 12)

Similar stitches:
Cretan stitch (p. 102)

THORN STITCH

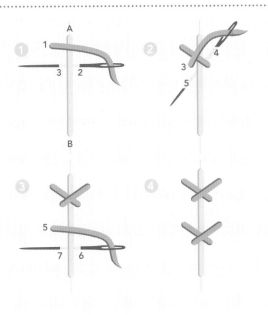

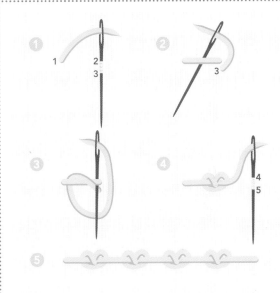

DOUBLE KNOT STITCH

Also known as: Palestrina stitch, Smyrna stitch and tied coral stitch

METHOD AND USES

This stitch consists of small, gradually widening crosses, which can be used to depict thorny branches or ferns.

Make a long, straight stitch from A to B. This is the thread to be couched. Working top to bottom, in the same or a contrasting colour, bring your needle up at 1, take a small stitch from 2 to 3 underneath your laid thread, then take your needle diagonally across and down at 4 to make the second arm of the cross. Emerge at 5 to begin the next stitch, crossing under the laid thread from 6 to 7, and complete the cross as before. Continue as required.

FABRIC

Plain- or even-weave fabrics. Use a hoop to avoid puckering.

 Related techniques:
Couching (p. 30), freestyle embroidery (p. 12)

 Similar stitches:
No notable matches

METHOD AND USES

Double knot stitch can either be used singly, or worked in rows as a pretty beaded filling stitch.

Work horizontally or vertically. Bring your needle up at 1, down at 2, then up at 3. Pull through. Now slip your needle under the straight stitch just created without piercing the fabric. Pull through gently – keep your stitches quite loose.

Next, pass your needle underneath the straight stitch again, keeping the previous stitch and the looped thread under the needle, as shown. Pull through, then take another small stitch between 4 and 5 to repeat. Space knots along your row as required.

FABRIC

Plain- or even-weave fabrics. Cotton pearl (perlé) creates a raised effect.

 Related techniques:
Freestyle embroidery (p. 12)

 Similar stitches:
Coral stitch (p. 101)

BASQUE STITCH

Also known as: twisted daisy border stitch

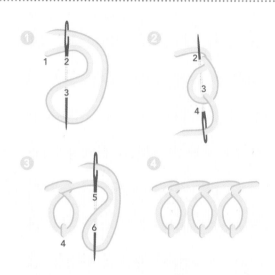

METHOD AND USES

This looped line stitch with a twist originated in Spain's Basque region, where it was usually worked in red thread on green fabric, or white on blue.

Working left to right, bring your needle up at 1. Arrange your thread in a question mark shape before inserting your needle at 2, just below the top loop. Emerge at 3 and pull through gently. Secure the loop with a small vertical stitch by inserting your needle at 4 and emerging again at 2.

Leave a small space then insert your needle at 5, emerging at 6, with the thread arranged as before, then repeat as desired along your row.

FABRIC

Plain-weave fabrics

Related techniques:
Freestyle embroidery (p. 12)

Similar stitches:
Knotted blanket stitch (p. 165)

PEKINESE STITCH

Also known as: Pekingese stitch, Chinese stitch, blind stitch, forbidden stitch, laced backstitch

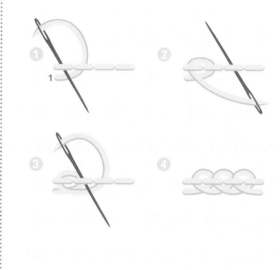

METHOD AND USES

Once commonly used in Chinese embroidery, this stitch was worked on such a small scale that it hurt the stitcher's eyes – hence the alternative name, 'blind stitch'. It is used for outlines or as a filling stitch.

Work a row of backstitch. Next, bring your needle up at 1, then pass it under the second backstitch along, keeping your thread loose. (Using a blunt needle will help to avoid piercing the fabric.) Pass down under the first backstitch and, keeping the thread beneath your needle, pull through.

Continue along the backstitches, only inserting your needle through the fabric at the end of the row.

FABRIC

Plain- or even-weave fabrics

Related techniques:
Freestyle embroidery (p. 12)

Similar stitches:
Backstitch (p. 94)

SINGLE FEATHER STITCH
Also known as: slanted buttonhole stitch

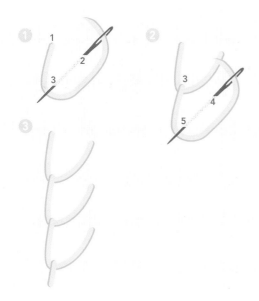

METHOD AND USES

Single feather stitch is similar to a blanket or buttonhole stitch (pp. 100 and 99) but with slanted arms. It is worked in a straight line or curve.

Working downwards, with your needle in a slanting position, come up at 1, down at 2, then up at 3. Loop your thread beneath your needle then pull through. For the next stitch, take your needle down at 4, up at 5, loop your thread under, as before and pull through again.

Continue downwards as required, then use a straight stitch to hold the last loop in place.

FABRIC

Plain- or even-weave fabrics

 Related techniques:
Freestyle embroidery (p. 12), smocking (p. 84)

 Similar stitches:
Closed feather stitch (p. 109), double feather stitch (p. 110), feather stitch (p. 97)

CLOSED FEATHER STITCH

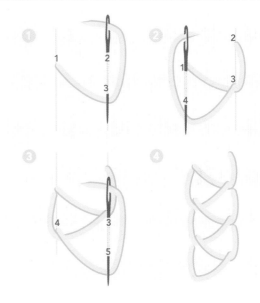

METHOD AND USES

Closed feather stitch is used to create wide, lacy borders, or to couch other threads and ribbons to a fabric's surface.

Bring your needle up at 1, down at 2 and up at 3, inside the loop of thread. Pull through. Loop the thread round to the left, then take your needle down just below 1 and up at 4, inside the loop. Pull through. Loop the thread now to the right and take your needle down just below 3 and up at 5 to begin the next set of stitches. Continue down your row. Note: each stitch touches the previous one but is not actually inserted in its loop.

FABRIC

Plain- or even-weave fabrics. Draw guidelines on plain weaves to keep stitches even.

 Related techniques:
Couching (p. 30), freestyle embroidery (p. 12)

 Similar stitches:
Double feather stitch (p. 110), feather stitch (p. 97), single feather stitch (p. 109)

DOUBLE FEATHER STITCH
Also known as: double coral stitch

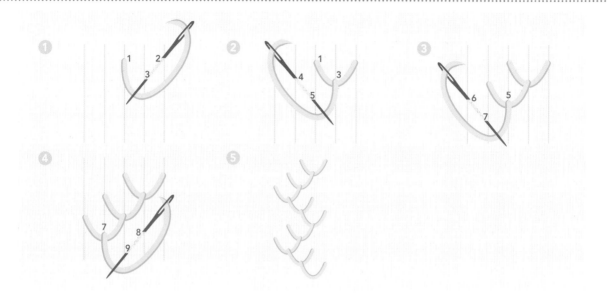

METHOD AND USES

This variation of feather stitch is used for decorative borders. It creates a feathery, branch-like line, which is perfect for depicting coral (as its other name suggests). It can also be used as a filling stitch when worked in multiple rows, and a variety of threads can be used to add different textures.

First mark your fabric with five parallel lines, then work downwards, as with feather stitch. Bring your needle up at 1 on the middle of the parallel lines, take your needle down again at 2 on a slant and up at 3, looping your thread beneath your needle. Pull through gently.

Next, working to the left, take your needle down at 4, slightly lower than 1, and back up at 5, looping your thread beneath your needle again. Finally, take your needle down at 6 and up at 7, again with your thread beneath your needle, then pull through.

Now continue back again to the right, starting by inserting your needle at 8 and emerging at 9, with your thread looped beneath your needle. Your needle should always point diagonally to the middle line. Secure the last stitch with a small, straight stitch.

FABRICS

Plain- or even-weave fabrics

Related techniques:
Freestyle embroidery (p. 12)

Similar stitches:
Closed feather stitch (p. 109), feather stitch (p. 97), single feather stitch (p. 109)

REVERSED FLY STITCH

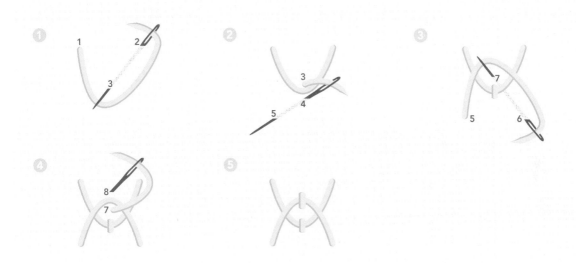

METHOD AND USES

Reversed fly stitch is formed by working sets of two fly stitches, one upside down and one on top of the other, in vertical rows. This is used as a filling stitch when worked solidly in rows, or it can be scattered for a more 'powdered' effect.

Bring your needle up at 1, down at 2 and up at 3. Your needle should be slanted and your thread should form a loop beneath your needle. Pull through gently. Now make a small, straight stitch from 3 to 4, at the base of the loop to hold it in place.

Next, bring your needle up at 5, below and to the left of the straight stitch you just formed. Take your needle down at 6 and up at 7, looping your thread beneath your needle. Pull through. Once again, make a small, straight stitch to hold the loop in place, from 7 to 8.

This stitch is usually worked all in one go, although if it is broken down into two passes, contrasting thread colours or thicknesses can be used.

FABRICS
Plain- or even-weave fabrics

Related techniques:
Freestyle embroidery (p. 12)

Similar stitches:
Closed fly stitch (p. 112), double fly stitch (p. 113),
fly stitch (p. 101)

CLOSED FLY STITCH

METHOD AND USES

This variation of fly stitch is created by working a series of basic fly stitches, packed closely together in a downwards direction to give a heavy line effect. It can be worked as a vertical line stitch. It can also be used as a filling stitch for narrow shapes if the width of the stitches is graduated.

First, work a fly stitch by bringing your needle up at 1, down at 2 and up at 3 on a slant, making a small, straight stitch to finish by inserting the needle at 4. Now prepare to make another fly stitch by bringing your needle up at 5 (just next to 1).

Next, loop round to insert your needle at 6, following the path of the previous fly stitch, and bring it up at 7, just below the small tying stitch of the previous stitch. Pull the

needle through and, once again, finish with a small, straight stitch by inserting your needle at 8. Emerge at 9 and continue to repeat stitches as required down your line.

FABRICS

Plain- or even-weave fabrics. Draw guidelines on plain weaves to keep stitches even.

Related techniques:
Freestyle embroidery (p. 12)

Similar stitches:
Double fly stitch (p. 113), fly stitch (p. 101),
reversed fly stitch (p. 111)

DOUBLE FLY STITCH

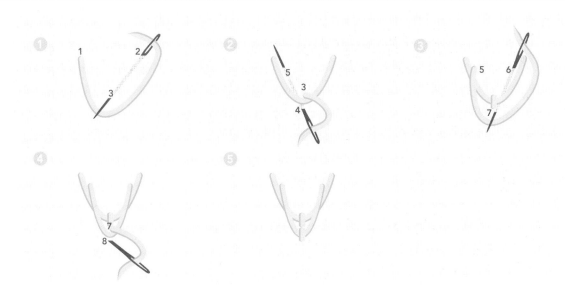

METHOD AND USES

Yet another variation of fly stitch, double fly stitch is created by working a row of vertically spaced fly stitches. A second set of fly stitches is then worked over the top. This stitch can be worked all at once using thread of a single colour, or in two passes, with the second worked in a contrasting colour. It is generally used for decorative borders.

Start by bringing your needle up at 1, down at 2 and then up at 3. Your needle should be inserted at a slant and your thread should form a loop beneath it. Pull through gently. Next, insert your needle at 4 to secure the stitch with a small, straight stitch, then bring it up at 5 to begin your next fly stitch. Pull through.

Now take your needle down at 6, up at 7 (just below 4), keeping the thread beneath your needle. Pull through. Again, secure this stitch with a small, straight stitch by taking the needle down at 8. Continue along your line.

FABRICS

Plain- or even-weave fabrics

Related techniques:
Freestyle embroidery (p. 12)

Similar stitches:
Closed fly stitch (p. 112), fly stitch (p. 101),
reversed fly stitch (p. 111)

LOOP STITCH
Also known as: knotted loop stitch

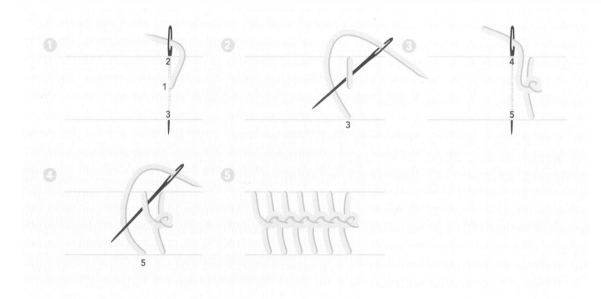

METHOD AND USES

This stitch is usually worked in a straight line, and sometimes on a curve. The stitch's centre has a raised, plaited appearance, which produces a fancy outline stitch when worked small. It can be worked on its own or in rows with interlocking arms to form a filling. Nice variations can be achieved, too, when you vary the distance between each stitch – it's great for a broken fence effect!

To keep your stitches even, draw two guidelines on your fabric. Starting on the right, bring your needle up at 1 down at 2, then up at 3. Next, pass your needle under the stitch just made between 1 and 2, without piercing the fabric. Your thread should be beneath the needle, as shown.

Next, take your needle down at 4 and up at 5, then pass it under the top stitch, keeping the thread beneath the needle, as before. When passing the needle under the top stitch, always keep the loop of your thread to the left of you. Repeat to the left as required.

FABRIC

Plain- or even-weave fabrics. Twisted threads, eg cotton pearl (perlé), emphasize the plaited effect.

Related techniques:
Freestyle embroidery (p. 12)

Similar stitches:
No notable matches

LADDER STITCH
Also known as: ladder hemstitch and step stitch

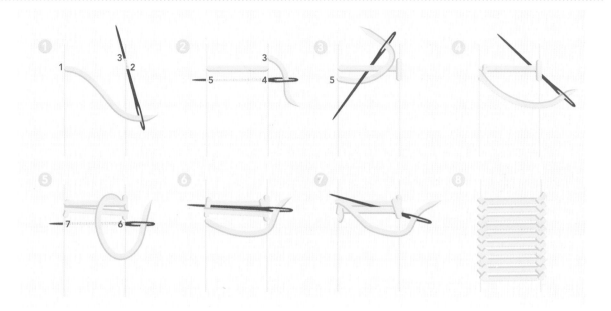

METHOD AND USES

You guessed it – this decorative stitch looks just like a ladder! It can be straight, curved or even used for fancy stems. It makes a nice border, too, with stitches either worked close together for a solid effect, or spaced further apart. Always stretch your fabric in a hoop first, since ladder stitch can tighten and distort the fabric.

Start by marking two parallel guidelines on the fabric. Working from top to bottom, and using a blunt needle to avoid piercing the fabric later on, come up at 1, down at 2, then up at 3, just above the stitch. Next, cross over the top of the end of this stitch to take the needle down at 4, then emerge at the opposite side again at 5.

Without piercing the fabric, pass your needle under the stitch from above. Then, working on the opposite side, pass the needle upwards under the crossed ends. Insert the needle at 6 and bring it up at 7, then pass the needle from right to left under the crossed ends of the stitch above on this side. Now on the opposite side, pass the needle upwards under the crossed ends of the stitch above.

Repeat these steps downwards to create a row of the desired length.

FABRIC

Plain- or even-weave fabrics. Cotton pearl (perlé) or soft cotton are best for a raised effect.

Related techniques:
Freestyle embroidery (p. 12)

Similar stitches:
Open chain stitch (p. 174)

PLAITED BRAID STITCH

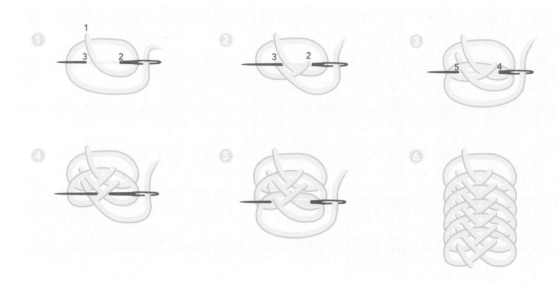

METHOD AND USES

This heavy line stitch is quite complex to work and so requires a lot of practice. It works well in metallic threads on clothing and furnishings, where a very heavy, raised, plaited effect is required. Plaited braid stitch should be worked in a single, solid thread so that it maintains its shape and does not become tangled.

Always work from top to bottom. Start by bringing your needle through to the right side of the fabric at 1. Loop your thread on the surface of your fabric and hold it in place with your thumb. Insert the needle at 2 and bring it up again at 3; your working thread should be beneath the tip of your needle. Pull through gently.

Next, thread your needle through the loop of thread, without piercing the fabric, as shown. Pull it through gently. Then, insert your needle at 4 and bring it up again at 5. Pull it through. Repeat steps 2 and 3 only down your line.

FABRIC

Plain-weave fabrics

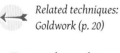

Related techniques:
Goldwork (p. 20)

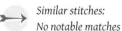

Similar stitches:
No notable matches

SORBELLO STITCH

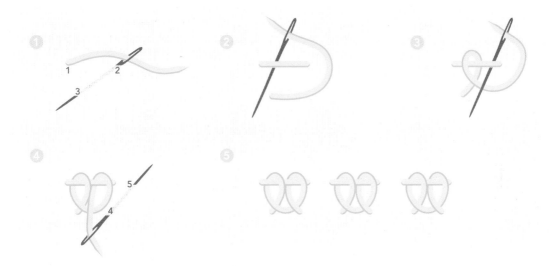

METHOD AND USES

Originating in the town of Sorbello in Italy, this line stitch was often used in Italian embroidery to fill geometric shapes, just like a cross-stitch is used in embroidery today. Sorbello stitch can be worked in straight or curving lines. It can also be worked individually as a filling stitch.

First, create a straight stitch by bringing your needle up at 1, down at 2 and up at 3. Next, pass your needle diagonally under the straight stitch you have just created, making sure that the needle does not go through the fabric. Loop your thread and insert your needle again under the straight stitch to the right of your first loop. The thread should be beneath the needle. Pull it through.

Now insert your needle at 4 and bring it up again at 5 to begin the next stitch. Continue working as many stitches as are required. Each stitch should be worked quite loosely.

FABRIC
Plain- or even-weave fabrics

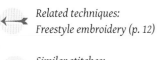

Related techniques:
Freestyle embroidery (p. 12)

Similar stitches:
Double knot stitch (p. 107)

7: CROSSED STITCHES

The collection of stitches known as crossed stitches, or cross-stitch, are produced by working one straight stitch over another to form a cross. The most popular form is the single cross-stitch, which is also one of the oldest of all embroidery stitches. It has been used for centuries to produce samplers – pieces of embroidery that were once commonly used for teaching children to embroider.

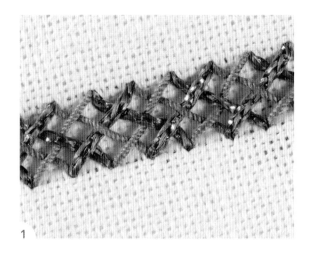

1

Examples of crossed stitches can be found in many cultures around the world, and you will discover a great many variations of the stitch in this chapter.

2

1 Double herringbone stitch (p. 127)

2 Raised herringbone stitch (p. 131)

3 Tied herringbone stitch (p. 126)

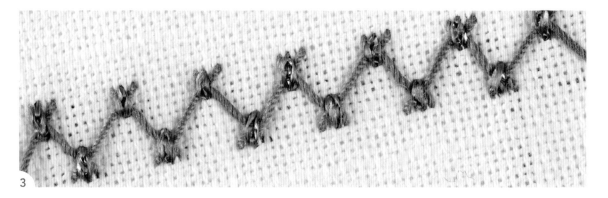

3

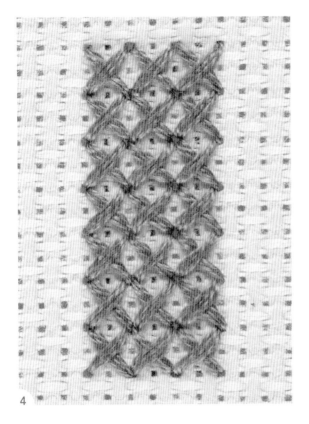

FABRICS: Crossed stitches are best worked on even-weave fabrics – such as even-weave linen and Aida cloth, ginghams and striped fabrics, due to the regular patterns produced by these stitches. They can also be worked on plain-weave fabric with the aid of waste canvas. Waste canvas is an open canvas fabric, with fibres held together with water-soluble glue. When damp, its threads are easy to pull away, leaving just your stitching remaining on the surface of the fabric.

THREADS: Embroidery cotton (six-stranded cotton) is most often used for these stitches.

NEEDLES: Crossed stitches are traditionally worked using a tapestry needle, though herringbone stitches can be worked on plain-weave fabrics using a crewel needle.

OTHER EQUIPMENT: You will need a small pair of sharp embroidery scissors and an embroidery hoop or frame to keep your fabric taut.

4 *Raised herringbone stitch (p. 131)*

5 *Three-quarter (left) and half (right) cross-stitch (pp. 120 and 121)*

6 *Single cross-stitch (p. 120)*

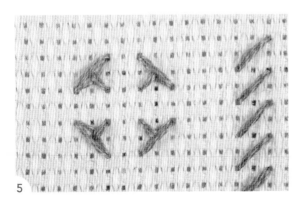

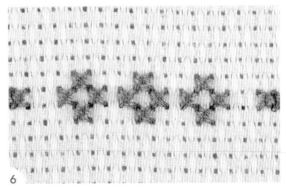

SINGLE CROSS-STITCH
Also known as: Berlin stitch, point de marque and sampler stitch

HALF CROSS-STITCH
Also known as: half stitch

Tip

Avoid half cross-stitch and tent stitch in the same piece – it will create an irregular surface as the method of working the two stitches is different.

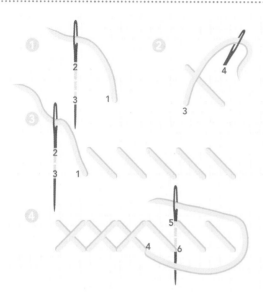

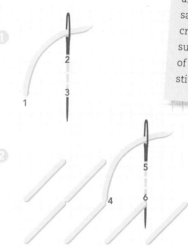

METHOD AND USES

A very old stitch, yet one of the easiest to learn, this is usually worked on even-weave fabrics, but can also be used as an isolated or filling stitch on plain weaves, or worked over single squares on gingham.

To work singly: Bring your needle up at 1, down at 2, then up at 3. Cross over to insert the needle at 4 for a cross. Or in rows: Bring your needle up at 1, down at 2, then up at 3 to start the next stitch to the left. Reverse direction and, working along the row, bring your needle up at 4, down at 5 and up at 6, to complete the crosses.

FABRIC

Usually even-weave fabrics, particularly Aida. Sometimes plain-weave fabrics and gingham.

Related techniques:
Blackwork (p. 40), cross-stitch (p. 42), Assisi (p. 46)

Similar stitches:
Double cross-stitch (p. 122), half cross-stitch (p. 120), marking cross-stitch (p. 123), three-quarter cross-stitch (p. 121), tied cross-stitch (p. 121)

METHOD AND USES

This diagonal stitch is always worked in the same direction and is used for lines and fillings, shading and to add depth to backgrounds in cross-stitch pictures.

Begin from the top left, working each row left to right. Bring your needle up at 1, down at 2, up at 3. Repeat as required. Turn your work upside down at the end of the row and continue working in the same way – up at 4, down at 5, then up at 6, touching the tips of the previous stitches. Half cross-stitch can be worked horizontally or vertically.

FABRIC

Even-weave fabrics, eg Aida or double (Penelope) canvas

Related techniques:
Blackwork (p. 40), cross-stitch (p. 42), canvaswork (p. 44), Assisi (p. 46)

Similar stitches:
Double cross-stitch (p. 122), marking cross-stitch (p. 123), single cross-stitch (p. 120), three-quarter cross-stitch (p. 121), tied cross-stitch (p. 121)

THREE-QUARTER CROSS-STITCH

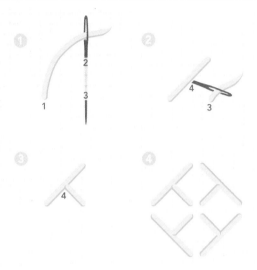

TIED CROSS-STITCH

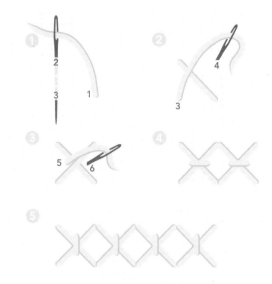

METHOD AND USES

Three-quarter cross-stitch combines a half cross-stitch and a quarter cross-stitch, and can be worked in any direction. It is commonly used to add extra detail to designs – particularly for corners, to create a rounded effect and slanted lines.

Bring your needle up at 1, down at 2 and up at 3 to create the half stitch. Next, take the needle down at 4 to complete the quarter stitch. Insert your needle into the centre of the half stitch you have just produced, either under or over the stitch.

FABRIC

Even-weave fabrics, eg Aida

 Related techniques:
Cross-stitch (p. 42)

 Similar stitches:
Double cross-stitch (p. 122), half cross-stitch (p. 120), marking cross-stitch (p. 123), single cross-stitch (p. 120), tied cross-stitch (p. 121)

METHOD AND USES

This stitch is tied at its centre with matching or contrasting thread. It may be worked large or small, as a single stitch, in lines, a chequerboard pattern, scattered or as a filling stitch. The tie stitch may also be worked in metallic threads.

Create a cross-stitch, coming up at 1, down at 2, up at 3, then crossing to pass down at 4. Bring your needle up at 5 and down at 6 to tie the centre. This tying stitch can be worked horizontally or vertically.

FABRIC

Even-weave fabrics, eg linen or Aida

 Related techniques:
Counted-thread work (p. 38)

 Similar stitches:
Double cross-stitch (p. 122), half cross-stitch (p. 120), marking cross-stitch (p. 123), single cross-stitch (p. 120), three-quarter cross-stitch (p. 121)

DOUBLE CROSS-STITCH

Also known as: leviathan stitch and star stitch

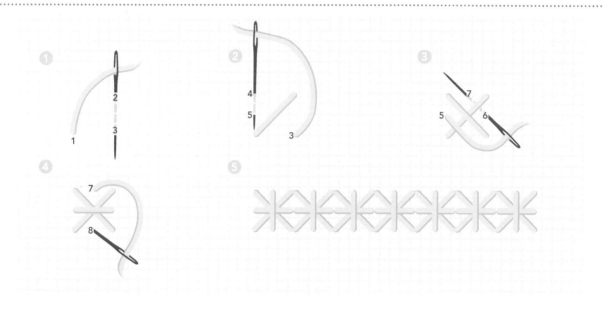

METHOD AND USES

Double cross-stitch is produced by combining a single cross-stitch and an upright cross-stitch. It can be worked singly, in rows to form a pattern, or scattered to fill a shape. It is also often used to represent stars or snowflakes in cross-stitch embroidery. This stitch works particularly well when worked in metallic threads.

Start by bringing your needle up at 1, down at 2 and up at 3. Next, pass over the diagonal stitch you have just created and take your needle down at 4, then up at 5 (halfway down) to form a cross-stitch.

To work the upright cross-stitch that sits on top of this, take your needle horizontally across the first cross-stitch.

Insert the needle at 6 and bring it up again at 7. Finish off this second cross by inserting the needle at 8, then repeat the whole sequence as required along your row.

FABRIC

Even-weave fabrics, eg linen or Aida

Related techniques:
Cross-stitch (p. 42)

Similar stitches:
Half cross-stitch (p. 120), marking cross-stitch (p. 123), single cross-stitch (p. 120), three-quarter cross-stitch (p. 121), tied cross-stitch (p. 121)

MARKING CROSS-STITCH

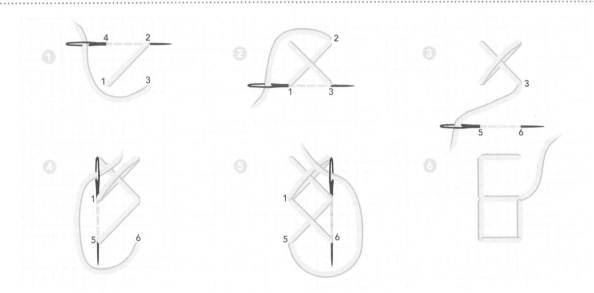

METHOD AND USES

This variation of cross-stitch forms a cross-stitch on one side of the fabric and a square of four stitches on the reverse side. Crosses are covered twice in order for the squares on the back to be produced. This results in a reversible pattern, which is why this stitch is used for lettering and monograms on household linens, where the back of the fabric will often be visible.

Begin by leaving a tail of thread. Bring your needle up at 1, down at 2, up at 3, down at 4 and up at 2 again. Take your needle down at 1 and up at 3 to begin the next stitch. Take the needle down at 5, up at 6. Pull through, then cross over to insert the needle again at 1, emerging at 5 to complete the second cross.

To finish, take the needle down again at 3 and up at 6 to begin the next repeat. Two cross-stitches are formed on the front; two squares on the back. Thread the tail end of the thread under the stitches to finish off neatly.

FABRIC
Plain- or even-weave fabrics; even weaves are easier

Related techniques:
Cross-stitch (p. 42)

Similar stitches:
Double cross-stitch (p. 122), half cross-stitch (p. 120), single cross-stitch (p. 120), three-quarter cross-stitch (p. 121), tied cross-stitch (p. 121)

LONG-ARMED CROSS-STITCH

Also known as: long-legged cross-stitch

UPRIGHT CROSS-STITCH

Also known as: St George cross-stitch

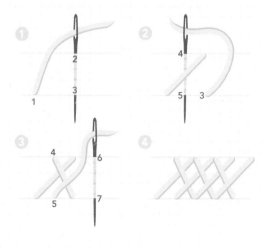

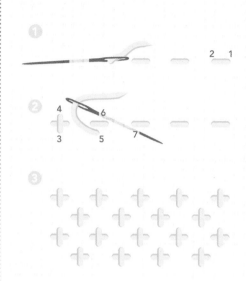

METHOD AND USES

As the name suggests, this stitch has one arm of its cross longer than the other. It is used in rows as a border or worked as a filling stitch.

Working from left to right, bring your needle up at 1, down at 2 and up at 3. Next, take your needle across and down at 4 then up at 5 to begin your next stitch. Cross over again to insert your needle at 6 and emerge at 7. Repeat as required to the right.

FABRIC

Plain- or even-weave fabrics. Draw guidelines on plain weaves to keep stitches even.

METHOD AND USES

This stitch is very easy to work – on its own, in rows or as a filling stitch.

Upright cross-stitch is worked in two stages. The first is a row of running stitches, worked from right to left. Bring your needle up at 1 and down at 2 and repeat as required. The second pass is now worked from left to right. Bring your needle up at 3 and down at 4 to form a vertical stitch, then up at 5 and down at 6 to form the next one, emerging at 7 to continue. Progress along the line until you have worked a vertical stitch over each horizontal one.

FABRIC

Plain- or even-weave fabrics

 Related techniques:
Freestyle embroidery (p. 12)

 Similar stitches:
No notable matches

 Related techniques:
Counted-thread work (p. 38)

 Similar stitches:
Double cross-stitch (p. 122)

STAR STITCH

Also known as: star filling stitch

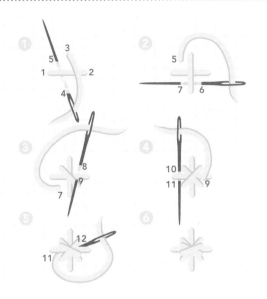

ERMINE STITCH

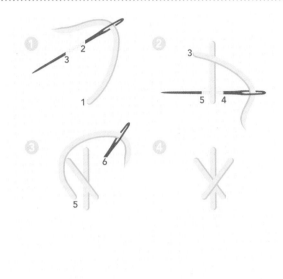

METHOD AND USES

Star stitch is worked singly, or used as a filling stitch, or for borders. It can be worked in one or two colours, and the centre cross-stitch may be worked in fine or metallic thread.

Work an upright cross-stitch by bringing your needle up at 1, down at 2, up at 3 and down at 4. Emerge at 5 to cover this with a cross-stitch – take the needle down at 6, up at 7, down at 8, then up at 9. Now tie the stitch with a small cross-stitch by passing down at 10, up at 11 and then down at 12.

FABRIC

Plain- or even-weave fabrics

 Related techniques:
Counted-thread work (p. 38), freestyle embroidery (p. 12)

 Similar stitches:
Single cross-stitch (p. 120), upright cross-stitch (p. 124)

METHOD AND USES

This series of straight stitches, stitched in black on white fabric, resembles an ermine's tail. The stitches can be worked evenly, randomly scattered or used as a filling stitch. Ermine stitch can also be worked at a larger scale in heavy thread as a single spot motif.

Bring your needle up at 1, down at 2, then up at 3. The overall stitch needs to be spaced wider at the top than at the bottom, so insert your needle at 4, closer to the vertical stitch than your position at 3. Emerge at 5, the same distance on the other side, then cross back to 6, keeping this diagonal symmetrical with the previous one.

FABRIC

Plain- or even-weave fabrics

 Related techniques:
Blackwork (p. 40)

 Similar stitches:
Straight stitch (p. 146)

TIED HERRINGBONE STITCH

Also known as: couched herringbone stitch

LACED HERRINGBONE STITCH

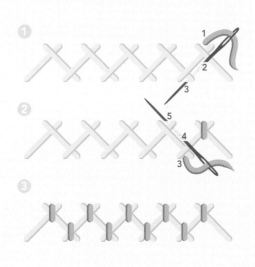

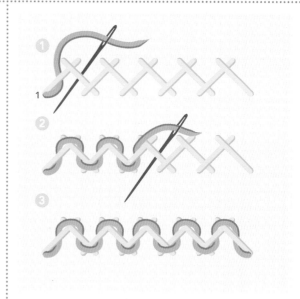

METHOD AND USES

This variation of herringbone stitch has its crossed ends tied down in a contrasting thread. It works particularly well for borders if the tying stitch is worked in metallic thread.

First, work a row of herringbone stitches. Next, working right to left in a contrasting thread, bring your needle up at 1 and down at 2 to form a small, vertical straight stitch over the first top crossed end. Bring your needle up at 3, down at 4 and up at 5 for the next tying stitch. Repeat.

FABRIC

Plain- or even-weave fabrics

METHOD AND USES

This stitch provides a really easy way to add decoration to plain herringbone stitches to create decorative borders.

Work a row of herringbone stitches. Using a blunt-ended needle, and a contrasting thread if desired, work left to right. Bring your needle up at 1, thread the needle under the first diagonal, then round and down under the second diagonal, forming a loop around the crossed ends. Do not pierce the fabric. Continue along your row, as shown.

FABRIC

Plain- or even-weave fabrics

 Related techniques:
Freestyle embroidery (p. 12)

 Similar stitches:
The following herringbone stitches: closed (p. 128), double (p. 127), herringbone (p. 100), interlaced (p. 130), laced (p. 126), ladder (p. 129), raised (p. 131), threaded (p. 127)

 Related techniques:
Freestyle embroidery (p. 12)

 Similar stitches:
The following herringbone stitches: closed (p. 128), double (p. 127), herringbone (p. 100), interlaced (p. 130), ladder (p. 129), raised (p. 131), threaded (p. 127), tied (p. 126)

THREADED HERRINGBONE STITCH

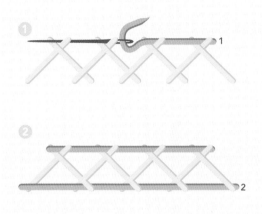

DOUBLE HERRINGBONE STITCH

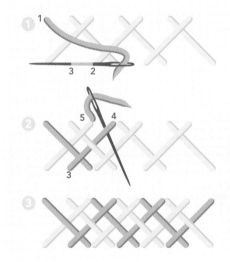

METHOD AND USES

Again, this stitch is used to add detail to herringbone stitch for decorative borders.

First, work a row of herringbone stitches. Using a blunt-ended needle, start on the top row, working right to left. Come up at 1, take the thread under the right diagonal above the crossed end and then over the left diagonal, as shown. Repeat along the row. To thread the second row, bring the needle up at 2 and work in the same way as before.

FABRIC

Plain- or even-weave fabrics

 Related techniques:
Freestyle embroidery (p. 12)

 Similar stitches:
The following herringbone stitches: closed (p. 128), double (p. 127), herringbone (p. 100), interlaced (p. 130), laced (p. 126), ladder (p. 129), raised (p. 131), tied (p. 126)

METHOD AND USES

Double herringbone stitch can be worked in contrasting colours to give a wide, two-colour border effect.

Working left to right, create a row of herringbone stitches. Using a contrasting thread, bring your needle up at 1, down at 2 and up at 3. Take your thread over the arm just created, then under the next arm from the previous row, as shown. Do not pierce the fabric. Insert your needle at 4, emerge at 5, then pass under the arm just created and over the next diagonal. Continue to the end of your row.

FABRIC

Plain- and even-weave fabrics. Draw guidelines on plain weaves to keep stitches even.

 Related techniques:
Freestyle embroidery (p. 12)

 Similar stitches:
The following herringbone stitches: closed (p. 128), herringbone (p. 100), interlaced (p. 130), laced (p. 126), ladder (p. 129), raised (p. 131), threaded (p. 127), tied (p. 126)

CLOSED HERRINGBONE STITCH
Also known as: shadow stitch

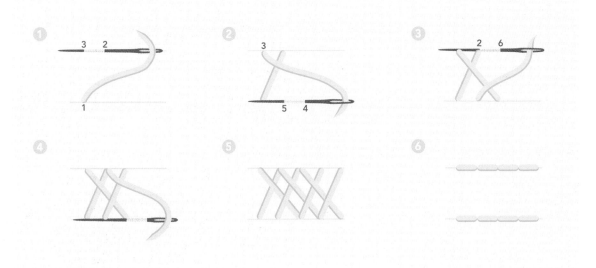

METHOD AND USES

Closed herringbone stitch is used both to make wide borders and also in shadow work.

Start by marking your fabric with two parallel lines. Working from left to right, bring your needle up at 1, down at 2, then up at 3. Pass over the top of the stitch just created, then on the bottom line insert your needle at 4 and emerge again at 5 to complete the first herringbone stitch. On the top line take the needle down at 6 and bring it up at 2. Repeat along your row.

The reverse side of your work will be two rows of backstitches. In shadow work, this stitch is worked on the back of the fabric – the front displays the backstitches, while the herringbone stitches are visible through the sheer fabric.

FABRIC

Plain- or even-weave fabrics; sheer fabrics for shadow work

Related techniques:
Shadow embroidery (p. 26)

Similar stitches:
The following herringbone stitches: double (p. 127), herringbone (p. 100), interlaced (p. 130), laced (p. 126), ladder (p. 129), raised (p. 131), threaded (p. 127), tied (p. 126)

HERRINGBONE LADDER STITCH
Also known as: double Pekinese stitch

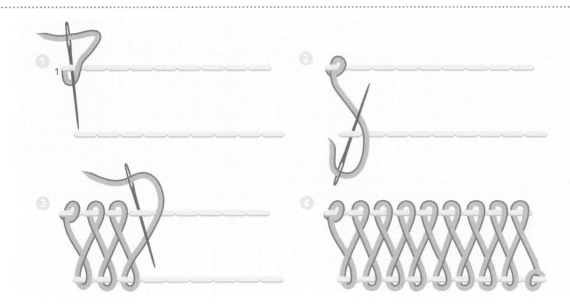

METHOD AND USES

This is generally used as a border stitch, but it can also be used as a filling stitch. It has a lovely open-lace effect, and it can be worked in two colours.

Create a foundation of two parallel lines of backstitch (p. 94), but make sure the stitches are not placed directly opposite each other (see Step 1)

Next, work the interlacing using a blunt-ended tapestry needle to avoid piercing the fabric. Bring your needle up at 1 at the left-hand end of the stitches. Loop the thread round and then slip it under the first stitch on the top line.

Keeping your thread under the needle, pull through. Next, thread your needle under the first stitch on the bottom row; the working thread should be beneath your needle again, and your needle should point to the centre of the design.

Continue along the backstitches, threading under the top then the bottom row until the full row is complete.

FABRIC

Plain- or even-weave fabrics. Draw guidelines on plain weaves to keep stitches even.

 Related techniques:
Freestyle embroidery (p. 12)

 Similar stitches:
The following herringbone stitches: closed (p. 128), double (p. 127), herringbone (p. 100), interlaced (p. 130), laced (p. 126), raised (p. 131), threaded (p. 127), tied (p. 126)

INTERLACED HERRINGBONE STITCH
Also known as: Armenian cross-stitch and interlacing stitch

METHOD AND USES

This stitch is always worked in a straight line. It is used as a wide, decorative border stitch, and works especially well when the interlacing thread is metallic.

Start by creating a row of double herringbone stitches. Work the stitches loosely. Next, begin the lacing using a blunt-ended needle to avoid piercing the fabric as you work. Starting on the left, bring your needle up at 1, slightly under the first cross. Thread your needle over the second arm of the first cross and under the first arm of the second cross. Loop it over and under the end of the cross.

Next, thread your needle under your lacing thread and under the first arm of the second cross. Continue along until you reach the final cross. Thread your needle around the middle of the end cross, then work back along the bottom row as for the top.

FABRIC

Plain- or even-weave fabrics. Draw guidelines on plain weaves to keep stitches even.

Related techniques:
Freestyle embroidery (p. 12)

Similar stitches:
The following herringbone stitches: closed (p. 128), double (p. 127), herringbone (p. 100), laced (p. 126), ladder (p. 129), raised (p. 131), threaded (p. 127), tied (p. 126)

RAISED HERRINGBONE STITCH

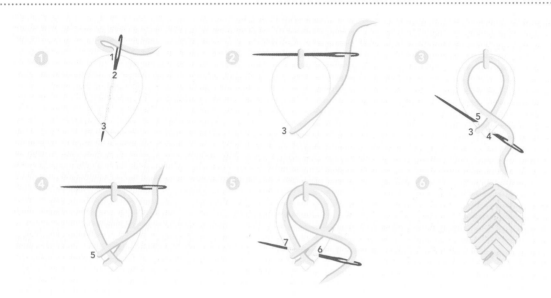

METHOD AND USES

This bold stitch is used to depict leaf and petal shapes. It can be worked in a variety of thicknesses, but works best in soft cotton or cotton pearl (perlé)-type threads. The thicker the thread, the more raised the effect. A blunt needle is used throughout to avoid piercing the fabric.

You may find it easier to mark a leaf or petal shape on your fabric with a marker pen before starting your stitches. Bring your needle up at 1 (the base of your leaf), down at 2 and up at 3. Pass your needle from right to left through the vertical stitch you have just created, taking care not to pierce the fabric. Next, insert your needle at 4 and bring it

up at 5 to begin the next stitch. Pass through the vertical stitch at the top again, then insert the needle at 6 on the right, emerging at 7 on the left.

Repeat this sequence, working gradually up the sides of the leaf until your entire shape is filled.

FABRIC
Plain- or even-weave fabrics

Related techniques:
Freestyle embroidery (p. 12)

Similar stitches:
The following herringbone stitches: closed (p. 128), double (p. 127), herringbone (p. 100), interlaced (p. 130), laced (p. 126), ladder (p. 129), threaded (p. 127), tied (p. 126)

8: ISOLATED STITCHES

Isolated stitches are those that are worked individually, rather than continuously. There are numerous variations; some are easy to work, while others require a lot of practice to perfect.

These stitches can be used on their own, applied randomly to add decorative elements to line stitches or scattered to form a filling. Most isolated stitches are raised in appearance and so add texture and interest to surface embroidery, acting as accents within flat areas of stitching.

1

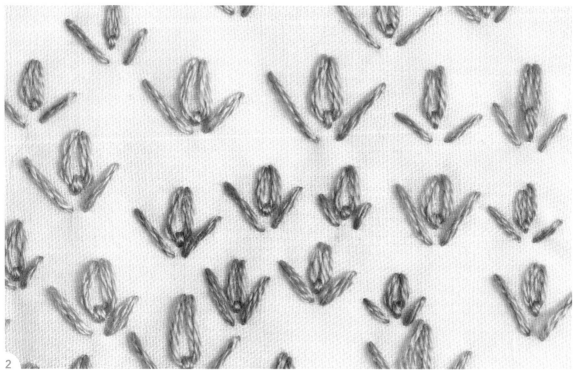
2

3

FABRICS: Isolated stitches can be worked on plain- or even-weave fabrics, such as Aida and canvas.

THREADS: Embroidery cotton (six-stranded cotton), cotton pearl (perlé), soft cotton, metallics and tapestry wool can all be used.

NEEDLES: Crewel needles are usually the needle of choice when working on plain fabric – however, some isolated stitches are better worked with a blunt-ended tapestry needle to avoid splitting the thread while working.

OTHER EQUIPMENT: You will need a small pair of sharp embroidery scissors and an embroidery hoop or frame to keep your fabric taut.

4

1 *A woven picot (p. 140)*

2 *Tête-de-boeuf stitch (p. 137)*

3 *French knot (p. 134)*

4 *Bullion knot (p. 134)*

5 *God's eye stitch (p. 139)*

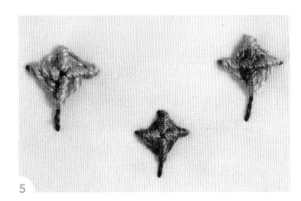

5

FRENCH KNOT

Also known as: French dot, knotted stitch and twisted knot stitch

BULLION KNOT

Also known as: caterpillar stitch, coil stitch, grub knot, worm stitch

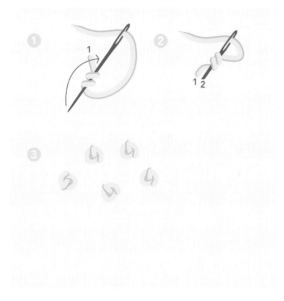

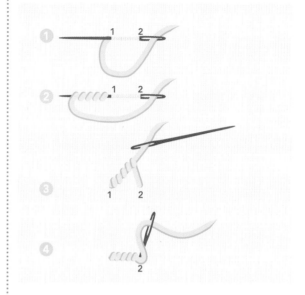

METHOD AND USES

Beginners often find this stitch tricky. In fact, it is quite easy, and worth mastering because it is so versatile – it can be scattered, packed tightly or evenly spaced, and worked in a variety of thread textures. It is used as an accent stitch or for filling or shading; it can also represent the centre of a flower, a simple dot or an eye.

Bring your needle up at 1. Holding the thread taut with your other hand, wind it around the needle twice. Keeping the thread taut, insert the needle at 2, just near 1. Pull through so the twists created form a knot on the fabric's surface. Pull gently or the knot may follow!

FABRIC

Plain- or even-weave fabrics

METHOD AND USES

Bullion knots give your work a lovely raised appearance, so are popular as an accent stitch, a powdering or a dense filling. They are also used in canvaswork on top of a flat area to add texture.

Using a blunt-ended needle to avoid splitting any threads, come up at 1, down at 2 (the required length of the knot) and up again at 1. Don't pull the needle through. Twist the thread around the needle – as many times as needed for the size of knot. Hold the twists and gently pull the needle and the thread through them, while pulling the thread towards 2 to tighten the twists. Insert the needle at 2 and pull through.

FABRIC

Plain- or even-weave fabrics

Related techniques:
Surface embroidery (p. 10)

Similar stitches:
Chinese knot (p. 135), colonial knot (p. 136)

Related techniques:
Canvaswork (p. 44), surface embroidery (p. 10)

Similar stitches:
French knot (p. 134)

CHINESE KNOT

Also known as: blind knot, forbidden knot and Peking knot

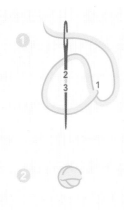

METHOD AND USES

This easy-to-work stitch is similar to the French knot (left), but flatter. It appears often in Chinese embroideries as a filling stitch, worked very small and close together. It is also worked in rows to create textured borders, or as an accent stitch.

Bring your needle to the front of your fabric at 1. Take it down at 2 and up at 3, then loop your thread around the needle, as shown. Hold the loop down with your thumb and pull through gently. Repeat as required.

FABRIC

Plain- or even-weave fabrics. Stranded cotton or silk gives a flatter appearance; tapestry wool or cotton pearl (perlé) gives a raised effect.

Related techniques:
Freestyle embroidery (p. 12), canvaswork (p. 44)

Similar stitches:
French knot (p. 134), colonial knot (p. 136)

FOUR-LEGGED KNOT

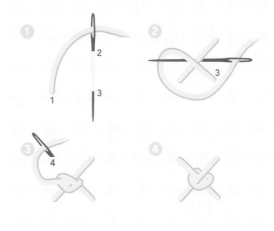

METHOD AND USES

A four-legged knot resembles a cross-stitch with a knot at the centre. It is used as an accent stitch, a filling stitch or is worked in rows to form a pattern or border.

Start by bringing your needle to the front of the fabric at 1. Take your needle down at 2 and up at 3 to form a diagonal straight stitch. Next, take your needle under the first diagonal stitch, looping the thread as shown; do not pierce the fabric. Pull through gently to form a knot. To finish insert your needle at 4.

FABRIC

Plain- or even-weave fabrics

Related techniques:
Freestyle embroidery (p. 12)

Similar stitches:
No notable matches

COLONIAL KNOT

Also known as: figure-of-eight knot

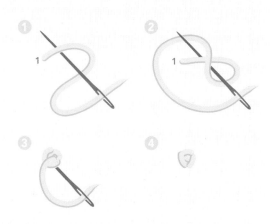

SQUARE BOSS STITCH

Also known as: raised knot

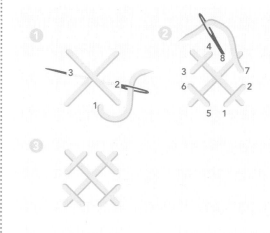

METHOD AND USES

The colonial knot is similar to a French knot, but here the thread is wrapped around the needle in a figure of eight.

Bring your needle up at 1 and make a backwards 'S' with the thread, as shown. Next, wrap your thread around your needle to complete a figure of eight. Pull the long end of the thread to tighten it at the needle tip, then insert the needle near to where your thread first emerged. Keeping the thread taut, pull through gently.

FABRIC

Plain-weave fabrics

METHOD AND USES

Square boss stitch can be used as an isolated stitch where extra colour and texture is needed, worked in rows or scattered to form a pretty knotted filling.

First, work a cross-stitch, then cover each arm of the cross-stitch with a straight stitch. Bring your needle up at 1, down at 2 and up at 3 to create the first straight stitch (step 1), then work a straight stitch to cross each arm – up at 1, down at 2; up at 3, down at 4; up at 5, down at 6; up at 7, down at 8 – keeping the straight stitches closer to the middle than the ends (step 2).

FABRIC

Mostly even-weave fabrics, including Aida. If using plain weaves, stitches must be kept even.

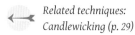

Related techniques:
Candlewicking (p. 29)

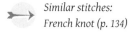

Similar stitches:
French knot (p. 134)

Related techniques:
Counted-thread work (p. 38)

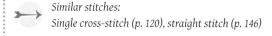

Similar stitches:
Single cross-stitch (p. 120), straight stitch (p. 146)

DETACHED WHEATEAR STITCH

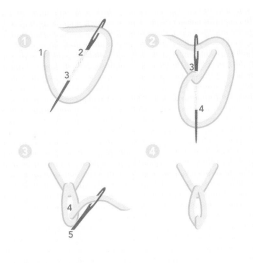

TÊTE-DE-BOEUF STITCH

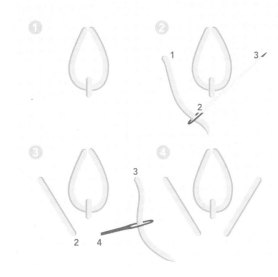

METHOD AND USES

Sometimes confused with tête-de-boeuf (right), this combines a fly and lazy daisy stitch to produce a filling stitch that can be scattered randomly or evenly. It is also used for foliage or, predictably enough, ears of wheat!

Work in any direction. Bring your needle up at 1, down at 2, up at 3. Pull through, leaving a loop of thread on the fabric to create the fly stitch. Now make a lazy daisy stitch. Insert your needle again at 3, leaving another loop, then emerge at 4, inside the second loop. Insert the needle again at 5 to form a small, straight stitch to secure the loop.

FABRIC

Plain- or even-weave fabrics

METHOD AND USES

This attractive filling stitch, shaped like a bull's head, can be scattered evenly or randomly. It combines a lazy daisy stitch and two straight stitches. It can also be arranged in alternating rows to create diagonal lines, or worked in two colours to create tiny buds.

Start with a lazy daisy stitch. Next, work a diagonal straight stitch on each side of this. Bring your needle up at 1, down at 2, then up at 3 and down at 4. Repeat as often as required.

FABRIC

Plain- or even-weave fabrics

 Related techniques:
Freestyle embroidery (p. 12)

 Similar stitches:
Fly stitch (p. 101), lazy daisy stitch (p. 96)

 Related techniques:
Freestyle embroidery (p. 12)

 Similar stitches:
Lazy daisy stitch (p. 96)

CUP STITCH

Also known as: raised cup stitch

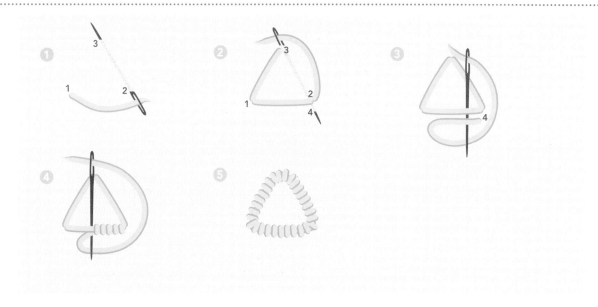

METHOD AND USES

Cup stitch is a decorative motif stitch, worked singly or one inside another in two or three different colours to create small flowers. Cup stitch is also used to add texture and depth to flat areas in canvaswork. A foundation of three stitches is worked to form a triangle, then a series of loop stitches is worked over these stitches and packed tightly around the triangle to give a three-dimensional effect.

For the triangle, bring your needle up at 1, down at 2, then up at 3. Insert the needle again back at 1, then emerge at 2 and take it back down at 3 to complete the three sides. Emerge at 4, slightly below 2.

The loop stitches will require a blunt needle to avoid piercing the fabric. Pass under the first bar, then continue clockwise around the triangle, packing your stitches tightly to form a circle. When you have finished, insert your needle back through the fabric.

FABRIC

Plain- or even-weave fabrics. Firm thread makes the stitch stand out from the fabric.

Related techniques:
Freestyle embroidery (p. 12), canvaswork (p. 44)

Similar stitches:
No notable matches

GOD'S EYE STITCH

METHOD AND USES

This stitch was inspired by *ojo de dios* – tokens made by the Huichole Indians of Mexico by weaving a wooden cross with colourful threads and wools to symbolize God's watchful eye. The God's eye stitch is created in a similar way, simply using a cross of straight stitches woven with a spiral of backstitches. It is used as an isolated stitch or as a heavy filling stitch.

Form the initial cross by bringing your needle up at 1, down at 2, up at 3 and down at 4. Next, weave the arms of the cross with backstitches. Bring your needle up above the crossbar, just to the left of the vertical arm, then pass it back over the top of the cross's vertical arm and under the horizontal stitch, as shown. Do not pierce the fabric. Continue working around each arm until the top part of the cross is covered. Finish by inserting the needle back through the fabric.

FABRIC

Plain- or even-weave fabrics. Cotton pearl (perlé) is best; wool threads give a textured effect.

Related techniques:
Freestyle embroidery (p. 12)

Similar stitches:
Woven circles (p. 141)

WOVEN PICOT

METHOD AND USES

This stitch is used to create flower petals and foliage, or worked as a decorative edging stitch.

Insert a ball-headed dressmaker's pin vertically into your fabric to use as a guide. Bring your needle up at 1, down at 2, then up at 3. The loop of thread should be around the head of your pin, as shown. Loop the thread around the pin head again, then, moving from right to left, pass the needle under, over, under these loops. Do not pierce your fabric.

Now work back the other way, passing your needle over, under and over the loops as you travel to the right. Repeat these two steps to fill your shape, packing the stitches close together as you go. Finally, insert your needle back through the fabric to finish off, then remove the pin. Your stitch should only be attached to the fabric at the base.

FABRIC

Plain- or even-weave fabrics. Use a firm thread, eg cotton pearl (perlé).

Related techniques:
Freestyle embroidery (p. 12)

Similar stitches:
No notable matches

WOVEN CIRCLES

Also known as: ribbed spider's web, spider's web, woven spoke stitch and woven wheel

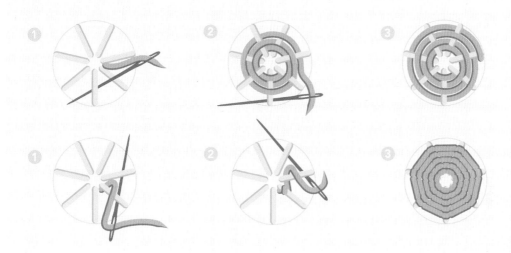

METHOD AND USES

This small, circular stitch has a raised appearance and can be used as a spot motif and also for spider's webs and flower heads, either with the spokes left around the edges or completely covered. There are two different versions of this stitch: the woven kind and the ribbed (whipped) kind.

The woven kind: Draw a circle with a dot in the middle as a guide to keep your spokes even. Bring your needle up at the outside of the circle, then insert it at the centre. Create an odd number of 'spokes' around your circle. With a blunt needle, come up in between two spokes, near the centre of the circle, then pass your thread over the first spoke, under the next and so on. Work round, packing the weaving closely. When done, insert your needle under the previous row and pull through to the back.

The ribbed kind: Begin by creating a foundation of radiating spokes as before – this time, either an odd or an even number. Bring your needle up near the centre, pass under the first spoke, back over and under the same spoke, as shown. Continue working this way around the circle, then finish off as before.

FABRIC

Plain- or even-weave fabrics

Related techniques:
Freestyle embroidery (p. 12)

Similar stitches:
God's eye stitch (p. 139)

9: STRAIGHT STITCHES

Straight stitch is one of the easiest stitches to work, using a simple up-and-down motion of the needle. It can be used to create individual stitches in various sizes, or worked in a continuous line, as for running stitch (p. 94). This is one of the plainest stitches. However, a row of running stitches can be pretty in its own right – and even more so when laced, whipped or interlaced with a contrasting thread.

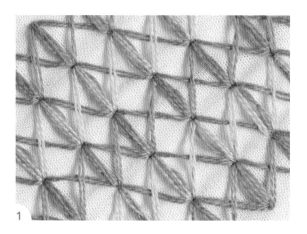

1

1 *Zig-zag stitch (p. 150)*

2 *Fern stitch (p. 147)*

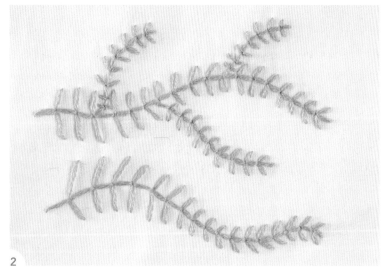

2

You will find that by using this simple stitch in a variety of ways and patterns, it is possible to build up a whole series of decorative stitches that can then be used to great effect within most styles of embroidery work.

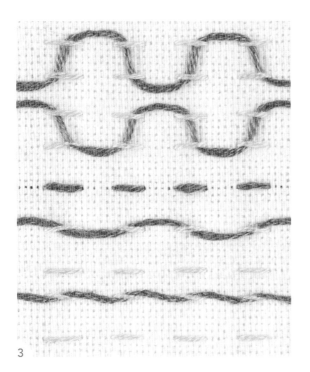

FABRICS: Straight stitches can be worked on plain-weave fabrics. Even-weave fabrics, such as even-weave linen or Aida cloth, are used when stitches are to be kept even.

THREADS: Embroidery cotton (six-stranded cotton), cotton pearl (perlé), soft cotton and silk threads may all be used. Metallic threads can be used for lacing, interlacing and whipping a row of straight stitches. Experimenting with combinations of threads and a simple straight stitch can build up areas of texture in a freestyle design.

NEEDLES: Crewel needles are usually the needle of choice when working on plain fabrics – they come in various sizes and have large eyes designed for threads of different thicknesses. Whipped, laced and interlaced running stitches are better worked with a blunt-ended tapestry needle to avoid splitting the threads of the base stitches while working.

OTHER EQUIPMENT: You will need a small pair of sharp embroidery scissors and an embroidery hoop or frame to keep your fabric taut. Fabric marker pens (fading or water-soluble) can be used to draw guidelines for keeping your straight stitches even.

3 *Laced (top) and whipped (bottom) running stitch (p. 144)*

4 *Brick stitch (p. 154)*

WHIPPED RUNNING STITCH
Also known as: cordonnet stitch

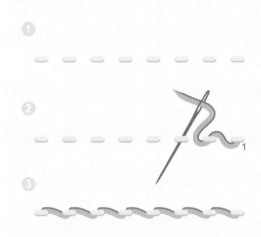

METHOD AND USES

This is a decorative outline stitch, used for straight or curved lines.

Working from right to left, create a foundation row of running stitches. Now, using the same or a contrasting colour, bring a blunt-ended tapestry needle up at 1, below the first stitch you created, and thread it over and under the second stitch. Continue along the row of stitches. Do not pass the needle back through your fabric until all stitches are completed.

FABRIC

Plain- or even-weave fabrics

Related techniques:
Freestyle embroidery (p. 12)

Similar stitches:
Interlaced running stitch (p. 145), laced running stitch (p. 144), running stitch (p. 94)

LACED RUNNING STITCH
Also known as: threaded running stitch

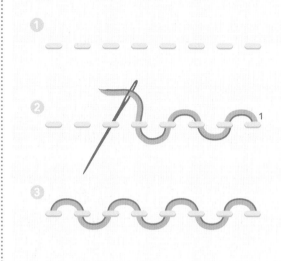

METHOD AND USES

As with whipped running stitch (left), this stitch can be worked straight or curved. It can also be used for decorative details.

Work a row of running stitches, right to left. Next, thread a blunt-ended tapestry needle with a contrasting colour and bring it up just below the first stitch at 1. Pass up and under the first stitch, down and under the second, up and under the third and so on. Insert your needle back through your fabric at the end of the row. Keep your thread slightly loose so the lacing has a slight arch to it.

FABRIC

Plain- or even-weave fabrics

Related techniques:
Freestyle embroidery (p. 12)

Similar stitches:
Interlaced running stitch (p. 145), running stitch (p. 94), whipped running stitch (p. 144)

INTERLACED RUNNING STITCH
Also known as: double laced running stitch

SEED STITCH
Also known as: seed filling stitch, seeding stitch, speckling stitch

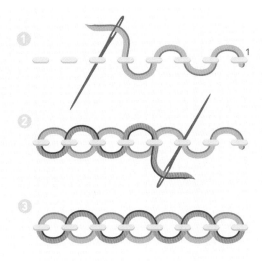

METHOD AND USES

This interlaced variation is best for wide outlines and decorative borders.

Begin as for laced running stitch (p. 144), first working a row of running stitches from right to left and then lacing along this row. For this stitch, however, the lacing is worked a second time, left to right.

Using the same thread as your first row of lacing, or a contrasting thread, work back along your row, filling in the spaces. Again, don't pull your lacing thread too tightly – keep your second pass even and flat.

FABRIC

Plain- or even-weave fabrics. A single thread, eg cotton pearl (perlé) or soft cotton, works well.

 Related techniques:
Freestyle embroidery (p. 12)

 Similar stitches:
Laced running stitch (p. 144), running stitch (p. 94), whipped running stitch (p. 144)

METHOD AND USES

These small, straight, seed-like stitches are created equal in length, then scattered irregularly but evenly to fill shapes or create patterns. They also add texture and interest to plain areas of stitching.

Two parallel seed stitches, as shown here, can be worked together to create a more raised, textured effect on the surface of your fabric. Working randomly in different directions, bring your needle up at 1, down at 2, up at 3 and down at 4.

FABRIC

Plain- or even-weave fabrics

 Related techniques:
Crewelwork (p. 18), freestyle embroidery (p. 12)

 Similar stitches:
Straight stitch (p. 146)

STRAIGHT STITCH
Also known as: stroke stitch

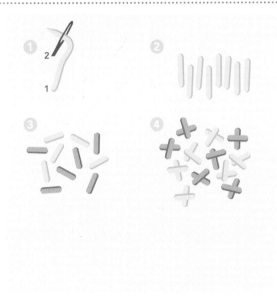

METHOD AND USES

This is the very easiest stitch to work of all, and versatile too. It adds both texture and interest. Try it with a green thread – it's great for depicting grass!

Working in any direction, bring your needle up at 1 and down at 2. Work as many stitches as required. Straight stitches can be worked over one another in different weights of thread and different shades. However, stitches should not be worked too large or they will look loose.

FABRIC

Plain- or even-weave fabrics

 Related techniques:
Freestyle embroidery (p. 12)

 Similar stitches:
Seed stitch (p. 145)

ARROWHEAD STITCH

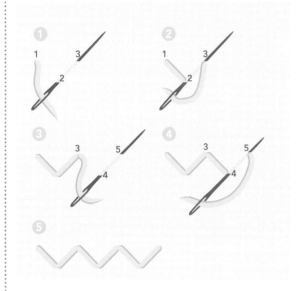

METHOD AND USES

This is a decorative line or filling stitch, formed by placing two straight stitches at right angles to each other, forming a series of 'V's. Stitches can be worked horizontally or vertically.

Working left to right, bring your needle up at 1, down at 2 and then up at 3. Take it down at 2 again and up at 3 to complete the first 'V'. Next, insert your needle at 4, emerge at 5, then pass from 4 to 5 again to complete the second 'V'. Repeat as required along your row.

FABRIC

Usually even-weave fabrics. Draw guidelines on plain weaves to keep stitches even.

 Related techniques:
Counted-thread work (p. 38)

 Similar stitches:
Zig-zag stitch (p. 150)

FERN STITCH

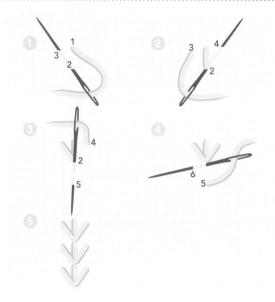

METHOD AND USES

This stitch consists of three straight stitches radiating out from the same hole. It can be worked in straight lines or curved, and is generally used to depict fern-like foliage.

Bring your needle up at 1, down at 2 and up at 3. Take it down at 2 again, then up at 4. Next, take it down at 2 and up at 5 to begin your next stitch. Bring your needle down at 2, up at 6 and down at 5. Repeat as required.

FABRIC

Plain- or even-weave fabrics. Draw guidelines on plain weaves to keep stitches even.

 Related techniques:
Freestyle embroidery (p. 12)

 Similar stitches:
Fly stitch (p. 101)

LEAF STITCH

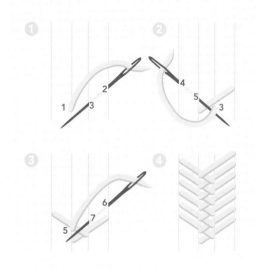

METHOD AND USES

Leaf stitch is used to add detail to leaf designs that have first been defined using stem stitch or backstitch. It makes decorative borders too.

Always work from the bottom up. Draw four guidelines. Bring your needle up at 1, down at 2, making a slanted stitch, then up at 3. Pull through. Take your needle down again at 4, then emerge at 5, diagonally below, and pull through once more. Next, insert your needle at 6, then come up at 7 to begin again. Repeat as required, making sure each stitch crosses the previous one.

FABRIC

Plain- or fine even-weave fabrics

 Related techniques:
Freestyle embroidery (p. 12)

 Similar stitches:
Vandyke stitch (p. 148)

VANDYKE STITCH

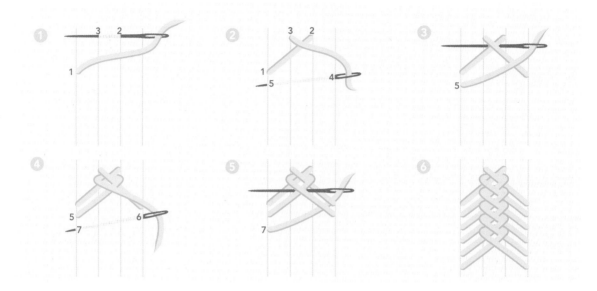

METHOD AND USES

The lovely plaited effect at the centre of this stitch works well for wide borders, or for filling small leaf shapes. The central plaited stitches should always be even, even though the length of the stitches can vary. If you are unable to count the threads in your fabric, begin by marking four parallel guidelines with a fabric marker pen.

Work from top to bottom. Bring your needle up through your fabric at 1, then take your thread across diagonally and insert it at 2, with your needle emerging at 3. Pull through. Next, insert your needle in the outer right-hand guideline at 4, in line with 1, then emerge at 5. Pull through. Now, without piercing the fabric, take your needle under

the centre cross and pull through gently. Insert your needle back through the fabric at 6 and out again at 7, ready to begin the next stitch, passing through the crossed stitches above, as before. The stitches are anchored at the outer edges only.

FABRIC

Plain- or even-weave fabrics

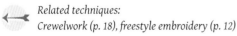

Related techniques:
Crewelwork (p. 18), freestyle embroidery (p. 12)

Similar stitches:
Leaf stitch (p. 147), loop stitch (p. 114)

BASKET STITCH (1)

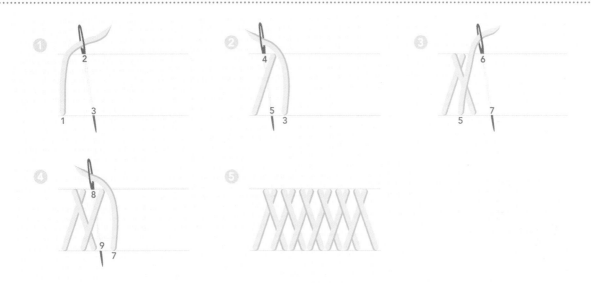

METHOD AND USES

Basket stitch is very similar in appearance to herringbone stitch. It can be worked both open and closed, and used for both borders and solid lines.

Begin by drawing two guidelines on your fabric to keep your stitches even, then follow this sequence carefully: Bring your needle to the front of the fabric at 1, then down at 2 on the top guideline. Bring your needle up on the bottom line at 3. Next, cross over the top of the previous stitch and take the needle down at 4, emerging at 5 on the bottom line. Cross back up again, over the top of the previous diagonal stitch, and insert the needle at 6 on the

top line, emerging at 7 on the bottom line. From 7, cross over the top of the previous stitch, and then take your needle down again at 8, emerging again at 9 to begin the sequence again. Repeat as required along your row.

FABRIC

Plain-weave fabrics

Related techniques:
Freestyle embroidery (p. 12)

Similar stitches:
Herringbone stitch (p. 100), long-armed cross-stitch (p. 124)

ZIG-ZAG STITCH

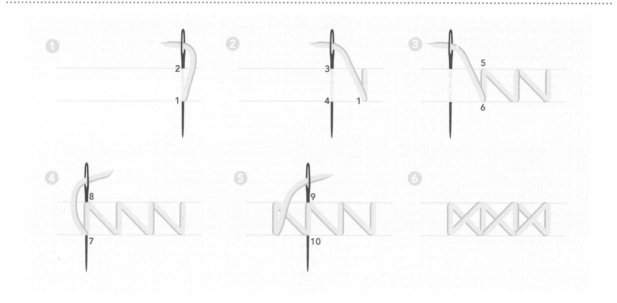

METHOD AND USES

This is a line or border stitch that can also be used as a filling stitch if worked closely in rows.

Start by working right to left, using two parallel guidelines. Bring your needle up at 1, down at 2, then up again at 1. Make a diagonal stitch by inserting it at 3 and emerging at 4. Insert again at 3 and emerge again at 4 before making another diagonal stitch by inserting the needle at 5, emerging at 6 and inserting again at 5. Repeat, emerging again at 6 before making another diagonal stitch.

Continue as desired along your row. At the end of the row, reverse direction.

Start by taking your needle up at 7 again, then down at 8, doubling up the vertical stitch here. Next, bring it up at 7 again, cross over the diagonal stitch to the right and insert your needle at 9, to emerge at 10. Continue these steps along to the right, filling in the zig-zags in the opposite direction to complete the row.

FABRIC

Plain- or even-weave fabrics

Related techniques:
Counted-thread work (p. 38), freestyle embroidery (p. 12)

Similar stitches:
Arrowhead stitch (p. 146)

DARNING STITCH
Also known as: tacking stitch

SATIN STITCH
Also known as: damask stitch

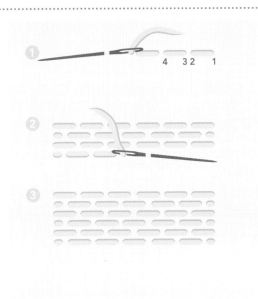

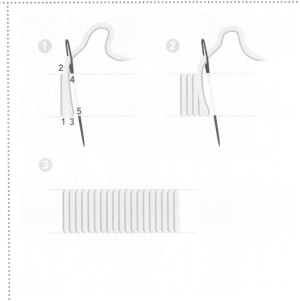

METHOD AND USES

Not the kind of darning used for mending! This is similar to running stitch but with tiny spaces between stitches. It is used as a filling or line stitch, or to create complex geometric borders.

Working right to left, bring your needle up at 1, down at 2, up at 3 and down at 4. Repeat as required. For a brick pattern, work a row of long, straight stitches right to left (eg five threads across with one thread's space in between). Work the next row left to right, beginning and ending with a small stitch and filling in the gaps with a long stitch.

FABRIC

Plain- or even-weave fabrics, including Aida

METHOD AND USES

One of the oldest stitches of all, this filling or line stitch consists of straight stitches worked close together, straight or slanted, to completely cover the fabric. It requires practice to keep your stitches even! This is used for filling small shapes; for wider shapes use long and short stitch.

Mark two parallel guidelines on your fabric. Bring your needle to the surface at 1, take it down at 2, then slide it under the fabric to emerge at 3. Take the needle down again at 4 and up at 5. All stitches must be even and flat.

FABRIC

Plain- or even-weave fabrics. A hoop will keep fabric taut.

Related techniques:
Broderie anglaise (p. 17), crewelwork (p. 18), freestyle embroidery (p. 12), whitework (p. 14)

Similar stitches:
Encroaching satin stitch (p. 153), long and short stitch (p. 154), padded satin stitch (p. 153), whipped satin stitch (p. 155)

Related techniques:
Crewelwork (p. 18), freestyle embroidery (p. 12)

Similar stitches:
Japanese darning (p. 152), running stitch (p. 94)

JAPANESE DARNING
Also known as: Japanese darning stitch

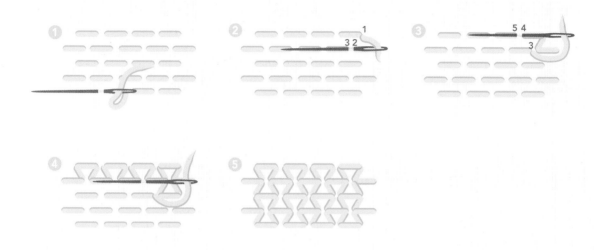

METHOD AND USES

Japanese darning is a decorative filling stitch, formed by first creating parallel rows of darning stitch and then adding diagonal stitches in between these to form a very distinctive pattern.

Working from right to left, create a row of darning stitches in a brick pattern (p. 151; there is no need here, though, to work a short stitch on the second row as shown on that page). Create as many rows as desired.

Next, connect your first two rows using diagonal stitches. Working from right to left, bring your needle up at 1, then pick up the fabric between the first two stitches on

the second row, between 2 and 3. Pull through and insert your needle again at 4, then bring it up at 5, picking up the fabric in the same way as before. Repeat along your row, then work in the same way along the next row. Repeat to fill your chosen area.

FABRIC

Plain- or even-weave fabrics, including Aida. Draw guidelines on plain weaves to keep stitches even.

 Related techniques:
Freestyle embroidery (p. 12)

 Similar stitches:
Darning stitch (p. 151), running stitch (p. 94)

PADDED SATIN STITCH

Also known as: raised satin stitch

ENCROACHING SATIN STITCH

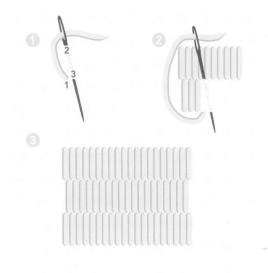

METHOD AND USES

This is similar to satin stitch. However, here a foundation row of chain stitch, split stitch or running stitches is worked first to create a 3-D effect. Draw your shape's outline on the fabric and work a row of chain stitches (p. 95) just inside this.

Next, bring your needle to the front at the top of your shape at 1, then take it down at 2. Keep working satin stitches over the top of your chain stitch. For a more padded effect, you could also work further satin stitches over the top of the previous ones in a diagonal direction.

FABRIC

Plain- or even-weave fabrics

 Related techniques:
Freestyle embroidery (p. 12), whitework (p. 14)

 Similar stitches:
Encroaching satin stitch (p. 153), long and short stitch (p. 154), satin stitch (p. 151), whipped satin stitch (p. 155)

METHOD AND USES

This filling stitch is useful for creating blended areas with subtle colour shifts.

Begin by working a row of vertical satin stitches (p. 151) from left to right, bringing your needle up at 1, down at 2 and up at 3 and continuing along your row. Next, create a second row of satin stitches, working each stitch in between the base of each of the stitches in the previous row.

FABRIC

Plain- or even-weave fabrics. Stranded cotton or silk thread with a slight sheen work well.

 Related techniques:
Crewelwork (p. 18), freestyle embroidery (p. 12)

 Similar stitches:
Long and short stitch (p. 154), padded satin stitch (p. 153), satin stitch (p. 151), whipped satin stitch (p. 155)

LONG AND SHORT STITCH

Also known as: embroidery stitch, shading stitch, tapestry stitch

BRICK STITCH (1)

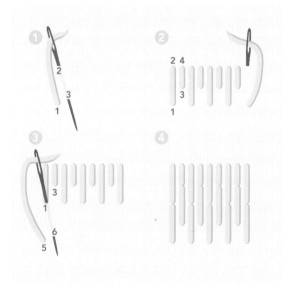

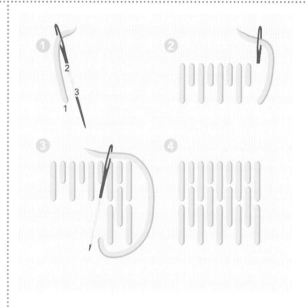

METHOD AND USES

This stitch provides a way to fill large shaded areas or irregular shapes. Bring your needle up at 1, down at 2, then up at 3. Take your needle down at 4 to complete a second, shorter stitch and then continue creating stitches of alternating lengths along your row.

The following rows use same-length stitches; it is their placement that gives a long/short appearance. Come up at 5, down at 1, piercing the base of the stitch above, then up at 6 and down at 3, again piercing the stitch above. Repeat. Work the stitches closely to cover the fabric completely.

FABRIC

Plain- or even-weave fabrics, including single-mesh (mono) canvas

Related techniques:
Crewelwork (p. 18), freestyle embroidery (p. 12)

Similar stitches:
Encroaching satin stitch (p. 153), padded satin stitch (p. 153), satin stitch (p. 151), whipped satin stitch (p. 155)

METHOD AND USES

This shaded filling stitch resembles laid bricks and is similar in appearance to long and short stitch. Here, however, the stitches do not pierce the bases of those in the previous row.

Working from left to right, create a row of long and short stitches (left), starting by coming up at 1, down at 2, then up at 3. Next, travelling right to left, fill in a second row, working even stitches to fill in the spaces of the previous row.

FABRIC

Plain- or even-weave fabrics, including Aida

Related techniques:
Crewelwork (p. 18), freestyle embroidery (p. 12)

Similar stitches:
Long and short stitch (p. 154)

PLATE STITCH

WHIPPED SATIN STITCH

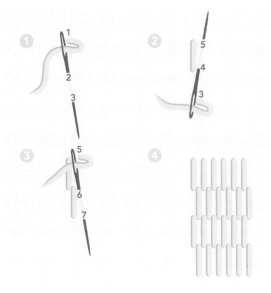

METHOD AND USES

These interlocking stitches are suited to flat areas of stitching. They do not entirely cover the fabric's surface.

Work all rows left to right. Bring your needle up at 1, down at 2 and up at 3. Pull through. Next take your needle down at 4, slightly above the base of the previous stitch. Pull through at 5. Next, insert your needle at 6, and emerge at 7 to begin again. Work your next row by placing each set of stitches in between the bases of those created in the previous row.

FABRIC

Plain- or even-weave fabrics. Mark three parallel guidelines if helpful.

 Related techniques:
Freestyle embroidery (p. 12)

 Similar stitches:
Encroaching satin stitch (p. 153), satin stitch (p. 151)

METHOD AND USES

Ordinary satin stitches can be 'whipped' with this stitch, using a contrasting thread, to create a raised or corded effect. The whipped stitches are worked diagonally, in the opposite direction to the satin stitches, and are evenly spaced.

First work a row of slanted satin stitches. Next, travelling in the opposite direction, work diagonal whipping stitches over and under the design.

FABRIC

Plain- or even-weave fabrics. A single thread, eg cotton pearl (perlé), works well.

 Related techniques:
Freestyle embroidery (p. 12)

 Similar stitches:
Encroaching satin stitch (p. 153), long and short stitch (p. 154) padded satin stitch (p. 153), satin stitch (p. 151)

10: BUTTONHOLE STITCHES

This series of stitches has been around for many years and is used in most styles of embroidery, including freestyle, cutwork, crewelwork, whitework, broderie anglaise, stumpwork and appliqué. Serious embroiderers should add these versatile stitches to their stitch arsenal.

All the stitches detailed in this chapter are worked by looping the thread around the needle and then securing the thread to the surface of the fabric. Buttonhole stitches can be used for many functional and decorative purposes – as filling, edging or line stitches, or for covering the raw edges of blankets, to name just a few.

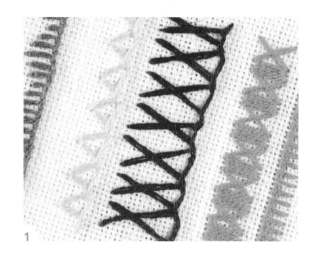

1 Crossed blanket stitch (p. 164)

2 Buttonhole flower (p. 161)

3 Antwerp edging stitch (p. 166)

4 Double blanket stitch (p. 163)

5 Long and short blanket stitch (p. 164)

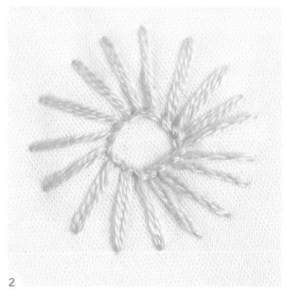

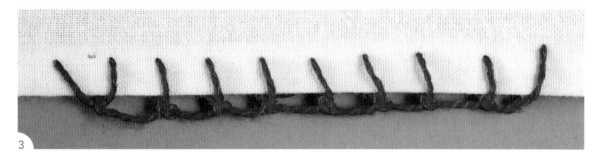

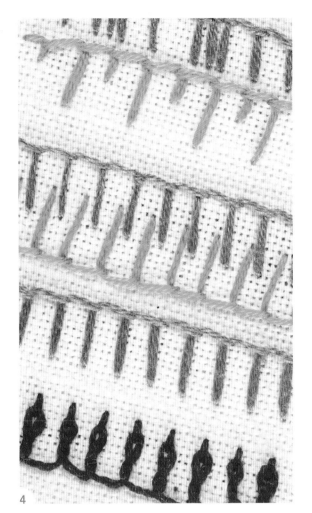

FABRICS: Buttonhole stitches can be worked on plain- or even-weave fabrics. Patterned fabrics or gingham can also be used.

THREADS: Embroidery cotton (six-stranded cotton), cotton pearl (perlé), stranded silk threads and crewel wools are all suitable – just as long as your thread is appropriate for your chosen fabric.

NEEDLES: Depending on the type of thread you are using, crewel needles can be employed for most of these stitches – they come in different sizes, have a large eye and are sharp. Sharply pointed chenille needles can be handy for heavier threads and fabrics, as they are thicker and have a larger eye. Tapestry needles are blunt-ended and so are helpful when working Ceylon stitch (p. 167).

OTHER EQUIPMENT: You will need a small pair of sharp embroidery scissors and an embroidery hoop or frame to keep your fabric taut. Fabric marker pens – either fading or water-soluble – are useful for marking guidelines on your fabric.

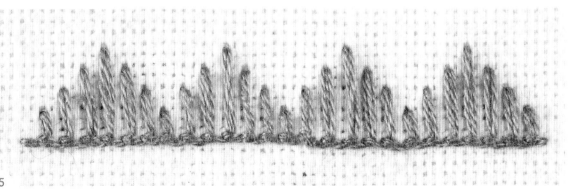

TAILOR'S BUTTONHOLE STITCH

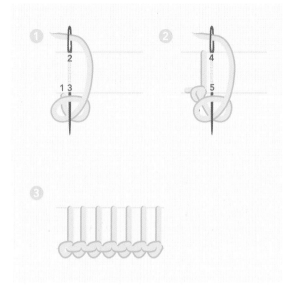

METHOD AND USES

Unlike plain buttonhole stitch, this has a strong, hard-wearing edge, which makes it suitable for heavy fabrics. For this reason it is used for making buttonholes on coats.

Draw two guidelines on your fabric. Working left to right, bring your needle up at 1, down at 2, then up at 3. Wrap your thread around the tip of your needle as shown and pull through gently. To work the next stitch, take your needle down at 4, up at 5, wrap the thread around as before and pull through. Repeat along your row.

FABRIC

Plain- or even-weave fabrics

Tip
Pull your thread up and then down to tighten the knot on the bottom line.

Related techniques:
Drawn-thread work (p. 49)

Similar stitches:
Buttonhole stitch (p. 99)

BUTTONHOLE WITH PICOT

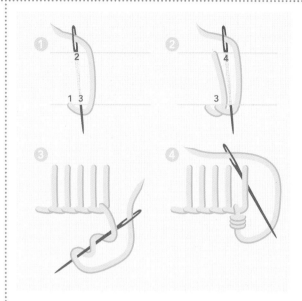

METHOD AND USES

This attractive line stitch can be worked straight or curved, with the stitches kept close or spaced slightly apart.

Working left to right, bring your needle up at 1, down at 2 and up at 3, keeping the thread beneath your needle. Pull through, then insert at 4 to repeat.

At the point where you require a picot, wrap your thread loosely around your needle, as shown; hold the twists in place with your thumb, then pull through to form a picot. Pass your needle under the previous stitch without piercing the fabric. With the thread under your needle, pull through.

FABRIC

Plain- or even-weave fabrics. Draw guidelines on plain weaves to keep stitches even.

Related techniques:
Cutwork (p. 32), freestyle embroidery (p. 12)

Similar stitches:
Buttonhole stitch (p. 99)

SINGLE BUTTONHOLE BAR
Also known as: detached buttonhole bar/stitch

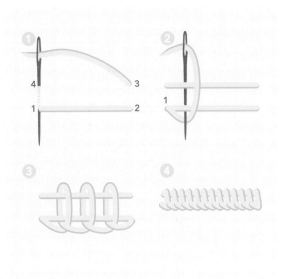

DOUBLE BUTTONHOLE BAR

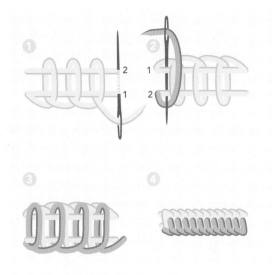

METHOD AND USES

Single buttonhole bars are good for adding lacy effects to your work. Start by working two horizontal straight stitches. Bring your needle up at 1, down at 2, up at 3, down at 4, then up again at the end of the first horizontal stitch.

Next, work a buttonhole stitch over the two horizontal threads without piercing the fabric below. Repeat, keeping all the buttonhole stitches packed closely together to form a solid bar.

FABRIC

Plain-weave fabrics

METHOD AND USES

This double version creates a more solid bar. As for the single buttonhole bar (left), create a foundation of two horizontal straight stitches and work a first row of buttonhole stitches over the top of these. At the end of the row insert your needle at 1, bring it up again at 2 and turn your work around.

Work a second row of interlocking buttonhole stitches in between the first row of stitches, without piercing the fabric. Insert your needle at the end of the row to take your thread to the back of the fabric.

FABRIC

Plain-weave fabrics. A firm thread, eg cotton pearl (perlé), gives the best results.

 Related techniques:
Cutwork (p. 32), freestyle embroidery (p. 12)

 Similar stitches:
Buttonhole stitch (p. 99), double buttonhole bar (p. 159)

 Related techniques:
Cutwork (p. 32)

 Similar stitches:
Buttonhole stitch (p. 99), single buttonhole bar (p. 159)

UP AND DOWN BUTTONHOLE STITCH

Also known as: mirrored buttonhole stitch and up and down blanket stitch

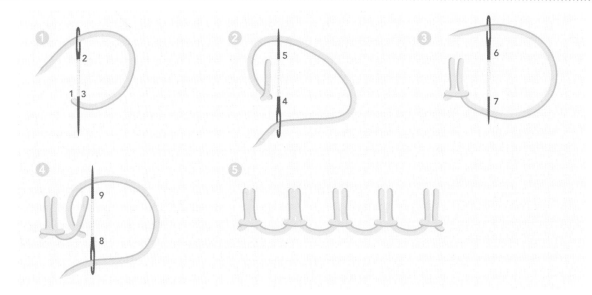

METHOD AND USES

This version of buttonhole stitch is very easy to work. It consists of two vertical buttonhole stitches crossed at the base with a bar. Each pair of stitches is then linked to the next with a loop. Up and down buttonhole stitch is used as a border, line or filling stitch.

Bring a blunt-ended needle up at 1, down at 2, then up again at 3. Loop your thread beneath the needle and pull through. Insert your needle nearby at 4, then up at 5 (level with 2). Again, loop your thread round and keep it under your needle as you pull through, pulling upwards and then downwards so that the stitch you create lies flat.

Leaving a gap, insert your needle at 6 and bring it up at 7. Loop the thread round and under the needle, then pull through as before. Insert the needle at 8, bring it up at 9, loop the thread and pull through. Repeat to create a row of the desired length.

FABRIC

Plain- or even-weave fabrics

Related techniques:
Freestyle embroidery (p. 12)

Similar stitches:
Blanket stitch (p. 100), buttonhole stitch (p. 99)

BUTTONHOLE WHEELS

Also known as: wheel stitch

METHOD AND USES

This stitch is used to depict flowers, wheels and petals. Regular buttonhole stitches are worked in a circle, with all vertical stitches passing through the central hole.

Mark a circle on your fabric then, working anti-clockwise, bring your needle up at 1, down at 2, then up at 3. Loop the thread beneath your needle and pull through. Continue working around the circle, then finish by taking your needle down next to the base of the very first stitch.

FABRIC

Plain- or even-weave fabrics. On even weaves a prominent hole will form; on plain weaves a stiletto tool (used to make holes in cutwork and broderie anglaise) may help.

Related techniques:
Freestyle embroidery (p. 12)

Similar stitches:
Buttonhole flowers (p. 161), buttonhole stitch (p. 99)

BUTTONHOLE FLOWERS

METHOD AND USES

Buttonhole flowers are similar to buttonhole wheels, and are also used to depict flowers and petals. With this stitch, however, the vertical stitches do not pass through the central hole.

Draw a large circle with a smaller one inside it. Working in a clockwise direction, bring your needle up at 1, down at 2, then back up again at 3. Loop the thread beneath your needle and pull through gently. Repeat all around your circle. Stitches can be kept even or can vary in length.

FABRIC

Plain- or even-weave fabrics

Related techniques:
Freestyle embroidery (p. 12)

Similar stitches:
Buttonhole stitch (p. 99), buttonhole wheels (p. 161)

BUTTONHOLE FILLING STITCH

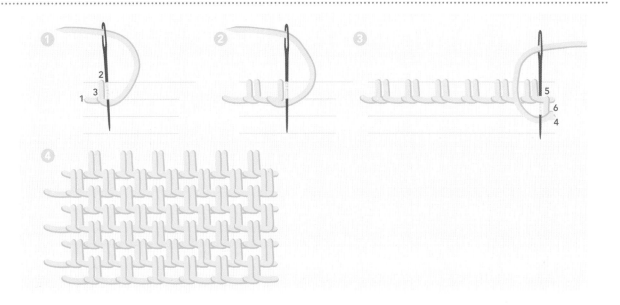

METHOD AND USES

Buttonhole filling stitch is an easy stitch to learn and can be used to produce lacy fillings for medium to large areas.

First, mark four horizontal guidelines on your fabric. Working from left to right, bring your needle up at 1, down at 2 and up at 3, then, keeping the thread beneath your needle, pull through, making a blanket stitch. Next, make a second blanket stitch close to the first. Repeat these two stitches to the right along your line.

Next, working back from right to left, bring your needle up at 4, down at 5 over the loop of the last stitch in the row above and then up at 6. With the thread beneath your needle, pull through to form a blanket stitch. Work another blanket stitch close to the first.

Work pairs of stitches in between the pairs of stitches in the row above. To begin a third row, work from left to right again. You do not have to stick to just two stitches; you can work three or four stitches together, too.

FABRIC

Plain- or even-weave fabrics

Related techniques:
Freestyle embroidery (p. 12)

Similar stitches:
Blanket stitch (p. 100), buttonhole stitch (p. 99)

DOUBLE BLANKET STITCH
Also known as: double buttonhole stitch

OVERLAPPING BLANKET STITCH
Also known as: encroaching blanket stitch

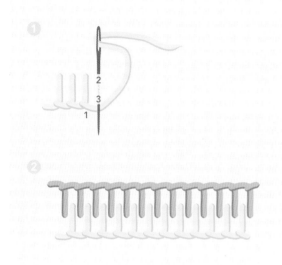

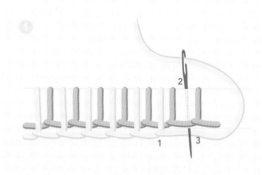

METHOD AND USES

This stitch consists of two parallel, interlocking lines of blanket stitch. It is worked straight or curved to produce wide lines and borders.

Working left to right, bring your needle up at 1, down at 2 and up at 3. With the thread beneath the needle, pull through. Repeat. At the end of the row, turn your work and create a second row in between your first row.

French knots (p. 134) can be worked between the spaces or a contrasting thread can be threaded through both rows to enhance the effect.

FABRIC

Plain- or even-weave fabrics

METHOD AND USES

As the name suggests, this consists of overlapping rows of blanket stitch, used to create wide borders.

Draw two guidelines, then work a row of blanket stitches, keeping the spaces between each stitch even. Change to a contrasting thread, then work a second row directly below the first, passing up at 1, down at 2, then up at 3, as shown, with the verticals of each stitch overlapping the previous row and slotting in between the spaces of each stitch, either to the left or to the right. Several rows can be worked in this way.

FABRIC

Plain- or even-weave fabrics

 Related techniques:
Freestyle embroidery (p. 12)

 Similar stitches:
Blanket stitch (p. 100), buttonhole stitch (p. 99)

 Related techniques:
Freestyle embroidery (p. 12)

 Similar stitches:
Blanket stitch (p. 100)

CROSSED BLANKET STITCH

Also known as: crossed buttonhole stitch

LONG AND SHORT BLANKET STITCH

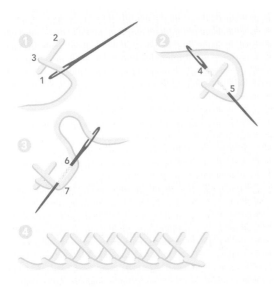

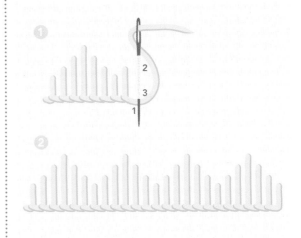

METHOD AND USES

Crossed blanket stitch consists of stitches that are worked in pairs but cross over one another. This is used as a line or filling stitch, and also to create attractive borders.

Working left to right, bring your needle up at 1, down at 2, then up at 3. Pull through. To work the second diagonal, take your needle down at 4 and then up at 5. Keeping the thread beneath your needle, pull through.

For the next stitch, insert the needle at 6 and cross to emerge at 7, by the base of the previous diagonal. Again, the loop of thread should be beneath your needle. Repeat step 2 to complete the stitch, then continue as required.

FABRIC

Plain- or even-weave fabrics

METHOD AND USES

Long and short blanket stitch is worked in the same way as regular blanket stitch, however the verticals of this stitch are either lengthened or shortened. Interesting patterns can be formed by creating stitches in repeated blocks of assorted lengths, as shown. Or you can work one row of long and one row of short blanket stitches. These patterns can then be used to create borders, outlines and line effects.

To complete a stitch, bring your needle up at 1, down at 2 and then up at 3. Keep the thread looped beneath your needle and then pull through. Progress along the row, working each stitch to your chosen length.

FABRIC

Plain- or even-weave fabrics

 Related techniques:
Freestyle embroidery (p. 12)

 Similar stitches:
Blanket stitch (p. 100)

 Related techniques:
Freestyle embroidery (p. 12)

 Similar stitches:
Blanket stitch (p. 100)

CLOSED BLANKET STITCH

Also known as: closed buttonhole stitch

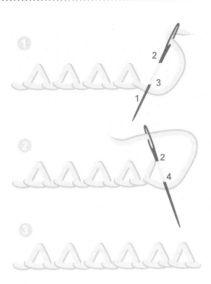

KNOTTED BLANKET STITCH

Also known as: knotted buttonhole stitch

METHOD AND USES

This is yet another version of blanket stitch. This one is similar to the basic stitch but here a pair of diagonal stitches are worked that enter the fabric through the same hole, forming a triangular shape. Closed blanket stitch is used as an edging, border or filling stitch.

Bring your needle up at 1, down at 2, then up again at 3. Keeping the thread beneath your needle, pull through. To create the second diagonal, move a short distance to the right, then insert the needle at 2 again, crossing diagonally underneath the fabric to emerge at 4 – again, keeping the thread beneath your needle. Pull through. Repeat these two stitches along your row.

FABRIC

Plain- or even-weave fabrics

 Related techniques:
Freestyle embroidery (p. 12)

 Similar stitches:
Blanket stitch (p. 100), buttonhole stitch (p. 99)

METHOD AND USES

This stitch takes a bit of practice, but it can be very striking. It is a decorative line stitch, which can be worked curved, straight or in circles. It can also be used for edging.

Mark two guidelines, bring your needle up at 1, then form a loop on the top guideline, as shown. It can be easier to wrap the thread around your index finger and then let it slip to the end of your finger, placing it on the fabric. Hold it in place with the thumb of your free hand.

Take your needle down at 2 and up at 3, keeping the loop beneath your needle. Tighten the thread around the needle before pulling it through gently, otherwise the vertical will be too slack. Repeat along your row.

FABRIC

Plain- or even-weave fabrics

 Related techniques:
Freestyle embroidery (p. 12)

 Similar stitches:
Antwerp edging stitch (p. 166), blanket stitch (p. 100)

ANTWERP EDGING STITCH

Also known as: knot stitch and knotted blanket stitch

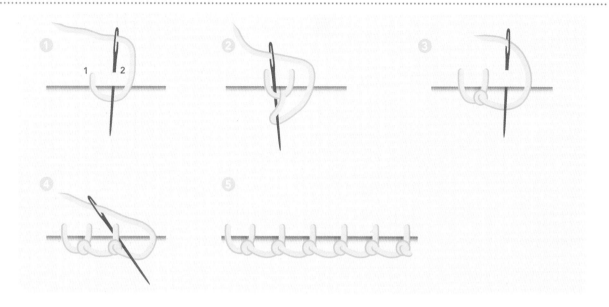

METHOD AND USES

Antwerp edging stitch adds a very pretty finish to plain-hemmed edges on all sorts of household linen items, from handkerchiefs to napkins, pillowcases and blankets. Although it can take a little practice, it is quite easy to work once you get the hang of it!

Working from left to right along the folded edge of your fabric (indicated by the horizontal line), bring your needle up at 1 and then down at 2, as shown. Then, keeping the thread beneath your needle, pull through, leaving a loop of thread. Now insert your needle inside the loop of thread you have just created and, keeping the thread in place beneath the tip of your needle, pull through gently to form

a knot. Repeat these steps to the right to form another stitch, then continue along the edge of the fabric as required to create a row of linked knots.

FABRIC

Plain-weave fabrics

Related techniques:
Freestyle embroidery (p. 12)

Similar stitches:
Knotted blanket stitch (p. 165)

CEYLON STITCH
Also known as: knitted stitch

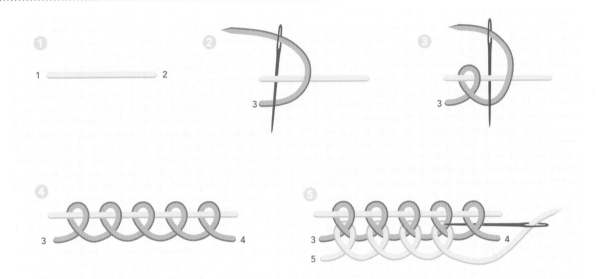

METHOD AND USES

This detached filling stitch is used to fill small and medium shapes. It can be worked with open stitches to create lacy patterns, or it can be worked closely together for a more 'knitted' appearance.

Begin by working a horizontal stitch at the top of your shape. Working left to right, bring your needle up at 1 and down at 2. Change to a blunt-ended needle and bring this up at 3, just below 1. Loop the thread over and under the horizontal stitch from above, keeping the thread beneath the tip of your needle. Do not pierce the fabric. Repeat this all along the horizontal stitch, keeping the loops even. Take the needle down through the fabric at 4, then up at 5.

Next, slip the needle under the two threads of the loop above from right to left, without piercing the fabric, and keeping the thread beneath your needle. Repeat this all along the row.

At the end of this second row, insert the needle into the fabric, as before, then bring it up again just below 5 to begin again. Try to keep your stitches quite loose so they lie flat and do not distort.

FABRIC
Plain- or even-weave fabrics

Related techniques:
Freestyle embroidery (p. 12), stumpwork (p. 37)

Similar stitches:
Buttonhole stitch (p. 99), Pekinese stitch (p. 108)

11: CHAIN STITCHES

The chain stitch has been around for hundreds of years and appears in the embroidery of many cultures. It originated in Persia and India, where it was worked on the right side of the fabric using a hook called an *ari*. In Western countries this became known as a 'tambour hook', which is why the version of chain stitch this tool produces is called 'tambour work'. Tambour work is worked on the reverse of the fabric using a frame.

Some early sewing machines were also able to produce a chain stitch – for example, the Cornely machine, which has been around since the mid-1800s.

1

2

1 *Feathered chain stitch (p. 171)*

2 *Heavy chain stitch (p. 179)*

3 *Raised chain stitch (p. 177)*

4 *Zig-zag chain stitch (p. 174)*

Nevertheless, a basic chain stitch (p. 95) is easy to work with a needle. It is useful for both straight and curved outlines, and as a solid filling. However, you needn't be restricted to the basics – there are many different versions of the stitch to discover in this chapter, including cable, feathered, heavy and raised variations.

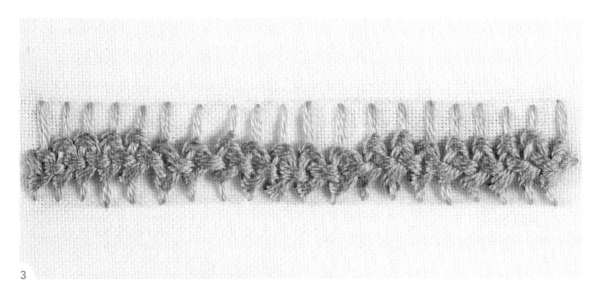

3

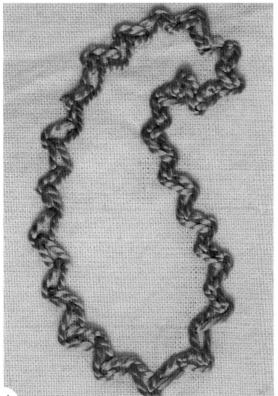

4

FABRICS: Chain stitches can be worked on plain- or even-weave fabrics.

THREADS: Embroidery cotton (six-stranded cotton), cotton pearl (perlé), soft embroidery cotton, metallic threads, tapestry wools and stranded silks can all be used.

NEEDLES: Crewel needles, with their sharp points and larger eyes, are generally used. However, if you are using a heavyweight fabric and thread, a thicker chenille needle can be a better choice.

OTHER EQUIPMENT: You will need a small pair of sharp embroidery scissors and an embroidery hoop or frame to keep your fabric taut. Fabric marker pens – fading or water-soluble – can be used to draw guidelines for keeping your stitches even.

CABLE CHAIN STITCH

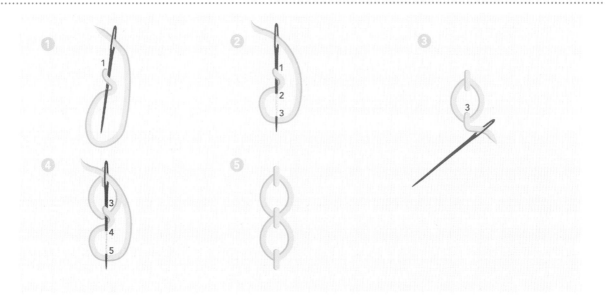

METHOD AND USES

This variation produces a series of chain stitches held together with links, following either a straight or curved line. It is formed in a similar way to regular chain stitch – however, here the thread is twisted around the tip of the needle between each loop of the chain before the needle is reinserted into the fabric. Use this stitch as a filling stitch, or to create lines, borders or zig-zag patterns.

Start by bringing your needle up at 1. Twist your thread around the tip of your needle. Next, insert your needle at 2 and bring it up a short distance away, at 3. Keeping the thread beneath your needle, pull through. To work the next stitch, once again twist your thread around the needle, insert it at 4, then bring it up again at 5. Keeping the thread beneath your needle as before, pull through. Repeat this sequence to produce a vertical row of the desired length.

FABRIC
Plain- or even-weave fabrics

Related techniques:
Freestyle embroidery (p. 12)

Similar stitches:
Chain stitch (p. 95), zig-zag chain stitch (p. 174)

FEATHERED CHAIN STITCH

Also known as: chained feather stitch

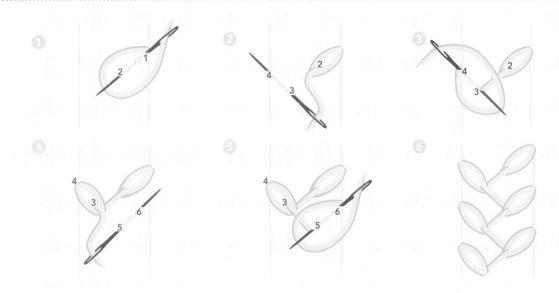

METHOD AND USES

Feathered chain stitch is worked in a zig-zag. It consists of small chain stitches at the end of straight stitches, and makes a nice wide line or border.

To begin, draw two vertical guidelines on your fabric. Working from the top, bring your needle up at 1. Make a small slanted chain stitch by inserting the needle again at 1, then bringing it up below and to the left at 2. Make sure the thread is beneath the needle, then pull through.

Next, insert the needle at 3 (a short distance away from 2), pointing the needle diagonally upwards, and bring it up at 4 (level with 2). Pull through, then take the needle back down again at 4, then up at 3, this time pointing diagonally downwards. Keeping the thread beneath the needle again,

pull through. Now take your needle down at 5 and up at 6 (level with 3), then start the next repeat by inserting the needle again at 6, with the thread looped under the needle as before, to emerge at 5.

Continue in this way, alternating from side to side until you reach the desired length, then finish the last chain with a small stitch.

FABRIC

Plain- or even-weave fabrics

Related techniques:
Freestyle embroidery (p. 12)

Similar stitches:
Chain stitch (p. 95)

BROAD CHAIN STITCH
Also known as: reverse chain stitch

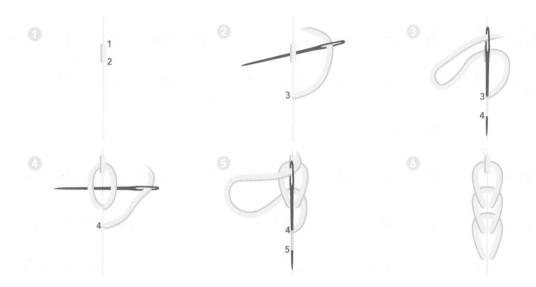

METHOD AND USES

A firm, round thread is ideal for working this heavy stitch – this will help it keep its shape. You can then take advantage of the weight by using this for broad lines or heavy shape outlines.

Mark a single guideline on the fabric to keep your stitches straight. Make a small, straight stitch by bringing your needle up at 1 and down at 2. This will anchor the following stitches.

Next, bring your needle up at 3, further down your line (the distance depends on how large you want your stitches to be). Pass your needle through the straight stitch at the top without piercing the fabric. Take the needle down

again at 3, then bring it up again at 4, further down. Return to pass your needle under the chain stitch just created – again, without piercing the fabric – then take it down again at 4, emerging at 5. Repeat this sequence to produce a row of the desired length.

FABRIC
Plain- or even-weave fabrics

Related techniques:
Freestyle embroidery (p. 12)

Similar stitches:
Chain stitch (p. 95), heavy chain stitch (p. 179)

DOUBLE CHAIN STITCH

Also known as: Turkmen stitch

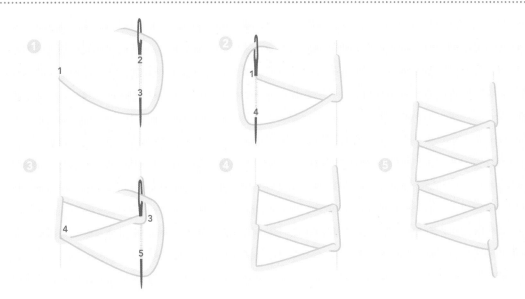

METHOD AND USES

This is a line or filling stitch, used for wide borders. It can be worked either straight or curved. You can also add extra interest by adding an isolated stitch, such as a French knot (p. 134), in the centre of each segment of a chain using a contrasting thread.

Begin by drawing two guidelines on your fabric. Working from top to bottom, bring the needle up at 1 on the left-hand guideline, down at 2, then up at 3 on the right-hand guideline. Loop the thread beneath your needle and pull through – not too tightly.

Next, take your needle to the left and insert it at 1 again, then bring it up at 4, just below. With the thread beneath the needle again, pull through. Insert your needle opposite again at 3, inside the chain, then bring it up at 5. With the thread beneath your needle, pull through.

Carry on working from side to side, inserting your needle inside each previous chain, then secure your last chain in place with a small stitch.

FABRIC

Plain- or even-weave fabrics

Related techniques:
Freestyle embroidery (p. 12)

Similar stitches:
Closed feather stitch (p. 109)

OPEN CHAIN STITCH
Also known as: ladder stitch and square chain stitch

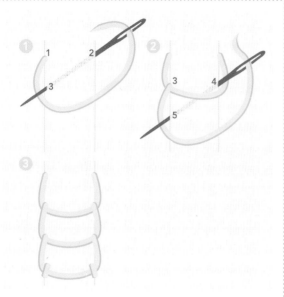

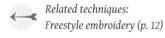

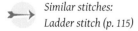

METHOD AND USES

This wide line or couching (p. 98) stitch creates a ladder-like effect. Work from top to bottom in any thread type.

Mark two guidelines on your fabric and then bring your needle up at 1. Insert the needle diagonally opposite at 2 on the right-hand guideline, then bring it up at 3 on the left-hand guideline. With the thread beneath the needle, pull through gently. Next, insert your needle at 4 (below 2) on a diagonal, inside the loop of thread, and bring it up again 5. Repeat downwards to create a line of stitches.

FABRIC
Plain- or even-weave fabrics

Related techniques:
Freestyle embroidery (p. 12)

Similar stitches:
Ladder stitch (p. 115)

ZIG-ZAG CHAIN STITCH
Also known as: Vandyke chain stitch

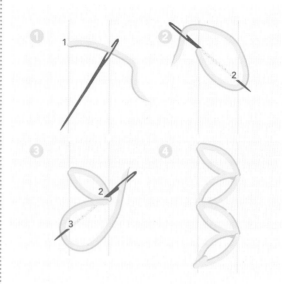

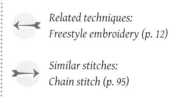

METHOD AND USES

The zig-zag of this stitch, which can be either curved or straight, is formed by using chain stitches set at right angles to each other. Zig-zag chain stitch can be used as a line, filling or outline stitch.

Mark your fabric with two parallel guidelines. Bring your needle up at 1. Insert it again at 1, then cross diagonally to emerge at 2. Keeping the thread beneath the needle, pull through. Insert your needle at 2 again and cross diagonally to emerge at 3. Again, pull through, with the thread beneath your needle. Continue down as required.

FABRIC
Plain- or even-weave fabrics

Related techniques:
Freestyle embroidery (p. 12)

Similar stitches:
Chain stitch (p. 95)

TWISTED CHAIN STITCH

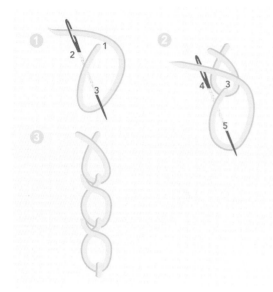

MAGIC CHAIN STITCH

Also known as: chequered chain stitch and magic stitch

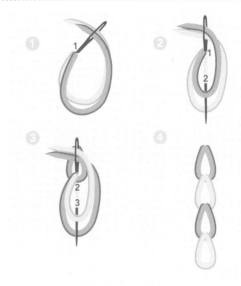

METHOD AND USES

The twisted, textured effect of this easy stitch works especially well for curved outlines. It can also be used as an isolated stitch, as for lazy daisy stitch.

Working downwards, bring your needle up at 1. Holding the thread down with the thumb of your free hand, insert your needle diagonally at 2 so that the threads cross over at the top of the loop. Bring the needle out again at 3 and pull through, keeping the thread beneath the needle tip. To work the next stitch insert the needle diagonally at 4 and emerge at 5, arranging the thread as before. Pull through and continue.

FABRIC

Plain- or even-weave fabrics. Cotton pearl (perlé) thread is best.

Related techniques:
Freestyle embroidery (p. 12)

Similar stitches:
Chain stitch (p. 95), lazy daisy stitch (p. 96)

METHOD AND USES

This line or filling stitch uses two contrasting threads alternately to make a chain stitch – a light and dark colour produce good results.

Working from the top, bring your needle up at 1. Hold both threads in place with the thumb of your free hand and insert the needle back at 1, forming a loop with your threads. Emerge at 2. Place one thread above the needle and one below, then pull through. Notice how the thread above the needle disappears. Work the second stitch in the same way, emerging at 3, but this time place the opposite colour above the needle.

FABRIC

Plain- or even-weave fabrics

Related techniques:
Freestyle embroidery (p. 12)

Similar stitches:
Chain stitch (p. 95)

ROSETTE CHAIN STITCH
Also known as: bead edging stitch

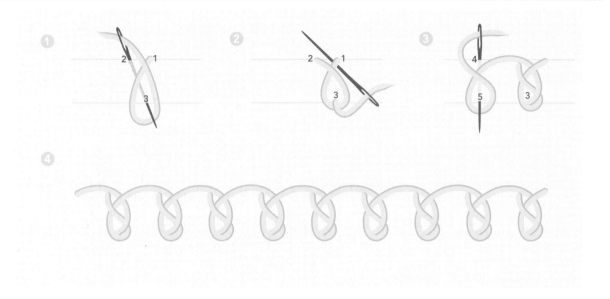

METHOD AND USES

This variation of chain stitch can be worked straight or in curves to produce lines, borders and edging. It can also be worked in a circle to make small floral motifs.

Start by drawing two parallel guidelines on your fabric. Working from right to left, bring your needle up at 1. Hold the thread down with the thumb of your free hand, then insert the needle to the left at 2, bringing it up again at 3. Loop the thread around your needle in an anti-clockwise direction, then pull through gently. Next, take your needle up and under the thread at 1, taking care not to pierce the fabric.

To begin the second stitch, move to the left a short distance, as shown. Insert your needle at 4, then bring it up again at 5, after looping the thread around it in an anti-clockwise direction again. Pull through and repeat along your line.

FABRIC
Plain- or even-weave fabrics

 Related techniques:
Freestyle embroidery (p. 12)

 Similar stitches:
No notable matches

RAISED CHAIN STITCH

Also known as: raised chain band

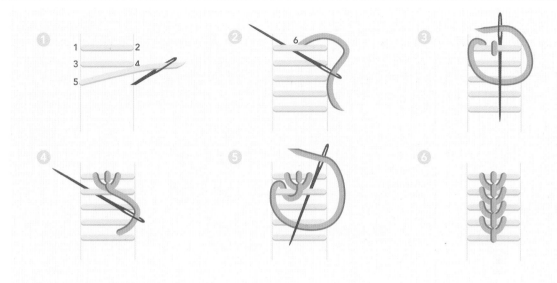

METHOD AND USES

Raised chain stitch can be worked in one or two colours for bands, lines and borders. It can also be highly effective worked side by side on a base of foundation stitches as a filling.

First work a horizontal ladder of straight stitches. Bring your needle up at 1, down at 2, up at 3, down at 4, up at 5 and so on.

Change to a blunt-ended needle (and contrasting thread, if desired) and bring your needle up at 6. Pass over and under the first horizontal stitch, without piercing the fabric. A small, straight stitch is formed in the centre. Pass under the horizontal stitch again on the right-hand side, making a loop, with your needle pointing downwards and the thread beneath it. Pull through. Pass the needle over

and under the second horizontal stitch to hold the first chain in place. Next, take the needle to the right and pass it under the second horizontal stitch. Keeping the thread beneath the needle, pull through.

Repeat this down the ladder. The needle does not enter the fabric until the very last chain, where you finish off with a small vertical stitch.

FABRIC

Plain- or even-weave fabrics

 *Related techniques:*
Freestyle embroidery (p. 12)

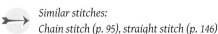 *Similar stitches:*
Chain stitch (p. 95), straight stitch (p. 146)

CRESTED CHAIN STITCH

Also known as: Spanish coral stitch

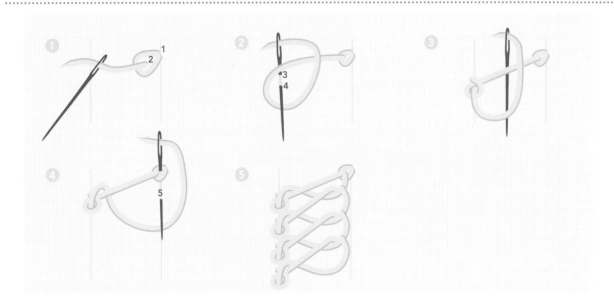

METHOD AND USES

This composite stitch combines a chain and a coral stitch, producing a ladder effect. It is a decorative line stitch that will follow a slight curve.

First mark two vertical guidelines on your fabric. Bring your needle up at 1 on the right-hand guideline and make a small chain stitch, finishing by emerging at 2. Take the thread diagonally across to the left-hand side. Hold the thread in place with your thumb and then pass your needle under and over the working thread, inserting it at 3 and emerging at 4. Pull through, keeping the thread beneath your needle to form a coral stitch.

Now take your needle and pass it under the diagonal thread, pointing the needle downwards. Then insert the needle inside the first chain stitch, on the right. Bring it up at 5 while keeping the thread beneath your needle, and pull through.

Finally, take the thread over to the left again and insert the needle slightly below the first coral stitch to begin the sequence again, repeating to produce a row of the desired length.

FABRIC

Plain- or even-weave fabrics. Use a firm thread.

Related techniques:
Freestyle embroidery (p. 12)

Similar stitches:
Chain stitch (p. 95), coral stitch (p. 101)

HEAVY CHAIN STITCH
Also known as: heavy braid chain stitch

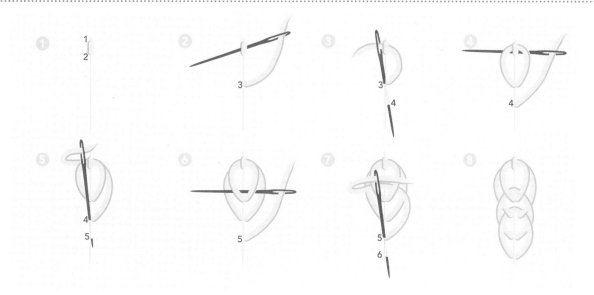

METHOD AND USES

Heavy chain stitch is worked in a similar way to broad chain stitch, although this stitch forms a much heavier line or outline.

Mark a single guideline on your fabric to keep your stitches straight. Make a small, straight stitch by bringing your needle up at 1 and down at 2. Next, bring your needle up at 3, further down your line, then pass it through the straight stitch at the top without piercing the fabric. Take the needle down again at 3, then bring it up again at 4, below. Now pass your needle through the straight stitch again before inserting it back at 4 and emerging at 5.

Next, pass your needle through the first chain stitch you made, returning to insert your needle at 5. Come up again at 6. Keep working in this way, by returning to pass your needle through the second chain stitch and back to 6, and so on to the end of your line.

FABRIC
Plain- or even-weave fabrics

Related techniques:
Freestyle embroidery (p. 12)

Similar stitches:
Broad chain stitch (p. 172), chain stitch (p. 95)

12: PULLED AND DRAWN STITCHES

The 16 stitches that appear in this chapter are used in either drawn-thread or drawn-fabric work.

Drawn-thread work (p. 49), as the name suggests, is formed by cutting and withdrawing threads from your fabric. This produces an open, lacy area in which stitches are then worked. Unlike drawn-thread work, drawn-fabric work (p. 50) involves no cutting; the threads are not removed from the fabric but rather 'pulled' (hence 'pulled stitches') to produce an openwork effect, which is why this is also sometimes referred to as 'openwork'.

Both of these are counted-thread techniques (literally, threads are counted before you insert your needle), usually worked in white thread on white fabric.

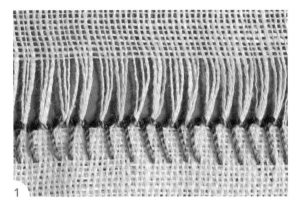

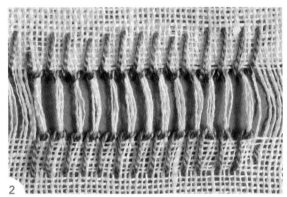

1 *Hemstitch (p. 189)*

2 *Ladder hemstitch (p. 190)*

3 *Overcast bars (p. 191)*

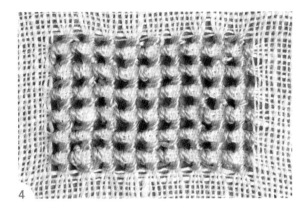

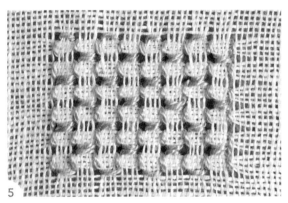

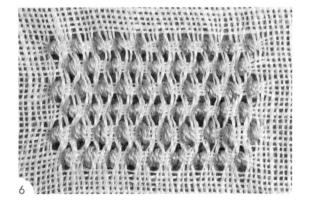

FABRICS: These stitches are worked on loosely woven or even-weave linen. Test your fabric edge first – see if the threads can easily be removed to be sure the fabric will hold pulled or drawn-thread work.

THREADS: The most popular thread for both types of work is cotton pearl (perlé).

NEEDLES: Pulled and drawn stitches are both usually worked with a blunt-ended tapestry needle to avoid splitting the threads of the fabric.

OTHER EQUIPMENT: You will need a small pair of sharp embroidery scissors and an embroidery hoop or frame.

4 *Punch stitch (p. 184)*
5 *Pulled honeycomb stitch (p. 185)*
6 *Coil stitch (p. 186)*

COBBLER STITCH

Also known as: cobbler filling stitch

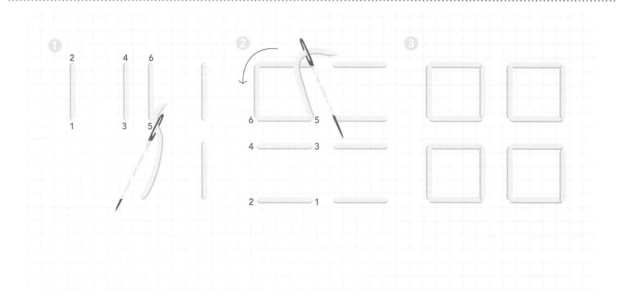

METHOD AND USES

This pulled stitch is worked in horizontal rows of vertical stitches. The stitches should be pulled tightly as they are made to create the desired open effect. Cobbler stitch is used as a filling stitch.

Using a blunt-ended tapestry needle, bring your needle up at 1, count four threads up, then insert the needle at 2. Now count four threads down and across to the right. Bring your needle up at this point, 3, then insert it four theads above, at 4. This forms the first square.

To work the second square, move two threads to the right and bring the needle up at 5 before inserting it four threads higher up, at 6. Repeat to create a row of the desired length.

To work a second row, work from right to left, leaving a space of two threads below the first row.

Now turn your work anti-clockwise so these first rows are lying horizontal rather than vertical. Work along in exactly the same way, filling in the gaps with vertical stitches to complete your squares.

FABRIC

Loosely woven or even-weave fabrics

Related techniques:
Drawn-fabric work (p. 50)

Similar stitches:
Pulled honeycomb stitch (p. 185), punch stitch (p. 184)

PIN STITCH

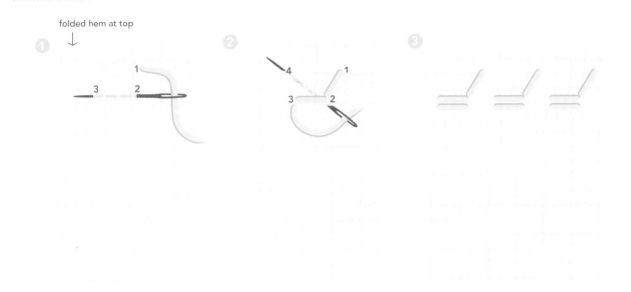

folded hem at top

METHOD AND USES

This pulled stitch, used for hemming, is worked in a similar way to hemstitch, where threads are wrapped in groups or clusters. However, no threads are withdrawn; they are just pulled together.

Fold your hem and tack it in place using running stitch. Work with the right side of fabric facing you – the hem edge should be at the top. Bring your needle up at 1 through the folded hem, down at 2 below the hem, then up at 3. Insert the needle back down at 2 and up again at 3. Repeat this once more, this time bringing the needle up at 4, catching the hem. Pull tightly so that the wrapped threads are pulled together, leaving a tiny hole. Begin the next repeat by inserting your needle at 3 again.

Finish by removing the tacking threads and securing the thread inside the hem.

FABRIC

Loosely woven or even-weave fabrics

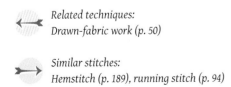

Related techniques:
Drawn-fabric work (p. 50)

Similar stitches:
Hemstitch (p. 189), running stitch (p. 94)

PUNCH STITCH

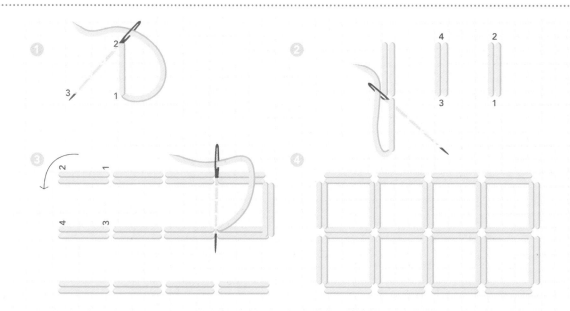

METHOD AND USES

Punch stitch is a pulled stitch, formed by working a series of straight stitches in a square formation; when pulled taut they leave regular dotted holes in the fabric. This is used as a filling stitch.

Begin on the right of the area to be worked. Bring your needle up at 1, count four threads up, then insert it at 2. Next, bring your needle up again at 1, just to the right of the first straight stitch. Take it down again at 2, then bring it up four threads down and to the left, at 3.

Now complete a second set of parallel stitches by inserting the needle at 4 (four threads up), then passing again from 3 to 4. Continue along as required.

Work your second row of stitches from left to right, directly below the previous row, placing the tops of each stitch in the same holes as the bottoms of the stitches in the previous row.

Next, turn your work anti-clockwise so that the vertical stitches are now horizontal, then fill in the gaps to form squares by working stitches in the same holes, starting from the right again.

FABRIC

Loosely woven or even-weave fabrics

Related techniques:
Drawn-fabric work (p. 50)

Similar stitches:
Cobbler stitch (p. 182), pulled honeycomb stitch (p. 185)

RINGED BACKSTITCH

PULLED HONEYCOMB STITCH
Also known as: honeycomb filling stitch and pulled brick stitch

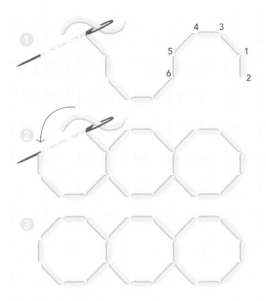

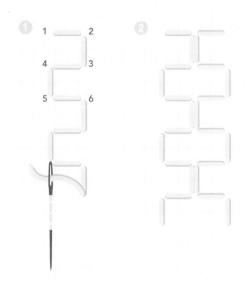

METHOD AND USES
Here, backstitches are worked in rings or half rings as a filling stitch or to decorate borders. The stitches need to be pulled tightly while working.

Bring your needle up at 1 and down at 2, making the first backstitch. Next, bring it up at 3, then back down at 1, up at 4, down at 3, up at 5, down at 4, up at 6, down at 5, and so on. Continue making a row of half rings, then turn your fabric round and work back in the same way to complete the rings.

FABRIC
Loosely woven or even-weave fabrics

METHOD AND USES
The brick-like effect of this stitch is best used for borders or as a filling. Stitches must be pulled tightly while working.

Working top to bottom, bring your needle up at 1, down at 2, up at 3, down at 2, up at 4, down at 3, up at 5, down at 4, up at 6, down at 5. Emerge at 6 to begin the next group.

Turn your fabric around and work in the same way for the following rows. Alternate vertical stitches are doubled and worked in the same holes, as shown.

FABRIC
Loosely woven or even-weave fabrics

Related techniques:
Drawn-fabric work (p. 50)

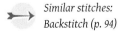

Similar stitches:
Backstitch (p. 94)

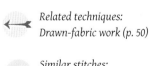

Related techniques:
Drawn-fabric work (p. 50)

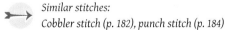

Similar stitches:
Cobbler stitch (p. 182), punch stitch (p. 184)

COIL STITCH

Also known as: coil filling stitch

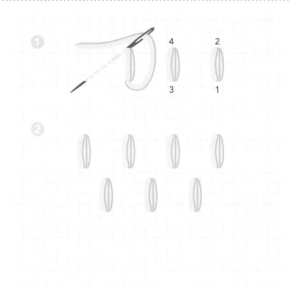

METHOD AND USES

This filling stitch consists of groups of three satin stitches, displayed in horizontal rows.

Starting on the right, bring your needle up at 1 and take it down at 2. Repeat twice more, working through the same holes. Move four threads to the left. Bring your needle up at 3 and take it down at 4; repeat twice. Continue creating groups of three along this row.

Work the second row of stitches from left to right, arranging the groups to sit in between those of the previous row, as shown.

FABRIC

Loosely woven or even-weave fabrics

 Related techniques:
Drawn-fabric work (p. 50)

 Similar stitches:
Satin stitch (p. 151)

ALGERIAN STITCH

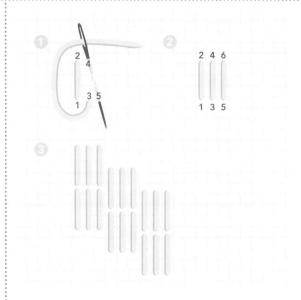

METHOD AND USES

Like coil stitch (left), Algerian stitch is a filling stitch that employs groups of three satin stitches. Here they are worked side by side to form a square.

Bring your needle up at 1, down at 2 (four threads up), then up at 3 to create the first stitch. Repeat this, passing down at 4, up at 5, then down at 6, pulling the stitches tightly as you go.

Begin working the next group two threads above or below the first group of stitches.

FABRIC

Loosely woven or even-weave fabrics

 Related techniques:
Drawn-fabric work (p. 50)

 Similar stitches:
Satin stitch (p. 151)

SINGLE FAGGOT STITCH

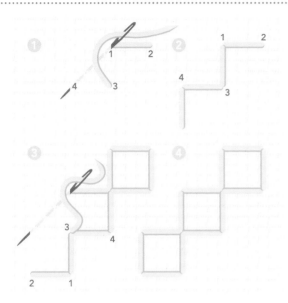

METHOD AND USES

This filling stitch uses a diagonal step formation to create a grid. Pull your stitches tightly while working.

Bring your needle up at 1, then insert it four threads to the right at 2. Bring it up again at 3 (four threads below 1), insert it at 1, then emerge at 4 (four threads to the left of 3). Insert it again at 3 to form another horizontal stitch.

Continue working stitches in this way until the end of the row. Now turn your work and complete the squares, inserting the needle in the holes made by the first row of stitches.

FABRIC

Loosely woven or even-weave fabrics

Related techniques:
Drawn-fabric work (p. 50)

Similar stitches:
Cobbler stitch (p. 182), pulled honeycomb stitch (p. 185), punch stitch (p. 184)

THREE-SIDED STITCH

Also known as: Bermuda faggoting and lace stitch

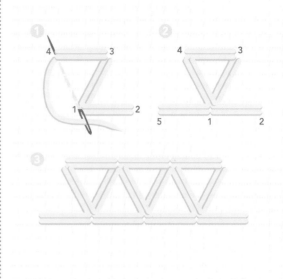

METHOD AND USES

A filling stitch that looks just like it sounds! Bring your needle up at 1, down at 2, then repeat. Pull your stitches tightly. Bring your needle up at 1 again, then insert it two threads across and four threads up at 3, midway between the first two horizontal stitches. Repeat.

Bring your needle up at 4 and make two stitches between 3 and 4. Now make two stitches diagonally between 4 and 1. Bring your needle up at 5 and work two stitches between 1 and 5. Emerge finally at 5 to work the next group.

FABRIC

Loosely woven, even-weave or plain-weave fabrics

Related techniques:
Drawn-fabric work (p. 50)

Similar stitches:
Four-sided stitch (p. 188)

FOUR-SIDED STITCH

WAVE FILLING STITCH

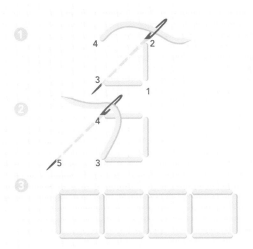

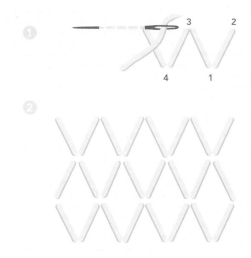

METHOD AND USES

Four-sided stitch is used for fillings and borders. Working from right to left, and counting four threads along for each stitch, bring your needle up at 1, down at 2, up at 3, down at 1, up at 4, down at 2, then up at 3. Now take your needle down at 4 to complete the square, and emerge at 5 ready to begin the next square to the left.

When the stitches are pulled tightly, tiny holes will appear at the ends of them.

FABRIC

Loosely woven or even-weave fabrics

METHOD AND USES

Wave filling stitch uses zig-zagging straight stitches to produce an open diamond effect – it's useful either as a filling stitch or for borders.

Working right to left, bring your needle up at 1 and down at 2. Next, bring it up at 3, then back down at 1 to create the first 'V' of your zig-zag. Bring the needle up at 4 to start the next 'V'. Repeat, travelling to the left.

To create the next row, turn your fabric and continue in exactly the same way. Pull all your stitches tightly.

FABRIC

Loosely woven or even-weave fabrics

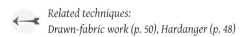

Related techniques:
Drawn-fabric work (p. 50), Hardanger (p. 48)

Similar stitches:
Three-sided stitch (p. 187)

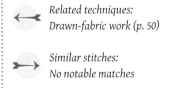

Related techniques:
Drawn-fabric work (p. 50)

Similar stitches:
No notable matches

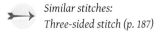

HEMSTITCH

Also known as: spoke stitch

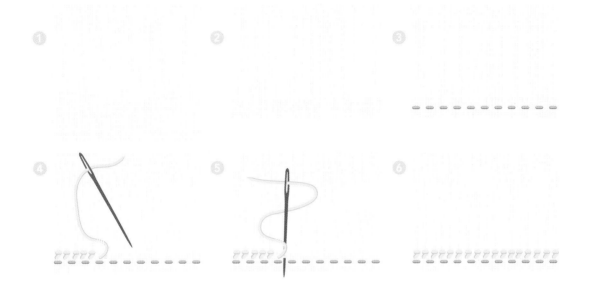

METHOD AND USES

This stitch does just as its name suggests – produces decorative hems and borders. It is traditionally worked in white thread on white linen, as are the following two variations: zig-zag and ladder hemstitch.

Remove the desired number of threads from your fabric (explained in detail on p. 230). If your stitching is to be placed above a hem, fold the fabric under, up to the level of the drawn threads and tack it in place using a running stitch, as shown in step 3.

Working from left to right, with the right side of your fabric facing you, knot your thread to secure it inside the folded hem, then bring your needle up through the fabric, just below the first vertical thread. Catching the hem in

place, pass the needle over four threads from left to right, then wrap it back under the same four threads from right to left.

Next, insert the needle at the same level but to the right of the encircled threads, then emerge again to the front, catching the hem. Pull through and draw the threads together before beginning the next cluster. Repeat.

Finish by securing the thread inside the hem and removing your tacking stitches.

FABRIC

Loosely woven or even-weave fabrics

Related techniques:
Drawn-thread work (p. 49)

Similar stitches:
Ladder hemstitch (p. 190), running stitch (p. 94),
serpentine stitch (p. 190)

SERPENTINE STITCH

Also known as: zig-zag hemstitch

LADDER HEMSTITCH

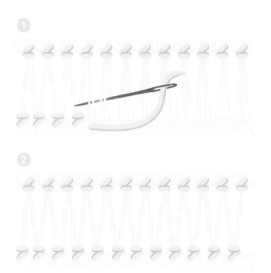

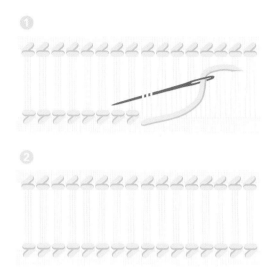

METHOD AND USES

In this variation of hemstitch, threads are gathered together at both top and bottom.

Follow the first four steps of hemstitch on the previous page, withdrawing your threads and tacking up your hem, then working a row of hemstitches from left to right. The clusters shown here contain four threads. However, the number of threads can vary for serpentine stitch, as long as it is an even number.

At the end of the row, turn your fabric and work a second row, this time dividing each bunch in two, picking up two threads from one group and two from the next to create a zig-zag effect.

FABRIC

Loosely woven or even-weave fabrics

 Related techniques:
Drawn-thread work (p. 49)

 Similar stitches:
Hemstitch (p. 189)

METHOD AND USES

Another hemstitch variation, this is worked by gathering in thread clusters at top and bottom to create a ladder effect.

Follow the first four steps of hemstitch on the previous page, withdrawing your threads and tacking up your hem, then working a row of hemstitches from left to right. The clusters shown here, however, contain three threads rather than four, as a variation.

As for serpentine stitch (left), turn your work at the end of the row so the top edge becomes the bottom edge, then gather the same groups of threads together.

FABRIC

Loosely woven or even-weave fabrics

 Related techniques:
Drawn-thread work (p. 49)

 Similar stitches:
Hemstitch (p. 189)

OVERCAST BARS

Also known as: corded clusters and twisted bars

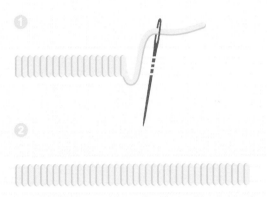

METHOD AND USES

These bars are formed by binding threads together with overcast stitches. They are worked either horizontally or vertically, and used as a filling stitch or to create borders.

Remove the required number of threads from your fabric (explained in detail on p. 230). Beginning on the left-hand side, count the number of threads you wish to group together, then pass your needle over and under these from top to bottom. Pack your stitches closely together to form a firm bar and repeat this until your group of threads is completely covered.

FABRIC

Loosely woven or even-weave fabrics

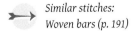

Related techniques:
Drawn-thread work (p. 49)

Similar stitches:
Woven bars (p. 191)

WOVEN BARS

Also known as: needleweaving clusters

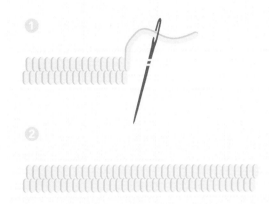

METHOD AND USES

These are similar to overcast bars, and are used in the same way. Here, though, an even number of threads are woven together to form a firm, flat bar.

Remove the required number of threads from your fabric (explained in detail on p. 230). Work each bar using an even number of threads (four here). From the left, pass your needle over and under the first two threads. Pull tightly. Next, pass your needle over and under the bottom two threads. Pull tightly again, packing the stitches closely together. Repeat, working alternate stitches until the bar is completely covered.

FABRIC

Loosely woven or even-weave fabrics

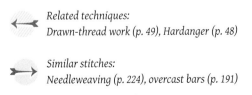

Related techniques:
Drawn-thread work (p. 49), Hardanger (p. 48)

Similar stitches:
Needleweaving (p. 224), overcast bars (p. 191)

Canvaswork stitches (sometimes called needlepoint) are often worked on canvas – hence the name. They employ a counted-thread technique – literally, the threads of the fabric are counted before the stitches are applied.

Canvaswork is often confused with tapestry, due to the fact that designs often completely cover the ground fabric.

1 *Leviathan stitch (p. 201)*

2 *Florentine stitch (p. 208)*

3 *Algerian eye stitch (p. 201)*

4 *Gobelin filling stitch (p. 204)*

5 *Pineapple stitch (p. 205)*

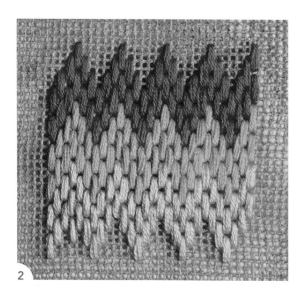

The stitches in this chapter can be used to decorate a variety of items, from wall hangings to cushions, bags and purses. Although several types of thread can be used, the most commonly chosen is wool.

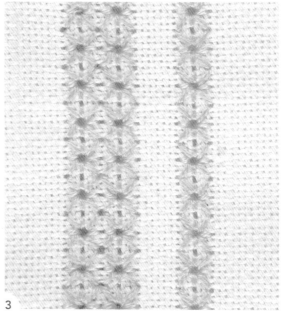

4

5

FABRICS: Canvas is the material traditionally used for these stitches. It comes in different gauges, which are measured in terms of mesh size, or number of threads per 2.5cm (1in) in each direction. The higher the mesh size, the finer the canvas.

Single-mesh (mono) canvas ranges from 10 count (coarse) to 22 count (fine). Double (Penelope) canvas, which is woven with pairs of threads, is available in a range from 7 to 10. Rug canvas is available in 3, 7 or 10. Plastic canvas is stiff and so is used for three-dimensional work. It is also great for beginners. This is available in 7, 10 and 14. Waste canvas (p. 119), which is used for working cross-stitch or canvaswork on plain-weave fabrics, is available in 8.5, 10, 14 and 18.

Canvas material is available either plain – for freehand designs or when following a counted-thread chart – or pre-stamped with a design.

THREADS: Canvaswork generally uses four-ply tapestry threads or two-ply crewel wools.

NEEDLES: A blunt-ended tapestry needle is used, since it has a large eye for holding thicker threads. These needles range in size from the biggest, 13 (for coarse work), down to the finest, 25 (for fine work).

OTHER EQUIPMENT: You will need a small pair of sharp embroidery scissors, plus fabric scissors for cutting your canvas. An embroidery frame will prevent the canvas distorting, and masking tape is used for binding the canvas edges.

TENT STITCH

Also known as: basketweave stitch, canvas stitch, Continental stitch, needlepoint stitch and petit point

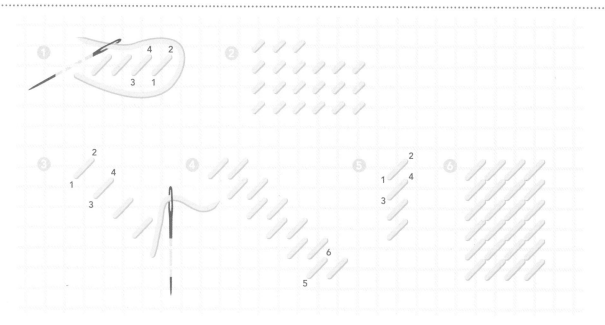

METHOD AND USES

This is the most popular and versatile of all canvaswork stitches, consisting of tiny stitches that all lie in the same direction. Use it on its own or in conjunction with other stitches, for backgrounds of all sizes or as an outline stitch. When worked in horizontal rows this is known as Continental stitch.

Working right to left, bring your needle up at 1, down at 2, up at 3 and down at 4 (step 1). Repeat. For the next row, either work left to right or turn your work and work right to left (step 2).

When worked diagonally, tent stitch is known as basketweave stitch. It is good for working large areas so that the canvas does not distort. From the top left, bring your needle up at 1, down at 2, up at 3 and down at 4

(step 3). Repeat. A hole is left between any diagonal stitches so that on the next row the stitches fit in between the first row, as shown by the row ending with the stitch between 5 and 6 (step 4). Work your stitches up and down the canvas.

Tent stitch can also be worked vertically. Working top to bottom, bring your needle up at 1, down at 2, up at 3, down at 4 and so on (step 5). Repeat, turning your work at the end of each row to work a block (step 6).

FABRIC
Single-mesh (mono) canvas

Related techniques:
Canvaswork (p. 44)

Similar stitches:
Slanted gobelin stitch (p. 204)

CASHMERE STITCH

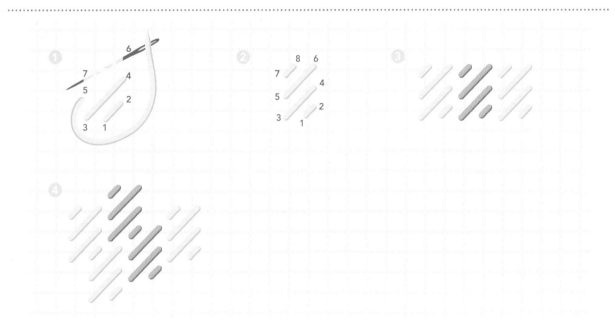

METHOD AND USES

Cashmere stitch is used for filling large background areas when quick coverage is needed. It is formed by working steep, vertical, straight stitches either horizontally or diagonally on the canvas.

To work a first block of stitches, bring your needle up at 1, down at 2 (passing over one canvas thread), up at 3 and down at 4 (over two threads), up at 5 and down at 6 (over two) and finally up at 7 and down at 8 (over one).

To create horizontal rows, continue to work from right to left, turning your work at the end of each block to create as many aligning blocks as required.

To create diagonal rows, first work down and to the right. Then return, working the following row from the bottom right to the top left, slotting your stitches in between those of the previous row, as shown.

FABRIC

Single-mesh (mono) canvas

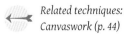

Related techniques:
Canvaswork (p. 44)

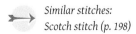

Similar stitches:
Scotch stitch (p. 198)

MILANESE STITCH

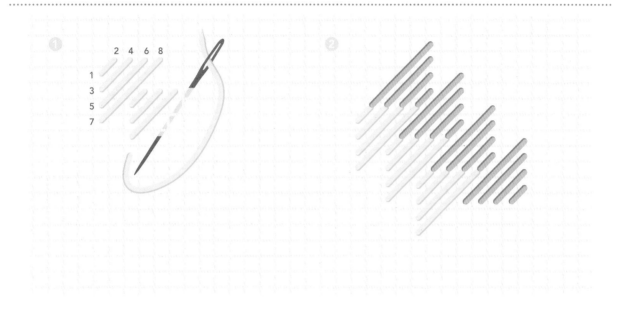

METHOD AND USES

This canvaswork stitch produces a bold triangular effect that works well in two or more colours, and is handy for creating backgrounds. A triangle of four stitches is worked in one direction, then subsequent rows are worked in the opposite direction, filling in the gaps.

Working from the top left, create four stitches that gradually lengthen by bringing your needle up at 1, down at 2, up at 3, down at 4, up at 5, down at 6, up at 7 and finally down at 8. Repeat these steps again, working diagonally downwards, to create the next triangle.

Now begin your next row from the bottom right upwards. Continue this procedure, working stitches diagonally up and down the canvas. As can be seen

above, the ends of the stitches in the new row use the same holes as the ends of the stitches in the previous row, so that the blocks sit snugly side by side.

FABRIC

Single-mesh (mono) or double (Penelope) canvas

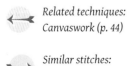

Related techniques:
Canvaswork (p. 44)

Similar stitches:
No notable matches

BRIGHTON STITCH

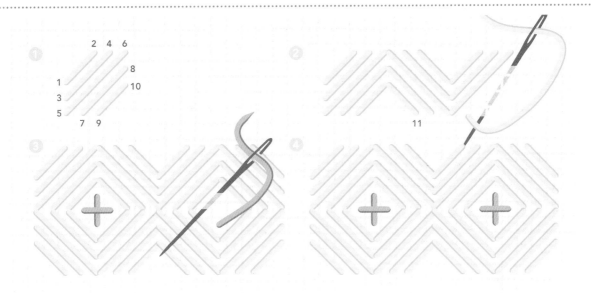

METHOD AND USES

Brighton stitch is used to work geometric backgrounds on medium to large areas. Five slanting stitches form blocks, which are then worked in opposing directions. When rows are worked, these blocks line up to form a series of diamonds, each finished off with a central upright cross-stitch.

Working from the top left, bring your needle up at 1 and down at 2 (passing over two threads), up at 3 and down at 4 (over three), up at 5 and down at 6 (over four), up at 7 and down at 8 (over three), then up at 9 and down at 10 (over two threads).

Emerge at 11 to begin the next block, working the mirror image of the block just created. Repeat this whole sequence to the right, then turn your work and create a second row in exactly the same way.

When your rows are complete, change to a contrasting colour and add an upright cross-stitch, as shown, to each central diamond.

FABRIC

Single-mesh (mono) canvas

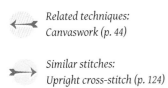

Related techniques:
Canvaswork (p. 44)

Similar stitches:
Upright cross-stitch (p. 124)

SCOTCH STITCH

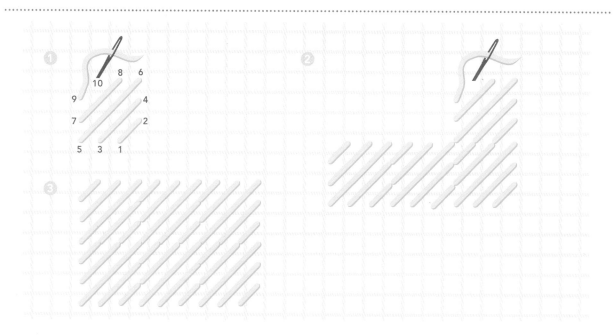

METHOD AND USES

Scotch stitch consists of five slanted stitches, worked in blocks and used to fill medium to large areas.

Start by travelling from right to left. Bring your needle up at 1 and down at 2 (passing over one thread of the canvas), up at 3 and down at 4 (over two threads), up at 5 and down at 6 (over three), up at 7 and down at 8 (over two) and finally up at 9 and down at 10 (over one) to complete the first block.

Repeat these five stitches to the left, then continue, producing as many blocks as required. When you reach the end of the row, turn your work and continue in the same way for the next row, working from right to left as before.

Scotch stitch can also be worked in diagonal rows, simply working down from top left to bottom right.

FABRIC

Single-mesh (mono) canvas

Related techniques:
Canvaswork (p. 44)

Similar stitches:
Cashmere stitch (p. 195), condensed Scotch stitch (p. 199)

CONDENSED SCOTCH STITCH

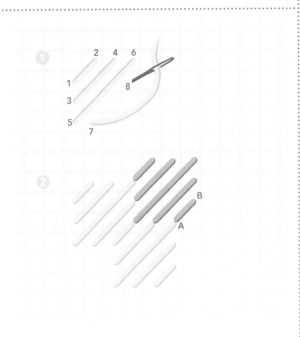

CHEQUER STITCH

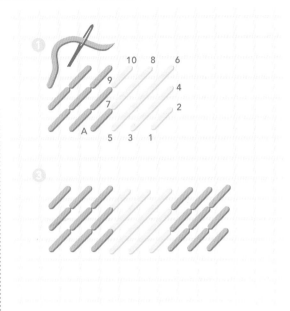

METHOD AND USES

The interlocking diagonal rows of this stitch are useful for medium to large areas of background.

Starting at the top left, bring your needle up at 1 and down at 2 (passing over one thread), up at 3 and down at 4 (two threads), up at 5 and down at 6 (three threads) and up at 7 and down at 8 (two threads). Work the next block of four to the right and down.

Work the next row from bottom right to top left, bringing your needle up at A and down at B to begin. Repeat up and down the canvas.

FABRIC

Single-mesh (mono) canvas

Related techniques:
Canvaswork (p. 44)

Similar stitches:
Scotch stitch (p. 198)

METHOD AND USES

A combination of Scotch stitch and tent stitch, chequer stitch is used for medium to large backgrounds; alternate colours create the chequerboard effect.

Work a block of Scotch stitch, right to left, bringing your needle up at 1, down at 2, up at 3, down at 4, up at 5, down at 6, up at 7, down at 8, up at 9, down at 10.

Next, work a block of nine tent stitches, bringing your needle up at (A) to start. Repeat these two blocks along your row, then turn your work and complete another row, working right to left again.

FABRIC

Single-mesh (mono) canvas

Related techniques:
Canvaswork (p. 44)

Similar stitches:
Scotch stitch (p. 198), tent stitch (p. 194)

MOORISH STITCH

METHOD AND USES

Condensed Scotch stitch is worked here with diagonal tent stitches to create a zig-zag pattern, which is used for filling medium to large areas.

Work a line of condensed Scotch stitch, bottom left to top right, bringing your needle up at 1, down at 2, up at 3, down at 4, up at 5, down at 6, then up at 7 and down at 8. Continue up and down the canvas, working lines in a downwards direction.

Next, work diagonal rows of tent stitch bottom left to top right in a contrasting colour, filling the gaps between each row of condensed Scotch stitch and using the same holes as before so that the ends of the new stitches meet the ends of those in the previous row.

FABRIC

Double (Penelope) canvas

Related techniques:
Canvaswork (p. 44)

Similar stitches:
Condensed Scotch stitch (p. 199), tent stitch (p. 194)

ALGERIAN EYE STITCH
Also known as: star stitch

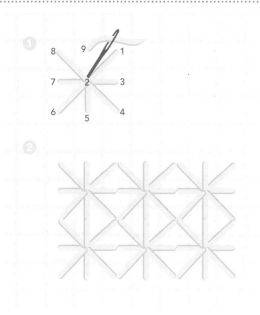

METHOD AND USES

This pretty stitch is popular for samplers. Eight stitches of alternating lengths radiate from the same central hole, forming a squared-up star.

Bring your needle up at 1 and down again at 2 (the centre hole). Come up again at each point, working your way around from 3 to 9, returning after each point to insert the needle at 2 to create the rays of the star. Stitch your rows from right to left, then from left to right

FABRIC

Single-mesh (mono) canvas. Use loosely woven linens for drawn-fabric work, where stitches must be pulled tight to form the central hole.

 Related techniques:
Drawn-fabric work (p. 50), canvaswork (p. 44)

 Similar stitches:
No notable matches

LEVIATHAN STITCH
Also known as: double cross-stitch and Smyrna cross-stitch

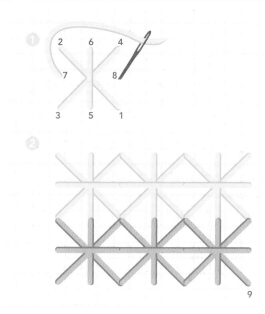

METHOD AND USES

This hardwearing yet attractive canvaswork stitch is useful for covering large areas. It consists of a large cross-stitch with an upright cross-stitch worked over the top of it.

Work the cross-stitch over four threads by bringing your needle up at 1, down at 2, up at 3 and then down at 4. Next, add the upright cross-stitch by bringing your needle up at 5, down at 6, up at 7, then down at 8. To work a second row, bring your needle up at 9, bottom right, as shown, to begin again.

Work your rows from left to right and then right to left. All your stitches must be worked in the same order.

FABRIC

Single-mesh (mono) canvas or even-weave fabrics

 Related techniques:
Canvaswork (p. 44)

 Similar stitches:
Single cross-stitch (p. 120), upright cross-stitch (p. 124)

RHODES STITCH

HUNGARIAN DIAMOND STITCH

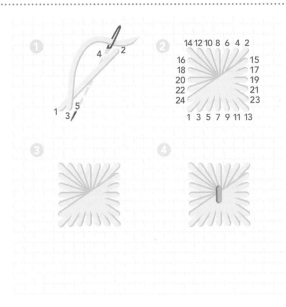

METHOD AND USES

This stitch forms a raised square block, which is used as a single motif stitch or for working medium to large areas and backgrounds.

Working anti-clockwise, bring your needle up at 1 and down at 2 (passing over 6 threads). Bring it up at 3, down at 4, up at 5, down at 6, up at 7, down at 8, up at 9, down at 10, and so on, following the diagram until you have covered the entire square.

For fairly large squares, you may add a tying stitch in the middle to hold everything in place.

FABRIC

Single-mesh (mono) canvas

METHOD AND USES

This stitch creates a diamond pattern, used for filling medium to large areas.

Bring your needle up at 1 and down at 2 (over two threads), up at 3 and down at 4 (four threads), up at 5 and down at 6 (six threads), up at 7 and down at 8 (four threads) and finally up at 9 and down at 10 (two threads). Leave one hole between each block. Start the next block at 11.

Work your next row from left to right, with the longest stitch of each block ending in the hole left empty in the previous row.

FABRIC

Single-mesh (mono) canvas

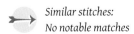
Related techniques: Canvaswork (p. 44)

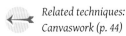
Similar stitches: No notable matches

Related techniques: Canvaswork (p. 44)

Similar stitches: No notable matches

CUSHION STITCH

Also known as: squares pattern and flat stitch

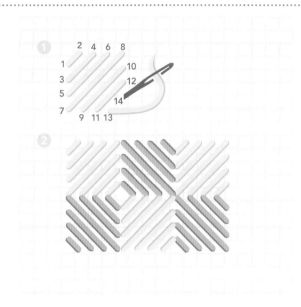

METHOD AND USES

Cushion stitch is used to fill backgrounds and medium to large areas. Blocks of seven slanted stitches are worked in either direction.

Starting top left, bring your needle up at 1 and down at 2 (over one thread), up at 3 and down at 4 (two threads), up at 5 and down at 6 (three threads), up at 7 and down at 8 (four threads), up at 9 and down at 10 (three threads), up at 11 and down at 12 (two threads) and up at 13 and down at 14 (one thread).

Work the next block of stitches slanting in the opposite direction, and continue along your row as required.

FABRIC

Single-mesh (mono) canvas

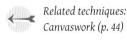

Related techniques:
Canvaswork (p. 44)

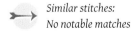

Similar stitches:
No notable matches

MOSAIC STITCH

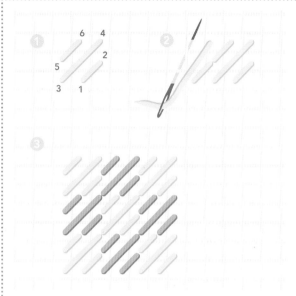

METHOD AND USES

This tiny, quick and easy stitch can be used to create detailed patterns in various colours, in imitation of the tiles it is named after.

Starting on the right-hand side, bring your needle up at 1 and down at 2 (passing over one thread), up at 3 and down at 4 (over two threads) and up at 5 and down at 6 (over one thread).

Work rows from right to left, turning your work at the end of each row. For diagonal rows, start from the top right and work downwards.

FABRIC

Single-mesh (mono) or double (Penelope) canvas

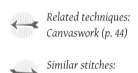

Related techniques:
Canvaswork (p. 44)

Similar stitches:
No notable matches

SLANTED GOBELIN STITCH
Also known as: oblique gobelin stitch

GOBELIN FILLING STITCH

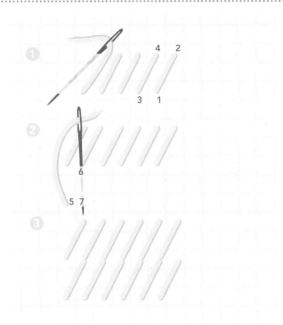

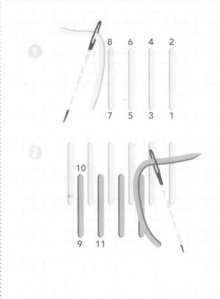

METHOD AND USES

This quick and easy filling stitch consists of small slanting stitches worked in horizontal rows. It provides a smooth, flat surface over large background areas.

Bring your needle up at 1, down at 2, up at 3 and down at 4, working each stitch over two threads. Repeat.

Work your stitches from right to left then left to right (up at 5, down at 6, up at 7, and so on). For your second row, the tops of your stitches should meet the bases of those in the previous row.

METHOD AND USES

This is another quick and easy stitch to use for filling shapes and backgrounds.

Travelling right to left, and working each stitch over six threads, bring your needle up at 1 and down at 2, up at 3 and down at 4, up at 5 and down at 6, up at 7 and down at 8, leaving a space between each stitch. Repeat to the left.

For the next row, working left to right, bring your needle up at 9, down at 10, then up at 11, halfway up (three threads) in between your first row of stitches.

FABRIC
Single-mesh (mono) canvas

FABRIC
Single-mesh (mono) canvas

 Related techniques:
Canvaswork (p. 44)

 Similar stitches:
Gobelin filling stitch (p. 204), tent stitch (p. 194), upright gobelin stitch (p. 205)

 Related techniques:
Canvaswork (p. 44)

 Similar stitches:
Slanted gobelin stitch (p. 204), upright gobelin stitch (p. 205)

UPRIGHT GOBELIN STITCH

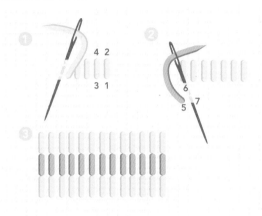

PINEAPPLE STITCH

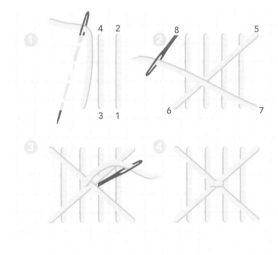

METHOD AND USES

This quick-to-work stitch produces rows of horizontal straight stitches with a ridge-like effect, useful for filling backgrounds and medium to large areas. The stitches are worked over two threads here; however, they can be worked over as many as five.

From the right, bring your needle up at 1, down at 2, up at 3 and down at 4. Repeat.

Work the next row left to right, starting by bringing the needle up at 5, down at 6 and up at 7, connecting with the base of each stitch in the row above as you go.

FABRIC
Single-mesh (mono) canvas

 Related techniques:
Canvaswork (p. 44)

 Similar stitches:
Gobelin filling stitch (p. 204), slanted gobelin stitch
(p. 204)

METHOD AND USES

Pineapple stitch is a filling stitch, used for covering large areas and backgrounds.

Work four straight stitches vertically over four threads. Take the needle up at 1, down at 2, up at 3, down at 4, then repeat to make four stitches. Next, work a cross-stitch (p. 120) over the top of these, crossing from corner to corner over five threads. Take the needle up at 5, down at 6, up at 7 and down at 8. Finally, tie the middle of the stitch down with a small, straight stitch, worked horizontally over one thread. The cross-stitch can be worked in a contrasting colour to the base stitches and the central tying stitch.

FABRIC
Single-mesh (mono) canvas

 Related techniques:
Canvaswork (p. 44)

 Similar stitches:
No notable matches

BYZANTINE STITCH

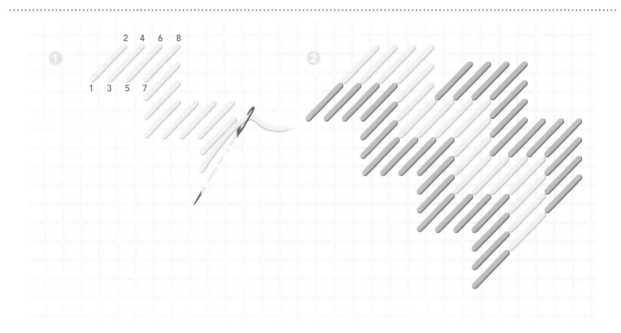

METHOD AND USES

This stitch creates a zig-zag pattern that resembles a woven or brocade fabric. It can be worked in one or alternating colours for a striped effect and, being quick to work, it is very useful for filling large areas and backgrounds.

Slanted stitches are worked in step formation; for example, here, four stitches are worked horizontally, followed by three stitches that progress vertically, then three horizontal and so on, starting at the top left-hand corner and travelling down to the right. Each stitch is worked over two threads.

Bring your needle up at 1 and down at 2, up at 3 and down at 4, up at 5 and down at 6, then up at 7 and down at 8 for the first set of four. Next, work three stitches vertically, directly under the last horizontally placed stitch.

Carry on working up and down the canvas diagonally. If there are any areas that remain uncovered, these can simply be filled in with some shorter stitches.

FABRIC

Single-mesh (mono) canvas

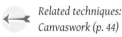

Related techniques:
Canvaswork (p. 44)

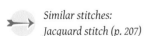

Similar stitches:
Jacquard stitch (p. 207)

JACQUARD STITCH

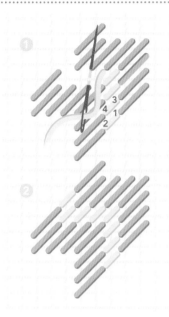

PARISIAN STITCH

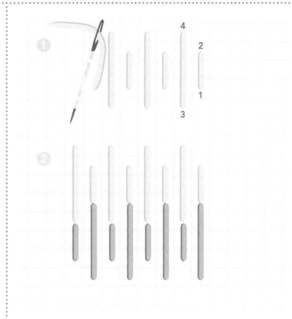

METHOD AND USES

Jacquard stitch combines diagonal rows of Byzantine stitch and tent stitch, often in different colours, to cover large areas and backgrounds.

First, work the area you wish to fill with Byzantine stitch, leaving one thread between each stepped row of stitches. Turn your work at the end of each row.

Next, return to fill in the gaps using tent stitch. Bring your needle up at 1 and down at 2, up at 3 and down at 4, repeating as you work from bottom right to top left.

FABRIC

Single-mesh (mono) or double (Penelope) canvas

Related techniques:
Canvaswork (p. 44)

Similar stitches:
Byzantine stitch (p. 206), tent stitch (p. 194)

METHOD AND USES

This is a very quick and easy stitch to work, so is often used as a filling stitch for backgrounds and medium to large areas. It consists of long, straight stitches worked over four or six horizontal threads, alternating with short stitches worked over two horizontal threads.

Working from right to left, bring your needle up at 1, down at 2, up at 3 and down at 4. Repeat this sequence along your row.

Work the next row from left to right, fitting the tops of your stitches into the bases of those in the previous row.

FABRIC

Single-mesh (mono) canvas

Related techniques:
Canvaswork (p. 44)

Similar stitches:
No notable matches

FLORENTINE STITCH

Also known as: Bargello stitch, cushion stitch, flame stitch and Irish stitch

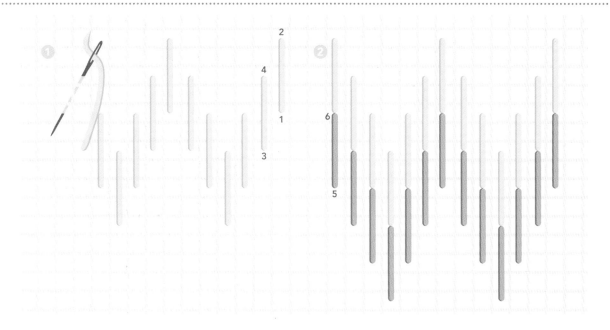

METHOD AND USES

This stitch takes its name from the type of work it is used for – Florentine work, or Bargello work, as it is also known. A series of long, straight stitches are worked in a zig-zag pattern, using various colourways, to produce a distinctive flame-like effect.

Begin in the centre of the canvas and work your stitches first to the left and then to the right of the centre. (The left-hand working is illustrated here.) Bring your needle up at 1 and down at 2 (passing over four threads). Work the next stitch two threads below this first stitch, bringing your needle up at 3 and down at 4. Keep working stitches in this zig-zag pattern, always shifting two threads above or below your previous stitch.

For the next row, change to a contrasting colour. Bring your needle up at 5 and down at 6. The tops of the stitches in this row should meet the bases of those of the previous row. Continue creating rows, using as many different colours as you like.

FABRIC

Single-mesh (mono) canvas

Related techniques:
Bargello work (p. 47), canvaswork (p. 44)

Similar stitches:
No notable matches

BRICK STITCH (2)

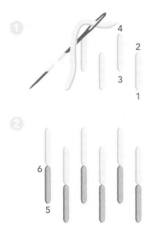

METHOD AND USES

This stitch consists of small stitches worked over two threads. Stitches are worked in a zig-zag formation, producing a filling stitch that adds a textured effect to backgrounds and medium to large areas.

From the right, bring your needle up at 1, down at 2, up at 3 and down at 4. Repeat this sequence to the left.

For the next row, start at the left and work back in the same way (up at 5, down at 6, and so on), fitting the tops of your stitches into the holes that hold the bases of those in the previous row.

FABRIC

Single-mesh (mono) canvas

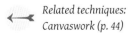
Related techniques: Canvaswork (p. 44)

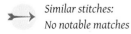
Similar stitches: No notable matches

GREEK STITCH
Also known as: Greek cross-stitch

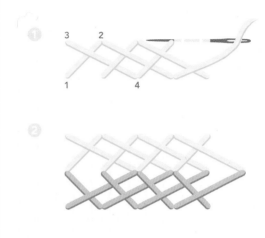

METHOD AND USES

Greek stitch is used to fill large areas and backgrounds. It consists of a short slanted stitch and a long slanted stitch, worked together in a cross. Rows of stitches are worked horizontally slanting one way and then the opposite way.

Bring your needle up at 1 and down at 2 (passing over two threads) and then up at 3 and down at 4 (over four threads). Repeat along your row. Turn your work at the end to work the second row of stitches.

FABRIC

Single-mesh (mono) or double (Penelope) canvas

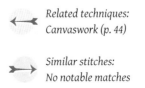
Related techniques: Canvaswork (p. 44)

Similar stitches: No notable matches

The assortment of stitches covered here are used with a range of different techniques. For instance, there are couching and laid-work stitches, which are used in freestyle embroidery, crewelwork and goldwork. Smocking stitches, such as honeycomb stitch, hold fabric gathers in place using decorative patterns; they are used predominantly for clothing. Both kloster blocks and needleweaving are used in Hardanger embroidery, while shisha stitch is used for the ancient art of shisha mirrorwork – attaching circular mirrors to fabric using a needle and thread.

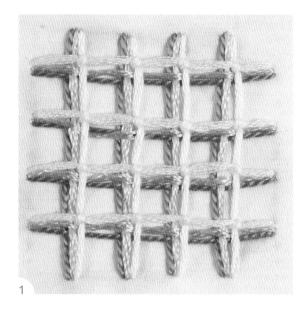

1

2

1 *Battlement filling (p. 218)*

2 *Square laid filling (p. 217)*

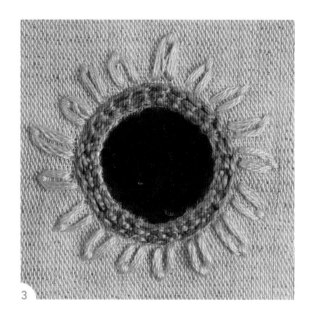

3

FABRICS: The stitches in this chapter can be worked on plain- or even-weave fabrics, including patterned fabrics such as gingham.

THREADS: Embroidery cotton (six-stranded cotton), cotton pearl (perlé), soft cotton, metallic thread and stranded silk can all be used.

NEEDLES: Crewel needles are usually the needle of choice when working on plain-weave fabric. Kloster blocks are better worked with a blunt-ended tapestry needle in order not to split the threads while working.

OTHER EQUIPMENT: You will need a small pair of sharp embroidery scissors, an embroidery hoop or frame to keep your fabric taut, a fabric marker pen and a tape measure.

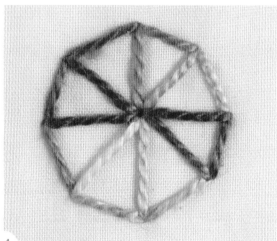

4

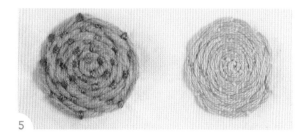

5

3 *Shisha stitch (p. 226)*

4 *Eyelet wheels (p. 222)*

5 *Couched circles (p. 216)*

BOKHARA COUCHING

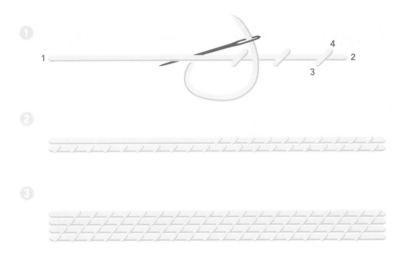

METHOD AND USES

Bokhara couching is worked using one continuous thread rather than laying a thread on the surface of the fabric to be couched. It is very easy to work, and is used for filling shapes of any size.

Working from left to right, bring your needle up at 1 and down at 2 to create a long, straight stitch over the area to be covered. Next, bring your needle up at 3 and down at 4 to create a small, slanted stitch over the top of the straight stitch, tying it in place. Continue along the straight stitch, placing even slanting stitches at regular intervals along its length.

The laid threads are worked close together and the slanting stitches can be worked in lines or patterns. The slanted stitches may be placed in between those of the previous row (as shown in step 2) or they may be placed so that they line up across adjacent rows.

FABRIC

Plain- or even-weave fabrics

Related techniques:
Couching and laid work (p. 30), goldwork (p. 20)

Similar stitches:
Romanian couching (p. 213)

ROMANIAN COUCHING

Also known as: antique stitch and Oriental stitch

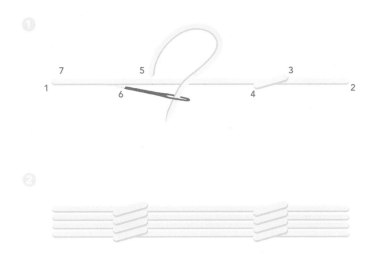

METHOD AND USES

Romanian couching is similar to Bokhara couching (left) in that it uses a continuous thread, which is first laid, then couched down by working back in the opposite direction. The tying stitches here, however, are a bit longer, and run along close to the foundation stitch. Romanian couching is also used for filling shapes of all sizes.

To keep your stitches even, you may wish to mark guidelines on the surface of your fabric with a fabric marker pen. Working from left to right, bring your needle up at 1 and down at 2 to create the first long stitch.

Next, return in the opposite direction, bringing your needle up at 3 and down at 4 to create the first tying stitch, then bring it up at 5 and down at 6 for the next, and up at 7 to continue along your line.

Work your laid stitches close together and position your tying stitches along them so that they lie grouped in rows to form the finished pattern.

FABRIC
Plain- or even-weave fabrics

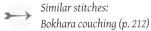

Related techniques:
Couching and laid work (p. 30), crewelwork (p. 18),
goldwork (p. 20)

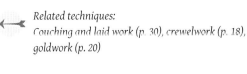

Similar stitches:
Bokhara couching (p. 212)

TRAILING COUCHING

Also known as: satin stitch couching and trailing stitch

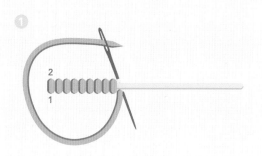

METHOD AND USES

For this stitch, threads are completely covered with satin stitches to produce a corded, raised effect. Trailing couching is used for straight and curved lines.

Working from the left-hand end of the line to be couched, bring your tying thread up at 1. Holding your fabric in your free hand and keeping the laid thread in place with the thumb of this hand, take your needle down and under at 2. Repeat along the line, working your satin stitches close together to cover the laid thread completely.

FABRIC

Plain- or even-weave fabrics

 Related techniques:
Freestyle embroidery (p. 12), whitework (p. 14)

 Similar stitches:
Satin stitch (p. 151)

PENDANT COUCHING

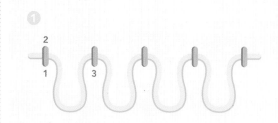

METHOD AND USES

Pendant couching creates a looped line or filling stitch by couching one or more laid threads to the surface of your fabric.

Bring the thread(s) to be couched to the end of your line and then bring your tying thread up at 1 and down at 2 to hold the laid thread securely in place. Make a loop in the laid thread, then come up at 3 to create another small tying stitch close to the first to hold the shape in place. Repeat this along your line.

FABRIC

Plain- or even-weave fabrics

 Related techniques:
Freestyle embroidery (p. 12)

 Similar stitches:
Puffy couching (p. 215)

PUFFY COUCHING
Also known as: bunched couching

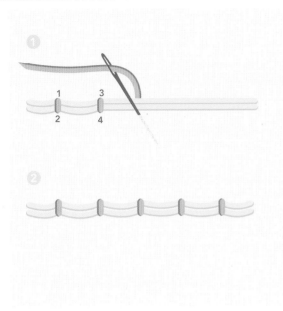

BASKET STITCH (2)

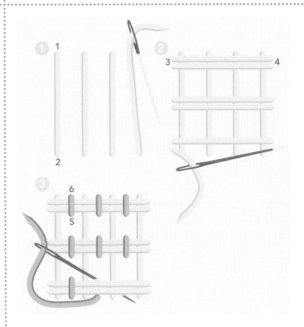

METHOD AND USES

Puffy couching bunches groups of laid threads together at intervals for a decorative 'beaded' effect. It is used as a line or outline stitch, worked either straight or curved.

Bring the threads to be couched to the end of your line. Hold these in place with the thumb of your free hand, then bring your tying thread up at 1. Take your needle over the laid threads and back down at 2, up again at 3 and down at 4.

Repeat this along the line, spacing the tying stitches evenly and pulling the tying thread tightly to create the bunched effect.

FABRIC
Plain- or even-weave fabrics

METHOD AND USES

This filling stitch is worked in a grid formation. Bring your needle up at 1, down at 2, and continue to create four vertical, evenly spaced stitches on the surface of your fabric. Next, come up at 3 and down at 4 to begin three evenly spaced sets of horizontal stitches over the top, with each set consisting of two stitches worked side by side.

Complete the grid by working from top to bottom and adding a vertical straight stitch over the sets of horizontal stitches in a contrasting colour, as shown, bringing your needle up at 5 and down at 6, and so on.

FABRIC
Plain- or even-weave fabrics

 Related techniques:
Freestyle embroidery (p. 12)

 Similar stitches:
Basic couching (p. 98)

 Related techniques:
Crewelwork (p. 18), laid work (p. 30)

 Similar stitches:
Battlement filling (p. 218), square laid filling (p. 217)

COUCHED CIRCLES

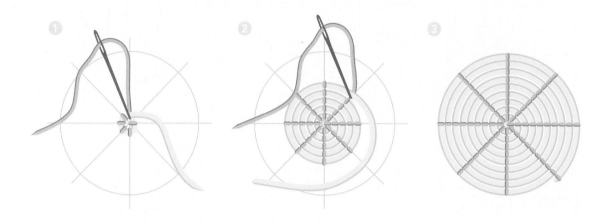

METHOD AND USES

This neat stitch is used to create flowers, wheels and decorative circles.

Begin by using a fabric marker pen to draw a circle on your fabric, divided up with either 8 or 12 regular radiating lines, or spokes.

First, bring the thread to be couched to the surface of your fabric at the centre of the circle. Start to coil this thread around neatly in a spiral then, as you go, couch it down with your tying thread at regular intervals, following the guidelines to form a spoke pattern. Always bring your needle up on the outside edge of the spiralled thread and then insert it again on the inner side, angling all your stitches towards the centre of the circle.

Once your spiralled circle reaches the desired size, take your laid thread to the wrong side of the fabric to finish off.

FABRIC

Plain- or even-weave fabrics

Related techniques:
Freestyle embroidery (p. 12)

Similar stitches:
Basic couching (p. 98)

SQUARE LAID FILLING

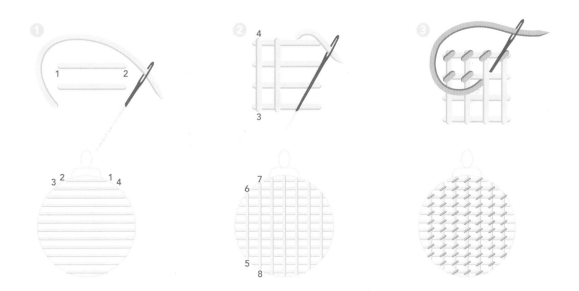

METHOD AND USES

This stitch is used to fill various shapes with a criss-crossed grid pattern.

To fill a square area, first, work a set of horizontal, straight stitches. Bring your needle up at 1 and down at 2, then repeat to create the basis of a square.

Next, work a series of vertical stitches over your horizontal stitches. Bring your needle up at 3 and down at 4. Repeat, spacing your stitches evenly to produce a neat grid. The stitch is finished off with the addition of a small, slanted tying stitch across each intersection.

The top example demonstrates a simple square, but this stitch can be adapted to fill any shape, as illustrated with the circle shown below it.

Work horizontal stitches across the circle, bringing your needle up at 1, down at 2, up at 3, then down at 4. Repeat to fill the shape, then work your vertical stitches by bringing your needle up at 5, down at 6, up at 7 and down at 8, and so on to complete the grid. Again, add a tying stitch to each intersection to complete the effect.

FABRIC

Plain- or even-weave fabrics

Related techniques:
Crewelwork (p. 18), laid work (p. 30)

Similar stitches:
Battlement filling (p. 218), couched filling stitch (p. 219)

BATTLEMENT FILLING

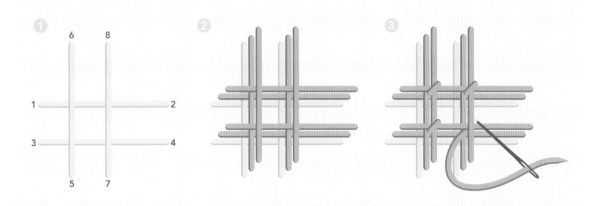

METHOD AND USES

This filling stitch uses overlaid sets of horizontal and vertical threads to form a dense, colourful grid. It is usually worked in three different colours, as shown here.

Begin by working your first grid. Bring your needle up at 1, down at 2, up at 3, then down at 4 to create the horizontal stitches. Next, work the vertical stitches over the top and slightly off-centre, coming up at 5, down at 6, up at 7, then down at 8.

Next, in your second colour, work another grid over the top of the first, but just above it and to the right so that they are lined up and nestle neatly together.

Now, in your third colour, work a final grid on top of the previous two. As before, this should be above and to the right of the previous grid.

Finish off by working small, slanted tying stitches in your third colour over each intersection of the top grid only to secure it in place.

FABRIC
Plain- or even-weave fabrics

Related techniques:
Crewelwork (p. 18), laid work (p. 30)

Similar stitches:
Couched filling stitch (p. 219), square laid filling (p. 217)

COUCHED FILLING STITCH

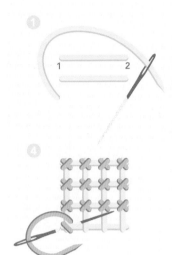

METHOD AND USES

Couched filling stitch is worked in the same way as square laid filling, creating an even grid of horizontal and vertical parallel stitches. However, for this stitch, when the grid is complete, cross-stitches are worked over each intersection using a contrasting colour.

Start by bringing your needle up at 1 and down at 2, then continue to complete a square of four stitches. Next, bring the needle up at 3 and down at 4 to begin a set of four vertical stitches, placed over the top of the horizontal ones.

Now, using a contrasting thread, complete a cross-stitch (p. 120) over each intersection, as shown, to finish off the stitch.

FABRIC

Plain- or even-weave fabrics

 Related techniques:
Crewelwork (p. 18), laid work (p. 30)

 Similar stitches:
Battlement filling (p. 218), square laid filling (p. 217)

HONEYCOMB STITCH

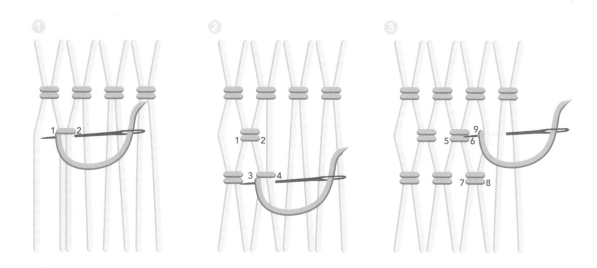

METHOD AND USES

Honeycomb stitch is used in smocking to produce an even, all-over dotted pattern.

Start by gathering your fabric into tubes (explained in detail on p.228). Now, working from left to right, bring your needle up at 1. Take a small stitch, picking up the first tube and the next to the right, then insert the needle at 2 to bind the two tubes together. Emerge at 1 again and pull the thread tightly.

Next, take your needle down at 2 again, then slip it downwards through the tube to emerge at 3. Take another small stitch across two tubes from 3 to 4. Repeat the stitch, then slip your needle upwards through this tube to emerge at 5 to create the next two stitches between 5 and 6. Slip your needle downwards to emerge at 7, create two stitches between 7 and 8, then slip the needle up to emerge at 9 and begin again.

FABRIC

Plain-weave fabrics, including gingham

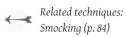

Related techniques:
Smocking (p. 84)

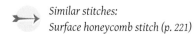

Similar stitches:
Surface honeycomb stitch (p. 221)

SURFACE HONEYCOMB STITCH

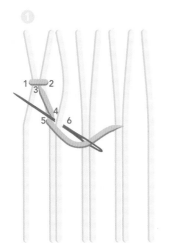

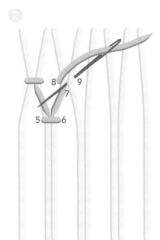

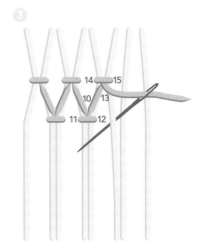

METHOD AND USES

This stitch is worked in a similar way to regular honeycomb stitch (left), and also looks very like chevron stitch (p. 103).

Start by gathering your fabric into tubes as for honeycomb stitch (explained in detail on p. 228).

Now, working from left to right, bring your needle up at 1. Take a small stitch across two tubes, taking the needle down at 2, then emerge at 3, between the tubes and below the stitch you have just created. Now, instead of passing the needle through the tube as for the regular honeycomb stitch, pass it over the top of it. Take the needle down at 4, on the right-hand side of the right tube, then emerge at 5.

Now stitch across two tubes as before, from 5 to 6, then emerge at 4 again, in the middle of the two joined tubes and above the stitch just created.

Pass the needle upwards over the right tube to insert it at 7, then emerge at 8 to complete a small stitch from 8 to 9. Pass downwards to complete the next set, working through 10 to 12, then up for another from 13 to 15, and so on.

FABRIC

Plain-weave fabrics, including gingham

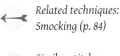

Related techniques:
Smocking (p. 84)

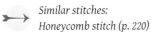

Similar stitches:
Honeycomb stitch (p. 220)

EYELET WHEELS

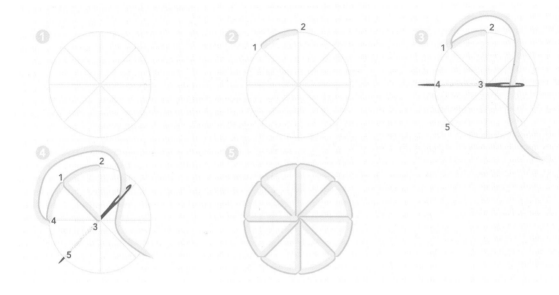

METHOD AND USES

Eyelet wheels are used for depicting wheels, flowers and even eyes. They can also be used as a filling stitch, worked in fine thread to form a lacy pattern.

Start by marking your fabric with a circle and then divide it up with any number of radiating lines. Next, bring your needle up at 1 on the perimeter, down at 2 and then up at 1 again. Now cross over to take the thread down at 3 in the centre, then emerge at 4 to the right. Take the needle back down at 1 once more, up at 4, back down at the centre, 3, and this time up at 5 further round the circle.

Continue working around the circle, alternating these backstitches and stitches in to the centre until all the spokes have been completed.

FABRIC

Plain- or even-weave fabrics

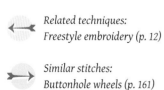

Related techniques:
Freestyle embroidery (p. 12)

Similar stitches:
Buttonhole wheels (p. 161)

TURKEY WORK
Also known as: Ghiordes knot stitch, rya stitch and turkey stitch

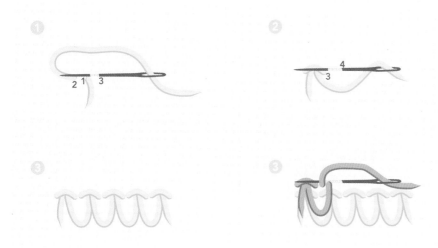

METHOD AND USES

Turkey work is an example of a pile stitch – formed by working loops close together, which may then also be cut and trimmed (as is done with this stitch). Pile stitches are generally used for rug making, but they also often appear in three-dimensional needlework too.

Starting at the bottom left, take your needle down at 1, leaving a tail of thread on the surface of the fabric. Bring your needle up at 2 and down at 3, keeping the thread above your needle. Bring your needle out again at 1 and pull through.

Now take your needle down at 4 and up again at 3, leaving a loop of thread behind as you begin the next stitch. Continue to the right.

At the end of your row, cut the thread, leaving a short tail to match the first one, then begin your next row on the left, above the previous row. When your rows are complete, cut your loops and trim them to size to create a fluffy finish.

FABRIC

Plain- or even-weave fabrics; single-mesh (mono) and double (Penelope) canvas

Related techniques:
Stumpwork (p. 37)

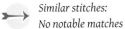

Similar stitches:
No notable matches

NEEDLEWEAVING

①

②

METHOD AND USES

Needleweaving is worked in a similar way to woven bars, where an even number of threads are woven together to form a firm, flat bar.

Start by removing the required number of threads from your fabric (explained in detail on p. 230). Each woven bar is then worked over eight threads in two sets of four.

Beginning on the right, work as for woven bars. Pass your needle over the first group of four threads and then under and over the second group of four threads in a weaving action. Pull the thread tightly as you go to pack the stitches closely together.

Halfway down your threads, shift to the left to work a woven bar over the second and third group of four stitches, and then continue downwards in the same way before repeating the whole process to the left.

FABRIC

Even-weave fabrics

Related techniques:
Drawn-thread work (p. 49), Hardanger (p. 48)

Similar stitches:
Overcast bars (p. 191), woven bars (p. 191)

KLOSTER BLOCK

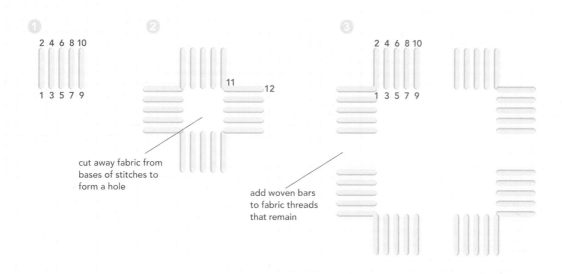

cut away fabric from bases of stitches to form a hole

add woven bars to fabric threads that remain

METHOD AND USES

Kloster blocks are used to produce geometric designs, either on their own or in combination with other decorative stitches, such as woven or overcast bars. Each block consists of five satin stitches (p. 151) worked over four threads, and whole blocks are then placed opposite one another. The firm ends of the stitches secure the cut edges of the fabric when the threads are removed (p. 230).

Bring your needle up at 1 and down at 2, up at 3 and down at 4, up at 5 and down at 6, up at 7 and down at 8 and finally up at 9 and down at 10 for the first kloster block.

To work a set of four opposing blocks, bring your needle up at 11 and down at 12 to work the first horizontal stitch of the adjacent block, as shown, then continue, working the remaining blocks as mirror images to form a square. Remove the fabric from the middle square.

This arrangement of blocks can then be varied to produce a range of different patterns, as shown in the example above. Woven bars (p. 191) are then added to any threads remaining between the blocks.

FABRIC

Even-weave fabrics

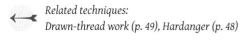

Related techniques:
Drawn-thread work (p. 49), Hardanger (p. 48)

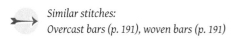

Similar stitches:
Overcast bars (p. 191), woven bars (p. 191)

SHISHA STITCH

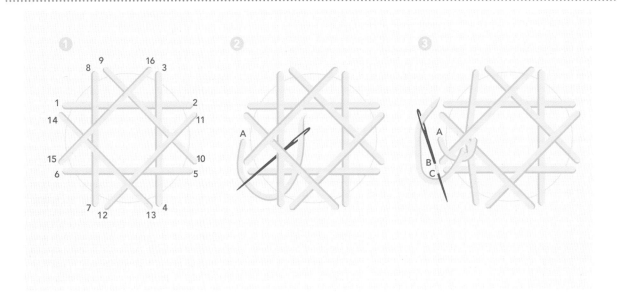

METHOD AND USES

Shisha mirrorwork is the ancient Indian technique of attaching circular mirrors to fabric (*shisha* means 'little glass'). Shisha mirrors are available from specialist needlework shops; however, you can improvise with coins or large sequins.

Begin by creating a base of straight stitches. Lay the mirror on your fabric and bring your needle up at 1 and down at 2 to make the first horizontal stitch. Next, bring your needle up at 3, to the left of 2 and down at 4. Bring your needle up at 5, to the right of 4 and down at 6. Continue, following the sequence shown above.

Now you need to make buttonhole stitches all around the mirror to pull the straight stitches to the sides. Bring your needle up at A. Slip it under the crossed foundation stitches and, keeping the thread beneath your needle, pull through tightly. Next, take a small, slanted stitch close to the edge of the mirror from B to C. Keep the thread beneath your needle and pull through tightly.

Work around the mirror, alternating between these two steps. The buttonhole stitches should cover the foundation stitches completely, pulling them to the edges to create a frame for the mirror.

FABRIC
Plain-weave fabrics

Related techniques:
Buttonhole stitch (p. 99)

Similar stitches:
No notable matches

PREPARING FABRIC FOR SMOCKING

Before embroidering fabric with smocking stitches, the fabric must first be gathered into narrow tubes. The fabric should be reasonably lightweight and drape well. Cotton and silk are suitable, either plain or patterned. Smocking can also be worked on fabrics that have a regular spot or check pattern, such as gingham. The pattern of the fabric itself can then be used instead of drawing a grid of dots.

If using plain fabric, prepare the cloth by marking a series of dots, in a grid formation, on the reverse side. You can do this by using a fabric marker pen and a ruler, but the easiest and quickest method is to buy an iron-on transfer. Transfers usually come in blue dots for light fabrics and yellow dots for darker fabrics.

STEP 1

Place the transfer face down on the wrong side of the fabric. You can pin or tack the corners if you want to make sure the transfer doesn't move. The dots should be in line with the grain of the fabric. Carefully press with a hot iron, then peel up a corner of the paper to check that the dots have transferred properly. Remove the paper. The dots will wash out with soap and water.

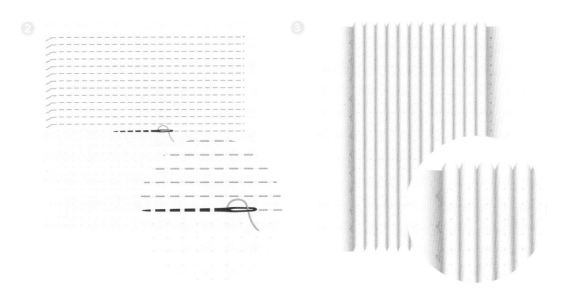

STEP 2

Using a cotton thread, work lines of tacking stitches (running stitch, p. 94), starting top right. Work each line with a knotted thread. Take a small stitch at each dot. At the end of each line, leave a long tail of thread.

STEP 3

Pull all the tail ends of the threads up evenly so that the fabric 'concertinas' into tubes. Smocking gathers in fabric to one-third of its original size, so make sure that your fabric is three times wider than the final width required.

You are now ready to work smocking stitches, such as surface honeycomb stitch (p. 221), on the right side of the fabric. Remove the tacking threads once the smocking stitches are complete; the smocking stitches secure the folds.

PREPARING A DRAWN-THREAD BORDER

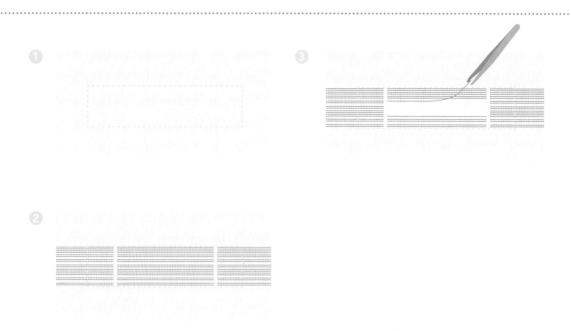

Before embroidering fabric with hemstitches (see p.189 for the basic version), the border of your fabric must be prepared by following the steps below.

STEP 1
First, decide on the size and depth of border you require. Using even-weave fabric, measure and tack the position of the border using running stitch (p. 94) and a cotton thread. If you are working a hem fold, hem and tack your fabric in place (p. 189).

STEP 2
Next, using small, sharp scissors, carefully snip the horizontal threads of the fabric 5cm (2in) in from each side of your marked border.

STEP 3
Using tweezers, carefully withdraw these horizontal threads from the middle section of your border, clearing them all the way up to the edges of your tacking stitches at top and bottom. Next, using a blunt needle tip, unweave the threads at each side of your border until you reach the edge of your tacking threads.

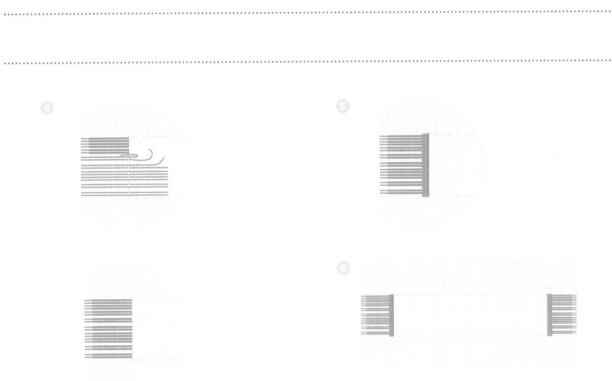

STEP 4
Fold these threads back.

STEP 5
Secure the threads with buttonhole stitch (p. 99). You can then simply trim the loose thread ends or weave them back into the fabric on the outside of the border to conceal them.

STEP 6
You are now ready to work hemstitches. When preparing your hem, make sure there is an even number of vertical threads along the width of your border.

GLOSSARY

Aida cloth – an even-weave fabric with regularly spaced holes used for cross-stitch embroidery.

appliqué – the application of fabric shapes to another fabric by hand stitching, fusing or machine stitching.

Assisi work – a *counted-thread* embroidery technique in which the background is worked in cross-stitch with the motif left unstitched.

Bargello – a type of canvaswork that uses a long, straight stitch called 'Florentine stitch', which forms a zig-zag or flame-like pattern. Also known as Florentine work.

beading needle – a long, sharp, thin needle with a round eye used for sewing beads and sequins.

beadwork – any type of surface decoration that uses beads and sequins.

betweens – small needles with a round eye used for quilting. Also known as quilting needles.

blackwork – a *counted-thread* embroidery technique, which is worked in small repeating patterns in black thread.

Brazilian embroidery – a type of embroidery originating in Brazil using rayon threads.

broderie anglaise – a type of *cutwork* embroidery, which creates small eyelet holes to form floral patterns. Usually worked in white thread on white cotton fabric.

calico – a plain-weave cotton fabric available in a variety of weights (known in the US as 'muslin').

candlewicking – a type of whitework embroidery that forms knots of thread on the surface of the fabric using a colonial knot stitch (p. 136).

canvas – an evenly woven mesh with an even number of holes per 2.5cm (1in) in each direction.

canvaswork – any type of embroidery that is worked on evenly woven canvas mesh. Also known as needlepoint.

chenille needle – a large-eyed needle with a sharp point used for thick threads.

chicken scratch – a type of *counted-thread* embroidery worked on gingham fabric.

colourfastness – a thread or fabric is colourfast if the colour does not bleed or run when washed.

corded quilting – a type of *quilting* in which two parallel lines are stitched around a design and then threaded with a wool cord to form a relief effect on the front of the fabric. Also known as Italian quilting.

cotton pearl (perlé) – a twisted, glossy cotton thread used for most types of embroidery.

couching – a method of attaching a thick thread or cord to fabric by stitching (tying) it down with another thinner thread.

count – the count of a fabric (even weave, canvas or Aida) is how many holes or threads there are per 2.5cm (1in).

counted-thread work – any embroidery technique that counts the holes or threads of the fabric (even weave, canvas or Aida) to work stitches.

crazy patchwork – a type of *patchwork* where randomly sized patches are sewn together to resemble crazy paving.

crewel needle – a sharp needle with a large eye used for crewelwork and most surface embroidery techniques.

crewel wool – a two-ply woollen thread, available in different shades.

cross-stitch – a type of *counted-thread* embroidery usually worked on Aida cloth.

cutwork – a type of *freestyle embroidery* where areas of fabric are stitched using a buttonhole stitch (p. 99) and then cut away to leave holes in the fabric.

double canvas – a very stable canvas, which is woven with two pairs of threads in each direction. Also known as Penelope canvas.

drawn-fabric work – a type of *counted-thread* embroidery often confused with drawn-thread work. Here, the stitches are pulled together to create an open effect rather than withdrawn altogether from the fabric.

drawn-thread work – a type of *counted-thread* embroidery where threads are withdrawn from the fabric to create open areas, which are then embellished with stitching.

embroidery cotton – consists of six strands of fine threads grouped together in a skein. Any number of threads can be used together in the needle. It is suitable for most types of *freestyle embroidery*. Also known as six-stranded cotton.

embroidery hoop – used to keep your fabric taut and prevent puckering of stitches while embroidering.

even-weave fabric – a fabric with the same number of threads per 2.5cm (1in), either vertically or horizontally. Used for *counted-thread* work.

fabric stabilizer – used to support lightweight or stretchy fabrics while stitching. Once stitching is complete, the stabiliser is torn away.

feed dogs – a set of toothed bars under the presser foot of a sewing machine used to control the fabric passing underneath the presser foot in order to create an even stitch.

Florentine work – see Bargello.

free machine/free-motion embroidery – the technique of free stitching using a sewing machine with the *feed dogs* lowered or covered. The embroiderer is then able to move the fabric freely in any direction.

freestyle embroidery – embroidery that is worked freely on the surface of the fabric, by following a design or pattern rather than counting threads.

fused appliqué – see fusible web.

fusible web – a non-woven fabric with a paper backing that, when heated with an iron, bonds one fabric to another. Particularly used in *appliqué*.

goldwork – a type of surface embroidery, which uses metal threads that are *couched* or laid on the surface of the fabric.

Hardanger – a type of *counted-thread* embroidery, which uses *cutwork* and *drawn-thread work* to create open geometric designs.

Hawaiian appliqué – a type of appliqué originating in Hawaii, which creates silhouette designs of flat colours that are cut in a similar way to paper snowflakes.

Hedebo – a type of *cutwork* traditionally worked in white thread on white fabric.

huck embroidery – a type of surface darning worked on a special cloth, which has pairs of raised threads.

GLOSSARY

interfacing – a light- to heavyweight non-woven fabric, which is applied to the back of another fabric to prevent it distorting.

kloster blocks – five satin stitches (p. 151) are stitched in a block to form open designs used in *Hardanger*.

mono canvas – a strong woven single-mesh canvas used for canvaswork.

muslin – see calico.

net embroidery – a surface embroidery technique worked on net fabric or tulle.

non-woven fabric – a type of fabric that is formed by bonding or felting fibres together rather than the usual methods of weaving or knitting fabrics.

patchwork – the technique of piecing together small scraps of fabric into geometric patterns to form a cloth.

Penelope canvas – see double canvas.

Persian wool – a three-ply yarn that comes in skeins usually used for canvaswork.

plain-weave fabric – the most popular type of fabric for *freestyle embroidery*. The design must be transferred or drawn on the surface of the fabric before starting.

punch needle – an embroidery technique that uses a special hollow, pointed tool that is 'punched' through the back of the fabric to leave a loop of thread on the right side of the fabric.

quilting – three layers of fabric are stitched together either by hand or machine. The middle layer is always a layer of *wadding*.

redwork – a type of surface embroidery that uses red thread, usually in outline only.

ribbon work – a type of raised embroidery that uses silk ribbon instead of *embroidery cotton* to create designs.

seed beads – tiny glass beads used in bead embroidery.

shadow embroidery – embroidery worked on transparent fabric, which creates a shadow effect. A closed herringbone stitch (p. 128) is the main stitch used for this technique.

sharps – sharply pointed needles with a round eye used for general stitching and *appliqué*.

silk shading – a type of surface embroidery where threads of silk or even cotton are blended together on a silk background fabric to form shaded areas of light and dark. Often referred to as 'needle painting'.

smocking – the technique of gathering fabric and then decorating the gathered folds with stitches. Usually used around the yoke of a dress or shirt.

stiletto – a sharply pointed tool with a handle used for creating holes in fabric. Used for *couching*, *cutwork* and *broderie anglaise*.

stranded cotton – see embroidery cotton.

tacking – temporary stitching, usually a running stitch (p. 94), used to keep fabrics in place while working. The tacking stitches are removed once the work is finished. Also known as basting.

tapestry needle – blunt-ended needles with large eyes used for *counted-thread* embroidery techniques.

tapestry wool – a twisted, four-ply thread that is hard-wearing and usually used for *canvaswork* techniques.

tatting – a form of lace constructed out of a series of knots and loops.

vanishing muslin – a fabric that dissolves in water or with the application of heat, and so can be used as a removable foundation for free machine embroidery.

wadding – natural or synthetic padding material used for quilting. Also known as batting.

waste canvas – an even-weave fabric used as a guide for stitching cross-stitch designs onto plain-weave fabrics. When wet it can easily be removed using tweezers.

water-soluble fabric – see vanishing muslin.

weaver's cloth – a firmly woven fabric used for punch needle embroidery.

CONTRIBUTORS AND PHOTOGRAPHERS

CONTRIBUTORS

Alyssa Thomas
(Penguin & Fish)
penguinandfish.com
alyssa@penguinandfish.com

Amanda Cowell
(Wild Plums)
wildplums.etsy.com
violetplays@gmail.com

Amanda Miller
flexfamilyarts.blogspot.com

Amy B Friend
(During Quiet Time)
duringquiettime.blogspot.com
amybfriend@gmail.com

Angela Salisbury
(Sake Puppets)
sakepuppets.etsy.com
sakepuppets@gmail.com

Anne Bruvold
(Nuperelle)
nuperelle.net
solurab@online.no

Annet Spitteler
(Fat-Quarter)
fat-quarter.blogspot.com
annet.zoet@xs4all.nl

Becky Meece
flickr.com/photos/meeced
sbmeece@aol.com

Belle Coccinelle
bellecoccinelle.etsy.com
design@embroideryny.com

Bonnie P Dulude
(Pastiche Studio)
pastichestudio.etsy.com
bpdpastiche@hotmail.com

Brenda Kee
(bstudio)
bstudio.bigcartel.com
bstudio18@gmail.com

Carina Envoldsen-Harris
(Polka & Bloom)
shop.polkaandbloom.com
carinascraftblog@googlemail.com

Catherine Parsons
(Sweet Petite Shoppe)
sweetpetiteshoppe.etsy.com
catherineparsons_2@hotmail.com

Catherine Rosselle
catherinerosselle.com

Claudia Dominguez
(Deep Indigo)
deepindigo.etsy.com
acuarius70@yahoo.com

Corey Voder
gymcoree@gmail.com

Daria Lvovsky
(Art of Felting)
darialvovsky.etsy.com
dasha.lvovsky@gmail.com

Diem Chau
diemchau.com
diemgia@gmail.com

Eleanor Pigman
http://eleanorpigman.com
http://eleanorpigman.blogspot.co.uk

Emma How
(Sampaguita Quilts)
sampaguitaquilts.blogspot.com
eho16677@bigpond.net.au

Emily Mackey
(Maxemilia)
maxemilia.com
emily@maxemilia.com

Erin Flanagan Lind
(Harp & Thistle Stitchery)
harpandthistle.etsy.com
erin115@hotmail.com

Fiona Dix
lovefibre.com
lovefibre@gmail.com

Firuzan Goker
firuzangoker.etsy.com
ametistangel@hotmail.com

Janet Reddick
(Urban Farmhouse Chic)
urbanfarmhousechic.etsy.com
janetreddick@yahoo.com

Kajsa Wikman
(Syko)
syko.fi
kajsa.wikman@gmail.com

Karen Grenfell
(Mimi Love)
mimilove.etsy.com
mimi@mimilove.co.uk

Karen Ruane
(Contemporary Embroidery)
karenruane.blogspot.com
contemporaryembroidery@hotmail.com

Katie Pirson
flickr.com/people/katiepirson
katie@katiepirson.co.uk

Katherine Kennedy
(Swedish Weave Designs: all items
designed and created by Katherine
Kennedy of Swedish Weave Designs)
http://swedishweavedesigns.com
katherine@swedishweavedesigns.com

Katrien Van Deuren
(Pilli Pilli)
pillipilli.etsy.com
pillipillihandmade@gmail.com

Katrina Herron
(The Story of Kat)
thestoryofkat.etsy.com
thestoryofkat@gmail.com

Kiloran Greenan
(Kid Kiloran)
kidkiloran.etsy.com
kiloran@nyc.rr.com

Kristena Derrick
(Thimbly Things)
thimblythings.com
kristena12180@hotmail.com

Kristy Kizzee
etsy.com/shop/bombastitch
kristeekizzee@mac.com

Kumi Nakagame
(K-Style Shonan)
k-style-shonan.com
k.style.shonan@gmail.com

Laura Amiss
lauraamiss.com
laura@lauraamiss.com

Leslie Richardson Dryg
(Needle You)
needleyou.etsy.com
Lesliealan@comcast.net

Liz Bookey
etsy.com/shop/ThisTinyExperience

Lizzy Lansberry
(Laurelin)
laurelin.co.uk
lizzylansberry@hotmail.com

Loretta Holzberger
(Loretta's Custom Stitchery)
lorettascustomstitchery.com
LHolzberger@comcast.net

Lucy Portsmouth
(Magpies Laundry)
magpies-laundry.co.uk
lucy@magpies.laundry.co.uk

Marie Grace Smith
(Marie Grace Designs)
mariegracedesigns.com
mariegrace@mariegracedesigns.com

Mary Brown
(Mary Brown Designs)
marybrowndesigns.com
mary@marybrowndesigns.com

Mary Maulhardt Gaston
(Mary Made Me)
marymademe.etsy.com
mary.maul@gmail.com

Michele Outland
(Return to Me)
returntome.co.uk
michele@returntome.co.uk

Rose Waterrose
(Waterrose)
waterrose.etsy.com

Roslyn Mirrington
(Bloom)
bloomandblossom.blogspot.com
bloom97@bigpond.com

Sam Gillespie
(Incy Wincy Stitches)
incywincytogs.blogspot.com
incywincytogs@hotmail.co.uk

Sami Teasdale
http://teasemade.blogspot.co.uk

Sara Adnum
sladnum@gmail.com

Shannon Genova Scudder
(Giggly Mama)
gigglymama.etsy.com
Genova.scudder@gmail.com

Sonja Pharr Poor
(Stringplay)
stringplay.blogspot.com
spoor@bellsouth.net

Susan Bischoff
(Dolly Delicacies)
dollydelicacies.com
susanbischoff@gmail.com

Susie Cowie
susiecowie.com
susie.cowie@gmail.com

Tanya Grin
(Pillowation)
pillowation.etsy.com
tanyagrin.design@gmail.com

Viv Sliwka
(Hen's Teeth)
hensteethart.blogspot.com
viv_sliwka@hotmail.com

Yuki Sugashima
(Barefoot Shepherdess)
barefootshepherdess.typepad.com
barefootshepherdess@gmail.com

PHOTOGRAPHERS

Corey T Lind
New York, USA
p. 83

Heidi Adnum
heidiadnum.com
p. 29; p. 69, right

pSquared Photography
p2photo.co.uk
p. 15, centre and right; p. 21, left
and right; p. 33, right; p. 50

Rachel Lanzafame
USA
p. 10, image 3; p. 25, centre

INDEX

accessories 25, 27, 47, 60
Aida 42
Algerian eye stitch 201
Algerian stitch 186
altar cloths 21
Amish embroidery 51
antique stitch 213
Antwerp edging stitch 166
applied work 68
appliqué 54, 68–79
aprons 51
Armenian cross-stitch 130
arrowhead stitch 146
artworks 13, 21, 23, 25, 35, 46, 61, 82
Assisi 46

baby clothing 17, 85
baby quilts 63
backstitch 94
bags 23, 25, 27, 35, 43, 45–47,
   60–62, 85, 89
Bargello stitch 47, 208
basic couching 98
basic stitches 92–103
basket stitch 149, 215
basketweave stitch 194
Basque stitch 108
basting 56, 62, 68, 72
batting 56, 63
battlement filling 218
bead edging stitch 176
bead embroidery 24
beaded stitch 101
beadwork 24–25
bed hangings 18
bedding/bed linen 13, 16–17, 33, 53
bedspreads 14–15, 29, 31, 50, 57,
   59–63, 65–67, 69–73, 75–79
belts 45
Berlin stitch 120
Berlin wool work 44
Bermuda faggoting 187
blackwork 40–41
blanket stitch 100
blankets 15, 31, 52
blind knot 135
blind stitch 108
blocks 28, 48, 225
bodices 40
Bokhara couching 212
bookmarks 43, 45–46
boxes 37
bracelets 87
Brazilian embroidery 34
briar stitch 97
brick stitch 154, 209
Brighton stitch 197

broad chain stitch 172
broderie anglaise 17
brooches 83
bullion knot 134
bunched couching 215
buttonhole filling stitch 162
buttonhole flowers 161
buttonhole with picot 158
buttonhole stitches 99, 156–67
buttonhole wheels 161
Byzantine stitch 206

cable chain stitch 170
candlewicking 29
canvas embroidery 44–45
canvas stitch 194
caps 40
Carrickmacross 36
Cashmere stitch 195
caterpillar stitch 134
Ceylon stitch 167
chain stitches 95, 168–79
chained feather stitch 171
checker stitch 198
checkered chain stitch 175
chevron stitch 103
chicken scratch 51
Chinese knot 135
Chinese stitch 108
christening robes 14–15, 17
church vestments 21
closed blanket stitch 165
closed buttonhole stitch 165
closed Cretan stitch 102
closed feather stitch 109
closed fly stitch 112
closed herringbone stitch 128
clothing 13, 21, 25–27, 31, 33–34, 53–54, 57,
   59–60, 65–67, 69–72, 75, 77–78
coats 27
cobbler stitch 182
coil stitch 134, 186
collars 86
colonial knot 136
colour choice 26
colour tips 41
condensed Scotch stitch 198
Continental stitch 194
coral stitch 101
corded clusters 191
corded quilting 62
cordonnet stitch 144
costumes 35
cot quilts 17
couched circles 216
couched filling stitch 218
couched herringbone stitch 126

couching 30–31
counted-thread work 38–53
covered buttons 45
crazy patchwork 66
crested chain stitch 178
Cretan stitch 102
crewelwork 18–19
cro-tatting 86
cross-stitch 42–43
crossed blanket stitch 164
crossed buttonhole stitch 164
crossed stitches 118–31
cup stitch 138
cushion stitch 203, 208
cushions 13, 15, 19, 21, 23, 29, 31, 34–35,
   41, 43, 45–47, 51–53, 60–62, 65–67, 69–73,
   75–79, 83, 85, 87, 89
cutwork 32–33

daisy stitch 96
damask stitch 151
Danish work 53
darning stitch 151
decorative couching stitches 31
decorative objects 37, 45–46, 57, 59, 61, 79,
   82, 86–87, 89
depression lace 51
detached buttonhole bar 159
detached chain stitch 96
detached wheatear stitch 137
dishcloths 23, 28, 52
doilies 86
double blanket stitch 163
double buttonhole bar 159
double chain stitch 173
double coral stitch 110
double cross-stitch 122, 201
double feather stitch 110
double fly stitch 112
double herringbone stitch 127
double knot stitch 107
double laced running stitch 145
double Pekinese stitch 129
double running stitch 99
drapes 18, 26, 52
drawn-fabric work 50
drawn-thread borders 230–31
drawn-thread work 49
dresses 33, 85
dry felting 88

earrings 87
ecclesiastical items 21
embellishers 88
embroidery stitch 154
encroaching blanket stitch 163
encroaching satin stitch 153
ermine stitch 125
eyelet embroidery 17
eyelet wheels 222

fabrics 12–37, 40–53, 56–79, 82–89, 93, 105, 119, 133, 143, 157, 169, 181, 193, 211
feather stitch 97
feathered chain stitch 171
feed dogs 22, 58, 74
fern stitch 147
figure eight knot 136
firescreens 19
flame stitch 47, 208
Florentine stitch 208
Florentine work 47
fly stitch 101
footstools 19
forbidden knot 135
forbidden stitch 108
four-legged knot stitch 135
four-sided stitch 188
free machine embroidery 22–23
free-motion embroidery 22
free-motion quilting 58
freestyle embroidery 12–13
French knot 134
furniture decorations 47
fused appliqué 77

garments see clothing
gathering 84
Ghiordes knot stitch 223
gingham 51
gingham lace 51
glossary 232–35
gobelin filling stitch 204
God's eye stitch 139
goldwork 20–21
gowns 27, 36
Greek stitch 209
grub knot 134

half cross-stitch 120
hand appliqué 68–69
hand quilting 56–57
handkerchiefs 14–15
Hardanger 48
hats 27
Hawaiian appliqué 73
heavy braid chain stitch 179
heavy chain stitch 179
Hedebo embroidery 53
heirloom pieces 14
hemstitch 109
herringbone ladder stitch 129
herringbone stitch 100
Holbein stitch 99
home décor 15, 19
honeycomb filling stitch 185
honeycomb stitch 220
hot water bottle covers 89

household items/linen 13, 17, 27, 49, 60
Huck embroidery 52
Hungarian diamond stitch 202
Hungarian point 47

interlaced herringbone stitch 130
interlaced running stitch 145
Irish stitch 208
isolated stitches 132–41
Italian quilting 62

jackets 67
Jacobean embroidery 18
Jacquard stitch 207
Japanese darning 152
jewellery 43, 79, 82, 85–87

Kensington outline stitch 95
Kloster blocks 48, 225
knitted stitch 167
knot stitch 166
knotted blanket stitch 165–66
knotted buttonhole stitch 165
knotted loop stitch 114
knotted stitch 101, 134

lace edgings 86
lace stitch 187
laced backstitch 108
laced herringbone stitch 126
laced running stitch 144
ladder hemstitch 190
ladder stitch 115, 174
laid work 30–31
lazy daisy stitch 96
leaf stitch 147
Leviathan stitch 122, 201
Limerick lace 36
line stitches 104–17
lingerie 26
long and short blanket stitch 164
long and short stitch 35, 154
long-armed cross-stitch 124
long-armed feather stitch 102
loop stitch 114

machine appliqué 74–75
machine quilting 58–59
macramé 86
Madeira work 17
magic chain stitch 175
marking cross-stitch 123
metal thread embroidery 20
Milanese stitch 196
mirror frames 37
Monk's cloth 52
Moorish stitch 200
mosaic stitch 203
Mountmellick 16

napkins 48–49
necklaces 87
needle care 59
needle felting 88–89
needle lace 82
needle painting 35
needle-turned appliqué 71
needlepoint 44–45
needlepoint stitches 192–209
needles 13–37, 40–53, 56–79, 82–89, 93, 105, 119, 133, 143, 157, 169, 181, 193, 211
needleweaving 224
needleweaving clusters 191
net embroidery 36
nightdresses 14, 16, 26
nightwear 17, 33, 36

oblique gobelin stitch 204
open buttonhole stitch 100
open chain stitch 174
open Cretan stitch 106
open loop stitch 101
openwork 50
Opus Anglicanum 20
Oriental stitch 213
ornaments 41, 43, 52–53, 65–67, 69–72, 75–78, 83
overcast bars 191
overlapping blanket stitch 163

padded satin stitch 153
Palestrina stitch 107
panels 37
Parisian stitch 207
patchwork 31, 54, 64–67
Pekinese stitch 108
Peking knot 135
pendant couching 214
penny squares 28
Persian stitch 102
petit point 44, 194
pictures 27, 34–35, 37, 41, 83, 88–89
pieced work 64
pillows/pillowcases 16, 28, 48–49, 51, 53
pin stitch 183
pincushions 52–53, 60, 65, 69, 75, 83
pineapple stitch 205
plain couching 98
plaited braid stitch 116
plate stitch 155
plunging 21
point de chaînette 95
point de marque 120
point de sable 94
puffy couching 215
pulled brick stitch 185
pulled and drawn stitches 180–91

INDEX

pulled honeycomb stitch 185
pulled work 50
punch needle 83
punch stitch 184
purses 23, 25, 43, 45–46, 60–62, 89

quilt blocks 28
quilting 54–63
quilting bees 54
quilts 17, 31

raised chain stitch 177
raised cup stitch 138
raised embroidery 37
raised herringbone stitch 131
raised knot 136
raised satin stitch 153
raw-edge appliqué 70
redwork 28
Renaissance cutwork 32
Reticella cutwork 32
reverse appliqué 78
reverse chain stitch 172
reversed fly stitch 111
Rhodes stitch 202
ribbed spider's web 141
ribbon work 27
Richelieu cutwork 32
ringed backstitch 185
rings 87
Romanian couching 213
rosette chain stitch 176
rugs 45, 83
running stitch 94
Russian cross-stitch 100
Russian embroidery 83
rya stitch 223

sachets 16, 26
St. George cross-stitch 124
sampler stitch 42, 120
samplers 41
sashiko quilting 60
satin stitch 151
satin stitch couching 214
scarves 85
Scotch stitch 198
scroll stitch 106
seed stitch 145
Seminole patchwork 67
serpentine stitch 190
shading stitch 154
shadow appliqué 72
shadow embroidery 26
shadow stitch 128
shawls 27
sheets 48–49

shirts 40, 53
shisha stitch 226–27
silk ribbon embroidery 27
silk shading 35
simple cross-stitch 120
single buttonhole bar 159
single chain stitch 96
single coral stitch 97
single faggot stitch 187
single feather stitch 109
single knotted line stitch 106
skirts 67
slanted buttonhole stitch 109
slanted gobelin stitch 204
smocking 84–85, 228–29
smocks 40, 84
Smyrna cross-stitch 201
Smyrna stitch 107
snowflake embroidery 51
Sorbello stitch 117
Spanish coral stitch 178
Spanish work 40
specialist equipment 23
speckling stitch 145
spider's web 141
split stitch 95
spoke stitch 189
square boss stitch 136
square chain stitch 174
square laid filling 217
stained-glass appliqué 76
star stitch 122, 125, 201
stem stitch 98
step stitch 115
stitch directory 94–227
straight stitches 142–55
stroke stitch 146
stuffed quilting 61
stumpwork 37
style directory 10–89
Suffolk puffs 79
surface embroidery 10–11
surface honeycomb stitch 221
Syon Cope 20

T-shirts 23
table linen 13, 15, 23, 28, 33, 35, 41, 43,
   52, 60, 75
table runners 52–53
tablecloths 14, 16, 48–51, 53, 70–72, 77–79
tablemats 16, 48–51
tailor's buttonhole stitch 158
tambour stitch 95
tapestry stitch 154
tatting 86–87
tea cozies 23
tent stitch 44, 194

tête-de-boeuf stitch 137
thorn stitch 107
threaded herringbone stitch 127
threaded running stitch 144
threads 12, 93, 105, 119, 133, 143, 157, 169,
   181, 193, 211
three-quarter cross-stitch 121
three-sided stitch 187
tied coral stitch 107
tied cross-stitch 121
tied herringbone stitch 126
tied quilting 63
towels 52
toys 57, 65
trailing couching 214
Trapunto quilting 61
tubes 84
tufting 29
Turkey redwork 28
Turkey work 223
Turkmen stitch 173
twisted bars 191
twisted chain stitch 175
twisted daisy border stitch 108
twisted knot stitch 134

undergarments/underwear 17, 36, 53
up and down buttonhole stitch 160
upholstery 18
upright cross-stitch 124
upright gobelin stitch 205

Vandyke chain stitch 174
Vandyke stitch 148
veils 36
Victoria and Albert Museum 20

wall hangings 19, 31, 57, 59, 65–67, 69–73, 75
wall panels 18
wave filling stitch 188
websites 236–37
wedding gowns 14, 36
wheel stitch 161
whipped running stitch 144
whipped satin stitch 155
whitework 14–15
working techniques 228–31
worm stitch 134
woven bars 191
woven circles 141
woven picot 140
woven spoke stitch 141

Y-stitch 101
yo-yos 79

zigzag chain stitch 174
zigzag stitch 150